C000098058

PUBLICATIONS
OF THE
ARMY RECORDS SOCIETY

VOL. 6

====

COLONEL SAMUEL BAGSHAWE
AND THE ARMY OF GEORGE II

1731–1762

The Army Records Society was founded in 1984 in order to publish original records describing the development, organisation, administration and activities of the British Army from early times.

Any person wishing to become a Member of the Society is requested to apply to the Hon. Secretary, c/o The National Army Museum, Royal Hospital Road, London, SW3 4HT. The annual subscription entitles the Member to receive a copy of each volume issued by the Society in that year, and to purchase back volumes at reduced prices. Current subscription details, whether for individuals living within the British Isles, for individuals living overseas, or for institutions, will be furnished on request.

The Council of the Army Records Society wish it to be clearly understood that they are not answerable for opinions or observations that may appear in the Society's publications. For these the responsibility rests entirely with the Editors of the several works.

Lieutenant-Colonel Samuel Bagshawe, 39th Regiment of Foot
(oil on canvas, artist unknown, *c.*1750)

Private Collection

COLONEL SAMUEL BAGSHAWE AND THE ARMY OF GEORGE II

1731–1762

EDITED BY
ALAN J. GUY

PUBLISHED BY
THE BODLEY HEAD
FOR THE
ARMY RECORDS SOCIETY
1990

First published 1990
© The Army Records Society 1990
The Bodley Head Ltd, 20 Vauxhall Bridge Road, London SW1V 2SA

A CIP catalogue record for this book
is available from the British Library

ISBN 0–370–31501–4

Typeset by J&L Composition Ltd, Filey, North Yorkshire
Printed in Great Britain by Mackays of Chatham PLC

ARMY RECORDS SOCIETY
COUNCIL FOR 1989–90

PRESIDENT
Field Marshal the Lord Carver GCB CBE DSO MC

VICE-PRESIDENT
The Rt Hon Sir Frank Cooper PC GCB CMG

COUNCILLORS
Professor John Gooch BA PhD FRHistS (*Chairman*)
Anthony Bennell MA BLitt
Professor Brian Bond MA FRHistS
David Chandler MA FRGS FRHistS
Lieutenant-General Sir Napier Crookenden KCB DSO OBE DL
General Sir Anthony Farrar-Hockley GBE KCB DSO MC BLitt
Alan Guy MA DPhil FRHistS
Tony Hayter BA PhD FRHistS
Keith Jeffery MA PhD FRHistS
Ian Roy MA DPhil FRHistS
Edward Spiers MA PhD FRHistS
Roderick Suddaby MA
Major-General Anthony Trythall CB MA DipEd

HONORARY SECRETARY
Ian Beckett BA PhD FRHistS

HONORARY TREASURER
Colonel John Power FCIS

To
John and Judy

Contents

Preface and Acknowledgements   ix

Introduction   1

Part 1 1713–1753 'I go abroad ... with great Advantages'   21
Part 2 1754–1758 'I want to obtain a few Thousand
                   pounds ...'   121
Part 3 1759–1763 'Every Regiment in Common
                   Occurrences has Equal Right to
                   favour and Protection ...'   199

Notes   273
Biographical Note of Correspondents   301
Bibliography   305
Index   311

Preface and Acknowledgements

Samuel Bagshawe of Ford Hall, the only son of Samuel Bagshawe and Frances Hardwar, was born, apparently, at Bromborough Court in May 1713. He became a Justice of the Peace for the County of Derby, Colonel of the 93rd Regiment of Infantry, MP for Tallagh, Co. Waterford, and Second in Command for some years of the East Indies. At the siege of l'Orient, in France, he lost a leg, and an eye in India where his constitution was shattered by the climate. He died on the 16th of August, 1762, and was buried in the chancel of Chapel-en-le-Frith church, on the 22nd of September following ...

This brief summary of the life and tribulations of Colonel Samuel Bagshawe forms the opening section of a 100-page biography by his descendant, W. H. G. Bagshawe, itself part of a much longer family history, *The Bagshawes of Ford*, published for private circulation as long ago as 1886. W. H. G's main purpose in writing the book was to reveal the hand of God at work in the lives of successive generations of Bagshawes (notable Derbyshire non-conformists), but he was a meticulous genealogist and a careful historian, bringing together at his ancestral home at Ford Hall not only many thousands of papers directly concerning the Bagshawes but also collections from families related to them, in particular, Samuel Bagshawe's in-laws, the Caldwells of Castle Caldwell, Co. Fermanagh.

At length, in 1950, the bulk of the Bagshawe Papers was deposited in the John Rylands University Library of Manchester (Deansgate) by Major F. E. G. Bagshawe. It was catalogued and listed by the then keeper of Manuscripts, Dr Frank Taylor, during 1953–55.

Although Samuel Bagshawe's papers are only a tiny part of the whole Bagshawe muniments, they still amount to over 3,500 items, ranging from military, family and estate correspondence to fragments of journals, regimental returns, muster rolls and accounts, wills and household and personal bills. It has only been possible to transcribe a small proportion of these documents, although many more are referred to in the introduction and commentaries. Yet more are transcribed, with spelling and punctuation modernized, in *The Bagshawes of Ford*, which, although very rare, remains essential reading for anyone interested in finding out more about the characters featured in this edition of the colonel's papers. The same is true of an important survey of the collection by James Hayes, 'The Military Papers of Colonel Samuel Bagshawe, 1713–1762', published in the *Bulletin of the John Rylands University Library of Manchester* in 1956–57.

It is a great pleasure for me to pay tribute at this point to the scholarship of Dr Taylor, Mr W. H. G. Bagshawe and Mr James Hayes, upon which this volume is based.

Samuel Bagshawe is not one of the resounding names of eighteenth century military history. He never served in Flanders, in Germany or North America. His plan to fight in Scotland during the '45 was thwarted, as he was too useful as a regimental administrator back at base. His service as a brigade major during the dismally conducted raid on Port l'Orient in 1746 was cut short when a cannon shot from the fortress shattered one of his legs. When Plassey was fought, he was homeward bound from India, totally blind in one eye and in danger of losing the other and his life into the bargain. It follows, therefore, that readers thirsting for glorious deeds and the rattle of musketry will be disappointed by much (though not all) of what follows. Rather, the unique strength of the Bagshawe papers lies in the close-in view they give of the less glamorous side of Georgian soldiering; the constant struggle to keep a unit 'fit for service' and in good administrative order, the ceaseless hunt for promotion and the problem of trying to keep up appearances on a less than adequate salary. The collection is also rich in the human comedy of regimental and domestic life, and the final choice and grouping of the letters owes much to a wish to make the most of this.

The great majority of the transcriptions have been made from documents in the John Rylands Library. Some important additional material has been taken from the Journal of Samuel Bagshawe's commanding officer in India, Colonel John Adlercron of the 39th Foot. This document, which is in the colonel's own hand, was part of a lot purchased at Sothebys on 24 July 1987 by the National Army Museum. One other document, Bagshawe's proposal to raise a regiment in 1759, has been transcribed from the Irish State Papers in the Public Record Office (Chancery Lane).

Every effort has been made in this edition of the Bagshawe Papers to reproduce the documents exactly as written, the result being that inconsistencies of spelling, punctuation, capitalization and sentence-structure abound. In my view, however, the style of the letters runs so close to the speech patterns of the correspondents (extending even to the Irish brogue of Lieutenant Francis Flood of the 93rd Foot in Part Three), that their distinctive appeal would be compromised by editorial interventions other than those absolutely necessary to aid understanding. In this connection, readers will note that the use of [sic] has been entirely avoided. Many of Colonel Bagshawe's letters survive only in draft form, and it was his custom to amend them up to three times on the same scrap of paper, variants of his first thoughts appearing above and below the line and in the margin. I have tried throughout to reconstruct the most cogent and colourful versions of his letters, the final forms of which will no doubt come to light from time to time, as they have in the Adlercron Journal. Most superscriptions have been left out, except where they are absolutely integral to the text or highlight the relationship between the correspondents. Substantial omissions are indicated by asterisks.

Many people and institutions have provided generous assistance in the preparation of this volume, in particular Mr M. C. Bagshawe. Two Directors of the National Army Museum, Mr William Reid and his successor, Mr Ian G. Robertson, have provided generous support to the project: excerpts from the Adlercron Journal appear by their kind permission. Dr Frank Taylor of the John Rylands Library introduced me to the Bagshawe papers more years ago than I care to remember and I am glad of this fresh opportunity to thank him for his kindness at that time. His successor as Keeper of Manuscripts, Miss Glenise Matheson, assisted by Miss Anne Young, ensured that not an instant of precious research time in Manchester was wasted. It has always been a delight to work in the wonderful Victorian 'gothick' library in Deansgate. Crown copyright material from the Public Record Office appears by kind permission of the Controller of Her Majesty's Stationery Office. I am, as ever, greatly in debt to the librarians and archivists of the Dorset Record Office, the British Library and the India Office Library and Records. Individual thanks for advice and support go first to my colleagues at the National Army Museum: Miss Liz Christie, Mrs Sylvia Hopkins, Miss Jenny Spencer-Smith and Dr Peter Boyden. My ill-written manuscript was painstakingly typed by Miss June Hicks, also of the National Army Museum. Important information from Ireland was provided by Mr John Cunningham of Belleek, Dr Ken Ferguson and Mr B. McKenna of the National Library of Ireland, Dublin. I am also grateful to Mr C. H. Gordon, Mr David Harding, Dr Tony Hayter, Dr Stephen Roberts, Dr Glenn Steppler, Dr Paul Thomas and Major-General Rex Whitworth for their advice and assistance. My dear wife Vivien and son Joe put up with my many long and inconvenient absences in Manchester during 1987; far too much time was spent with Samuel Bagshawe and his acquaintances that should have been spent with them. I owe them more than I can say. Two dear friends, John Clarke and Judy Sebba, opened their home to me in Manchester over a period of seven weeks. This book could not have been written without them, and to them it is dedicated.

Alan J. Guy
National Army Museum
August 1989

Introduction

1. Samuel Bagshawe's Army Review'd

The standing army that Samuel Bagshawe joined as a humble 'private centinel' in 1731 was still a relatively novel and unpopular feature of English life. As John, Lord Hervey, explained to the soldier-king George II in 1735, '... there is nothing so odious to men of all ranks and classes in this country as troops; that people who had not sense enough to count up to twenty, or to articulate ten words together on other subjects had their lessons so well to heart that they could talk like Ciceros on this topic, and never to an audience that did not chime in with their arguments.'[1]

The reasons for this state of affairs are not hard to find, for there was a basic dislike of professional military men and standing forces that predated even the Civil War.[2] In more recent times, enthusiasm for the great victories won by the Duke of Marlborough had all but evaporated, leaving only the memory of their huge human and financial cost. The alien and unpopular Hanoverian dynasty relied, in the final resort, on the bayonets of regular soldiers (candid politicians like Sir Robert Walpole admitted the fact). Hostile readings of the political scene merged with a 'country' ideology common to both sides of the Whig–Tory divide that viewed the relentless growth of the military machine during Queen Anne's War, and the opportunities this had given to ministers and courtiers to dispose of commissions and supply-contracts, with profound distaste. In town and country, the officers and men of the army, who were routinely obliged to play the unpopular roles of policemen or revenue officials, found themselves the target of criminal conspiracy or mob action, and this was as much the case in rural Hampshire as the turbulent city of Cork [15, 80]. Officership itself, despite its regular pay, honourable status and association with the sovereign, was tainted with the suspicion of peculation inseparable from proprietary command, and had only taken shape in career terms after 1697–98, when William III's government, unable to meet in full

I

debts owed to its officers, made much wider use of the institution of half-pay.[3]

The official reaction to this hostile climate was to trim military expenditure in time of peace to the lowest farthing, a policy which goes a long way to account for the massive career insecurity felt by Samuel Bagshawe and so many of his correspondents. For example, from 1743 to 1760, Bagshawe was an officer in the 39th Regiment of Foot, subsequently the Dorsetshire Regiment and one of the army's most senior and distinguished regiments of the line. Yet, it had escaped total disbandment in 1712–13 by only the narrowest of margins, and as the War of the Austrian Succession dragged to a close in 1748, some of its officers were predicting that the corps would either be broken or worse, in the light of its recent experience, converted to marines [48].[4]

The size of the army, and indeed the strength of individual units, varied dramatically throughout the period of Samuel Bagshawe's service, be it in response to wartime demands for manpower or the economic tyranny of peace. In 1715 for example, Parliament subsisted 15,851 officers and men in Britain itself, in the Mediterranean fortresses of Gibraltar and Minorca, in New York, Annapolis Royal (Nova Scotia), Placentia (Newfoundland), Bermuda, Jamaica and the Leeward Isles. During the 1730s, numbers stabilized around 26,000, rising to 76,516 at the height of the War of the Austrian Succession (1748). In the early 1750s the figure dropped back to just over 29,000 only to rise as high as 111,553 in the year of Bagshawe's death at the height of the Seven Years' War (1762). These fluctuations had a dramatic impact on the shape of the army and the job prospects of its officers, for even though numbers never fell to 1715 levels, it was at the back of everyone's mind that large-scale augmentations would inevitably be followed by massive reductions and it was a matter of overriding importance for a man to lever himself into permanent rank in an 'old corps' before the outbreak of peace.

Troop numbers stated so far take no account of 12,000 of His Majesty's '... natural born Subjects, commission and non-commission Officers' on the Irish establishment. Although the army in Ireland was maintained from Irish revenues and looked upon by Irish legislators as the bulwark of that country's defence, its main function was as a strategic reserve under the direction of the British Crown.[5] The 39th Foot was summoned from Ireland to England in 1744 and was kept on that Establishment until the Peace of Aix-la-Chapelle. In 1754 it was plucked from Cork and sent to the coast of Coromandel, the first royal regiment to be deployed in India.

The Irish Establishment of 12,000 had been fixed by the so-called 'Disbanding Act' of 1699 (10 William III, cap. 1), but in wartime this limit could be broken through; during 1756–57 Ireland supported an army of 17,000 and after a vote of credit in 1761, the Establishment climbed to 24,000 officers and men, including Bagshawe's own 'young corps', the 93rd Foot. Equally, when Irish units were transferred to the British Establishment, this could result in a dangerous shortage of trained men. In December 1745 there were under 7,000 effectives in Ireland, and when Commodore François Thurot raided Carrickfergus in February 1760 the defence of the whole of Ulster rested on four raw companies of the 62nd Foot with almost no ball ammunition [152].[6] In peacetime, at least, it was intended to buttress the minority Protestant interest in the sister kingdom by recruiting only English and Scottish Protestants. There were very few Irishmen in the 39th during Bagshawe's time in it,[7] and attempts to enlist them were frowned upon [12]. The restriction was relaxed in wartime (Bagshawe's 93rd was formed from Protestant Irishmen), but no Roman Catholics were taken until 1771.[8] Irishmen were to be found in large numbers in commissioned ranks at all times however. As Professor R. B. McDowell has commented, Irish Protestants were bred in what was still to some extent a frontier tradition. A commission carried social prestige, and as the Irish administration possessed a generous share of military patronage, particularly at the junior grades, it was relatively easy for a young gentleman with contacts to obtain an ensigncy or cornetcy in the rapidly expanding army. Several of the young men in Bagshawe's 93rd Foot were foisted on him by Dublin Castle and its influential hangers-on. It has been estimated that by mid-century, one in every four of His Majesty's commissioned officers was an Irishman.[9]

The army's standard administrative formation was the regiment, sub-divided into troops of horse and dragoons or companies of foot. As Samuel Bagshawe pursued his entire career in the infantry, from this point on the discussion will focus on the 'marching regiments' of foot – the line units that rotated through quarters at home or abroad, as distinct from the three regiments of Foot Guards based in the Metropolis and enjoying special conditions of service.

The marching foot made up by far the greatest part of the army at all times and experienced a much more demanding and unsettling pattern of service than their mounted brethren. Moreover, as Dr John Houlding has conclusively demonstrated, even to use terms like 'rotation' or 'pattern of service' before mid-century can be misleading. There was no regular system of reliefs even for the Mediterranean garrisons until 1749; an Empire-wide system did not begin until after the Seven Years' War. The 39th Foot was fortunate indeed when its expedition of 1731 against the insurgent negroes of Jamaica was terminated as early as March 1732,[10] for the 38th Foot languished in the Leeward Isles from 1716 to 1765. Even at home, regiments spent much of their time dispersed in company-strength and even smaller detachments, acting in aid of the revenue service or the civil power, or else strung out along lengthy lines of march, often wretchedly quartered in licensed premises amid a hostile populace. Small wonder that little could be attempted in the way of training other than basic arms drill. At first sight, conditions in Ireland were more auspicious: by 1740, many towns were well provided with barracks, while in any given year, half the foot was headquartered in Dublin and five other major garrisons: Galway, Limerick, Cork, Waterford and Kinsale, but service in the sister kingdom had its own disadvantages, as will be seen shortly.[11]

2. Regimental Organization

In the near total absence of any form of conscription, even during wartime,[12] army augmentations were based almost entirely on the regimental system and the semi-private enterprise of its recruiting officers. When men were needed, new units were raised, additional companies added to existing formations and the establishment of each company increased. During Samuel Bagshawe's time with the colours, the number of marching regiments climbed from 41 to as many as 126, many with more than one battalion. When peace returned the great majority of these 'young corps' were broken (Bagshawe's 93rd only survived him by a few months), and the companies of surviving units were reduced. Many of the surplus officers transferred to the half-pay list or sold out.

The wartime establishment of a battalion of foot comprised nine, ten or twelve companies each of 70 or 100 private men, two or three drummers, three or four corporals, three or four sergeants, an ensign, one or two lieutenants and a captain. In peacetime Britain, the rank and file were reduced to between 50 and 70 and in Ireland, where as many regiments as possible were packed on to the Establishment, to as few as 29 per company. These swingeing reductions went a long way towards off-setting the apparent training advantages offered in Ireland. However, units in Britain and Ireland retained as full a complement of commissioned officers as possible, to ensure that they could be quickly augmented by beat of drum in an emergency. The regimental structure was completed by topping and tailing it with field and staff officers.

In most instances, the senior field officer was a colonel proprietor. Some young corps 'raised for rank' during the Seven Years' War, as Bagshawe's 93rd Foot was, were headed by majors or lieutenant-colonels commandant,[13] but as Bagshawe was already a senior lieutenant-colonel by this time, he had a full colonelcy conferred upon him.[14] Many colonels were general officers, some of them of advanced age with shattered constitutions,[15] and they were rarely seen at regimental headquarters. Junior colonels appeared more frequently, and even led their men on active service, as John Adlercron did the 39th in 1754.[16] Absentee or not, however, the colonel was still seen as being '. . . at the head of a Family, and [you] are to do what you can to take care of it.'[17] It is possible that a number of the 39th's internal problems up until the appointment of Adlercron in 1752 can be traced to his predecessor Brigadier-General Edward Richbell's relative lack of interest in the corps. Adlercron's attempt to persuade Richbell to pay for deficiencies in the 39th's equipment involved Samuel Bagshawe in embarrassing correspondence with his old chief [71, 73, 75–77].

For much of the time, day-to-day command of a regiment devolved on the lieutenant-colonel, and according to Captain Samuel Bever of the 46th Foot, if he made good use of his authority he was virtually 'uncontroulable' and would be obeyed by officers and men alike '. . . with pleasure and resignation.'[18] In public and private correspondence, as in the case of Samuel Bagshawe who was the 39th's lieutenant-colonel from April 1749 to January 1760, it was the custom to refer to him as 'colonel', which can be confusing.

5

The lieutenant-colonel shared the burden of command with a third field officer, the major. It was the major's particular responsibility to drill the men and correct errors on parade, inspect the men's quarters and oversee the regiment's paperwork. Successive regulations for the attendance of officers insisted that either the lieutenant-colonel or the major should always be present at regimental headquarters, the implication being that one of them was often likely to be away. Lieutenant-Colonel Edward Windus and Major Robert Preston took it in turns to command the 93rd during Samuel Bagshawe's absences [190]. The lieutenant-colonel and the major were probably the most important influence on the management and general behaviour of a corps, and if one of them was a duffer, like poor 'tottering Major' Henry Fox of the 39th in the months leading up to his death in October 1747, there was little even the colonel could do about it. Accordingly, the first two Georges attached great importance to their field officers being men of service. Dr John Houlding has computed that in 1740 the lieutenant-colonels of foot had served an average of 27 years before attaining their present rank and majors 26 years. These figures, coming as they did at the end of a long peace, were exceptional, but even in 1759, with the Seven Years' War in full swing, the averages were still 13 and 17 years respectively.[19] So, although he often fretted over the failure of his schemes for preferment, Samuel Bagshawe's rise from second-lieutenant in General Bisset's 30th Foot in 1740 to lieutenant-colonel of the 39th in 1749 was relatively swift. (He had, of course, previously served seven years in the ranks.)

Captains of companies shouldered much of the burden of routine regimental administration. In fact, much of what is reckoned to be 'regimental history' in this period is in reality the achievement of this handful of men (including the field officers, who were captains in their own right). A captaincy was the first commissioned grade that offered a decent return on a man's investment of purchase money, labour and, not infrequently, blood. A captain's full pay per annum was £182. 10s. (plus dividends), but it was uncertain whether he would receive all of this. As in the case of the field officers, long service was the rule. In 1740, the captains of foot in Dr Houlding's sample had served an average of 19 years before getting their companies and in 1759 the figure was still as high as 10 years.[20] Once again, Bagshawe was ahead

of the pack, for the Duke of Devonshire obtained a captaincy for him
in just over two years from his first commission.

Even lieutenants often had years of service behind them before
attaining their present rank: as many as 11.5 years on average in 1740,
although this dropped to two years in 1759. During the 1730s, the
39th Foot became an exception to this general rule. The prospect of a
sickly campaign in Jamaica led to a flurry of sales and exchanges
among the captains and lieutenants, with the result that Houlding's
1740 sample reveals that the unit's ten lieutenants had obtained their
commissions after an average of only 3.5 years' service as ensigns (the
most junior commissioned grade), and that half the lieutenants had
served for only one year as ensigns before getting promotion.[21]

As mentioned, in addition to its field and company officers, each
regiment had its quota of staff officers. Some of them were specialists.
It was the chaplain's job to conduct divine service as prescribed in the
Articles of War, and undertake such tasks as schooling the regiment's
children, but the religious atmosphere of the Georgian army was
lukewarm – Bagshawe, a pious man, rarely refers to spiritual matters in
any formal sense – and the appointment was often nothing more than a
sinecure.[22] Regimental surgeons have received an equally unfavour-
able press; one recent commentator sees them as artisans rather than
scientists, out-ranked (and by implication despised) by every other
officer in the corps and indifferent to their patients' fate.[23] The 39th's
surgeon, William Kellett, was emphatically not of this breed; concern
for the men in his care radiates from his correspondence with Samuel
Bagshawe, and his methods, though terrifying to the modern reader,
were clearly up-to-date. He was well able to deal on equal terms with
the formidable Dr Andrew Munro, the East India Company's surgeon
at Fort St George, Madras [107, 116, 119]. Current research suggests
that there may have been many more like him.[24] The surgeon was
assisted by one or more surgeons' mates; the 39th took four mates to
the Coromandel coast in 1754 in anticipation of serious medical
problems.[25]

The remaining staff appointments – adjutant, quartermaster and
paymaster – were usually, though not invariably, held by subalterns in
addition to their company commissions. The adjutant was the major's
assistant; he superintended the drilling of the rank-and-file, particularly
the recruits [187], issued orders to the non-commissioned officers,

superintended punishments inflicted by regimental courts martial and took custody of the regimental books. His administrative burden could be considerable [41]. An adjutantcy was one of the few commissions considered appropriate for a man who had risen through the ranks. Joseph Kirkland, adjutant of Bagshawe's 93rd Foot, had been sergeant-major of the 39th.[26] The post of regimental quartermaster was also considered suitable for a senior sergeant. He took charge of regimental equipage, forage and rations, and when in garrison or quarters it was his responsibility to make sure that the men kept their billets in good condition. (There were no quartermasters in the regiments of foot on the Irish Establishment.) The status of the regimental paymaster was ambiguous, as he did not appear on the establishment. However, despite the fact that the paymaster was not a staff officer in the strictest sense of the term, he was indispensable.[27] He received money remitted to the corps by regimental agents in London or Dublin, negotiated with local tradesmen for credit or provisions and, within the unit, accounted with the captains and the proprietary colonel. By the custom of the army, the appointment was a regimental affair, as the paymaster was nominated by the captains, who then became responsible for any default. The colonel participated as captain of his own company, though it is hard to imagine the captains combining against their commander's nominee [90]. The duty was so vital that it was not uncommon to find captains and even field officers doing it; Samuel Bagshawe took on the paymastership of the 39th as a captain in April 1744 [13], and shared day-to-day responsibility with Lieutenant Archibald, 'Archy', Grant. Captain Francis Forde was appointed paymaster when the 39th sailed for India in 1754 and continued to do the job as major. Unfortunately, he proved to be a very negligent accountant [141]. Even a man who tackled the business diligently could end up a loser, as Bagshawe did in 1751.[28]

3. Proprietary Command

Samuel Bagshawe's pecuniary embarrassments, which lasted throughout his life and beyond, were inseparably tied to the institution of proprietary command. Attempts to explain this system make use of the handy metaphor of the regiment as a commercial enterprise. The officers, it is maintained, made their down payment by purchasing commissions. In return, they received regular pay in proportion to their investment, which was equivalent to the purchase of stock. At the proprietary grades of captain and colonel, officers pocketed dividends from the management of regimental funds in their care. By the time Bagshawe obtained command of the 93rd Foot however, the 'custom of the army' in this area had been severely dented by royal edict and a new attitude to public service, a trend which would be reinforced by the disastrous War of American Independence.[29] Captains' dividends from managing the 'non-effective' money of men vacant in their companies became strictly limited, while the profits made by proprietary colonels from clothing the men, appointing regimental agents and disposing of the occasional commission escaped relatively unscathed. It was Bagshawe's misfortune that neither he nor his regiment lasted long enough to take much advantage of this latter situation.[30] It is doubtful, in any case, whether the mercenary and speculative aspects of command below the rank of colonel had ever amounted to much in recent years. A hand-to-mouth system of regimental finance that relied shamelessly on the personal credit of individuals (from the Paymaster General down), whilst turning a blind eye to paroxysms of profit-taking on those rare occasions when there was a surplus in the regimental kitty, might have been tolerated in the peacetime army of the later Stuarts, but was hardly suited to an era of world wars. When William III failed to take the opportunity to reform the regimental economy presented by the collapse of the British Army in 1688–89, he condemned future captains to an existence in which debt would figure much more prominently than pickings.[31] For, in its habitual desire to conceal the true cost of the military establishment from the eye of Parliament, government continued to rely on the autonomous regimental structure to recruit, supply, clothe and equip large numbers of men – hazardous activities all, as Samuel Bagshawe and his colleagues were to discover.

The War Office in London was a minuscule organization at this period, and little help was available to regimental officers in what James Hayes has called the 'war of paperasserie and procedure' inseparable from proprietary command, other than that provided by the regimental agents.[32] Based in London or Dublin (for regiments in Ireland needed a separate agent on that Establishment), agents attended the War and Pay Offices, or, in Ireland, the offices of the

Chief Secretary and the Muster Master and Clerk of the Cheque, to resolve administrative problems and receive funds. Civilian servants of the proprietary colonels, they lobbied politicians, senior officers and civil servants on their patrons' behalf, remitted money to the corps and made up accounts in close consultation with the paymasters. They also dealt with regimental clothiers, accoutrement makers, sword cutlers, gunsmiths, insurers, carriers and other contractors. In addition to all this 'official' business, agents acted for the colonels and regimental officers in numerous private banking and speculative ventures, ranging from the purchase of commissions to lottery tickets and, in the best-organized firms, provided them, their patrons, friends and kinsfolk with a political and military information service. Some officers had taken up the profession of army agent. Samuel Bagshawe had dealings with several of them, notably Captain Theophilus Desbrisay of Cork Hill, Dublin and, in particular, Captain Thomas Levett of Warwick Street, Golden Square, London. Bagshawe first became acquainted with Levett in 1744, when the agent instructed him in the alarming intricacies of regimental paymastership [14]. Their business relation-ship blossomed into a friendship (Levett regularly put Bagshawe up on his visits to town), which even survived great difficulties over clearing the 39th's accounts after the War of the Austrian Succession, when both men sustained losses [59, 61, 62]. After 1721, when officers holding agencies were ordered to choose between them and their combat commissions, a young man intending to make a career in agency had to acquire the necessary expertise in one of the government offices, as secretary to a senior officer or as a clerk in an established firm. Bagshawe came into regular contact with the most important of these 'new men', John Calcraft of Channel Row, whom Colonel Adlercron appointed agent of the 39th in 1754. Under the patronage of Henry Fox (Secretary at War and Paymaster General), Calcraft built up an agency empire of over 60 regiments during the Seven Years' War. His letters to Bagshawe, particularly during 1758, when he was expecting his client to be given a colonelcy, give a good impression of his business methods. He could bring powerful influences to bear; Adlercron was probably bounced by Fox into appointing him.[33] Bagshawe, another potential colonel with little 'interest' of his own, was obliged to conform to the advice of his patrons, the Cavendish family and Sir Robert Wilmot,

long-time London secretary to successive Lords Lieutenant of Ireland
[126–29].[34]

4. Officers

In Samuel Bagshawe's time there were next to no opportunities for a
young man aspiring to a commission in the line to acquire a formal
military education in Great Britain; equally, the postulant did not have
to trouble his head about entrance qualifications. Moreover, although
this was at variance with trends in the other great professions, the law,
medicine, the ministry (and even the Royal Navy), it can be argued that
this did not matter a great deal. Weapons-systems were simple, drill
and tactics (at the level most officers were expected to carry them out)
were elementary, military accounting could only be learnt on duty and,
as long as officers were gentlemen or near imitations, there was no
need to study 'leadership.' The army's battlefield record was far from
discreditable; it did not disgrace the British name even alongside the
formidable regiments of Frederick the Great. Occasional disasters in
the field were not so much due to defects in the officers and men as to
a general lack of preparedness inherent in the way the army's
component parts were managed in peacetime, a factor which Dr John
Houlding has aptly termed 'the friction of peace'.[35]

A tradition of 'on-the-job' training, combined with the ethos of
long-service discussed earlier, resulted in an army of workaday officers
rather than military geniuses. Bagshawe considered that he had
studied his profession assiduously [113], but his military library at
Ford Hall contained only a few conventional titles, and the training he
valued most was acquired with the regiment.[36] He became increasingly
agitated when fate denied him opportunities to expand his military
education on active service [18, 113, 134].

James Hayes's London MA thesis of 1956 and a number of articles
derived from it still provide the starting points for any discussion of the
social background of early-Georgian officers.[37] It was a principle of
British public life that the best places in the military hierarchy were
reserved for men of birth and fortune. As Henry Pelham argued in 1744:

'I have always heard it admitted that our liberties can never be in
danger as long as they are entrusted to men of family and fortune,

and the reason is obvious as well as unanswerable. The security of property must always depend on the preservation of liberty. Under a despotic government there is neither property nor liberty, for every man's estate, as well as his life, depends upon the rapine of an arbitrary sovereign. Has not then a man of fortune more reason to avoid such a melancholy predicament than a man of no estate? Has it not always been with good reason urged that our liberties are in no danger from our standing army because it is commanded by men of the best families and fortunes?'[38]

This understanding of the potential threat posed by a standing army, together with a requirement to make use of it as an instrument of social control, ensured that those who dominated society in peacetime would lead the king's troops to war.[39] Peers of the realm, Members of Parliament and their close connexions clustered thickly in the upper ranks, as general officers, garrison governors and colonels of regiments. The majority of officers, lacking this group's superior patronage leverage, would be fortunate to progress beyond the rank of lieutenant-colonel. This group, which by the time of the Seven Years' War included representatives of families that had supplied the army with officers over several generations, comprised men from the middle ranks of society (sometimes cadets of good families that had branched out into trade and commerce), sons of the clergy, descendants of Huguenot refugees, a growing number of Scotsmen and Irishmen and a contingent of former non-commissioned officers. These officers lived with their battalions and, by dint of conscientious service, forged a formidable war machine. Compared with many of them, Samuel Bagshawe's status was advantageous, as might be inferred from his initially rapid promotion rate. He was heir to a Derbyshire gentleman with an estate valued at nearly £500 per annum. The powerful Cavendish clan, which was indebted to the Bagshawes for political services in Derbyshire, helped Samuel to three commissions gratis and, in later life, gave him a seat in the Irish Parliament. He married into an Irish gentry family, the Caldwells of Castle Caldwell, Co. Fermanagh, and eventually raised a regiment at his own expense. The reader should remind himself of these facts from time to time in order to counterpoint the note of gloom that resounds through so many of the letters in this collection.

Bagshawe's mixture of promotion by gift or by purchase (he was obliged to buy his lieutenant-colonelcy in the 39th in 1749 and effectively paid for his colonelcy in 1760 by levying the 93rd), was typical of the career pattern of many officers. Purchase vacancies arose when an officer sold out of the army or bought promotion in the regiment or outside. A free market in commissions had long ceased to exist. George I, who disapproved of the whole practice, had even managed to impose a tariff in 1720, and an officer was usually obliged to offer his commission to the man with the most seniority in the rank immediately beneath. If that man lacked either the funds or the desire to buy, the commission was offered to the next senior and so on. The purchaser got the rank, but not the seniority, becoming the most junior officer in his new grade for the time being. When a captain sold his commission a chain reaction began which could reach down to the youngest ensign and out into civilian life, where young gentlemen were queueing to join the army. These frequent and protracted negotiations were very unsettling for a regiment and its officers and contributed a great deal to men's sense of insecurity [18, 198]. The departing officer's purse was made up of the sum of the difference between one rank and the next [9]. Despite the existence of a tariff, there was a wide variation in the price of commissions. An old corps based at home was by far the most attractive proposition and priced accordingly, while a commission in a young corps like the 93rd, approaching the end of a war, was distinctly less attractive. Moreover, officers' continuing ability to influence the choice of their successors, even in the teeth of royal opposition, meant that payments on the side might be asked for [87–89]. It was often necessary to adjust prices on a regimental basis, subject to the colonel's approval [177]. These transactions were handled by the regimental agent in his capacity as banker to the officers.

Perhaps as many as one-third of vacancies however were filled without purchase. These were often death vacancies, in peacetime as well as on active service, when regimental seniority came into play, subject to the approval of the colonel and, ultimately, His Majesty. Sometimes, it was thought necessary to bring in an outsider, as when Matthews Sewell was commissioned major of the 39th in 1747 from the half-pay list. Junior commissions were often given without purchase. Samuel Bagshawe's first commissions were a gift from the

3rd Duke of Devonshire in his capacity as Lord Lieutenant of Ireland. This was also the case with many of what would now be called 'staff' appointments like Bagshawe's commission as major-of-brigade in the L'Orient expedition of 1746. In theory, what had not been purchased could not be sold, with the result that an officer's retirement to the half-pay list created new opportunities for promotion without purchase, as happened in a shake-out of superannuated officers in the 39th prior to the expedition to Indi1754.[40]

Peers and commoners rubbed shoulders in the regimental messes of Samuel Bagshawe's army without the snobbery of later decades. Even if a man was not initially a member of polite society, his commission gave him entry to it. Bagshawe's mess-mates in the 39th included the Hon. John Sempill (who became 12th Lord Sempill in 1746), and Rowland Lewis, whose brother was an apothecary on Tower Hill. Officers of the Guards sometimes indulged in an embryonic caste superiority at the expense of their brethren in the marching regiments (who responded by accusing them of shirking service), but there were as yet no 'crack' regiments in the army. Merit and service were valued more than wealth and ostentation, although by the time of Bagshawe's death the arrival of a new and much less engaging breed of officer was heralded by Lieutenant Francis Flood of the 93rd [201].[41]

Nonetheless, there existed in the army an obsessive concern with the aristocratic virtues of 'honour' and 'behaviour', which was frequently at odds with the printed *Articles of War* and turned the military condition into something like an endlessly prolonged initiation rite.[42] Samuel Bagshawe's life was untainted by the worst feature of the honour code and its alleged violations – the duel; indeed, the only reference to duelling discovered in the collection is Lieutenant William Dawkin's threat to cut Matthews Sewell's throat unless he treated him in a more gentlemanly manner [47]. But Bagshawe was constantly troubled by a fear that he might be seen to have 'misbehaved' in some way, attributing his failure to obtain a lucrative field command in India or lead the 93rd on active service to some hostile judgment on his character and capacity [36, 46, 89, 121, 189]. His stock response was to take advantage of the small size of the officer corps (there were only two or three hundred field officers), by submitting a formal memorial to the King, the Lords Justices of Ireland and, on one occasion, the East India Company's president and council at Fort St.

George, Madras [115, 140, 173]. In each case, he begged for some public acknowledgment of his pretensions that would re-affirm his status in the military world. Otherwise, the implication was that he would quit the service, and he certainly pondered this option more than once after inheriting Ford Hall in November 1756.

In fact, Bagshawe remained in the service until the end of his life. His action in raising the 93rd out of his own pocket after failing to obtain a colonelcy by seniority represents a renewed commitment to it, but in his initial reaction to an implied slur he was typical of his day. Convinced of their individual merit, British officers did not hesitate to call the actions of their commanders into question and quibble at their orders. They even went so far as to criticise the behaviour of the King whose red coat they wore so proudly.[43] Worse perhaps, their often insufferable sense of exclusiveness led to pointless clashes with people they were supposed to co-operate with. These included naval officers [39, 42], colonial Americans[44] and the 'meer Merchants' of the Honourable East India Company.[45]. It was a failure to appreciate the needs and interests of the latter group that caused Samuel Bagshawe and the officers of the 39th so many problems during their Indian expedition of 1754–58.

5. Rank-and-File

In recent years, the attention of scholars has shifted somewhat away from the army's officers towards the lower ranks and their women and children. It was once thought, by this writer among others, that sheer lack of information would make it difficult to reconstruct the lives of these hitherto neglected people. Happily, the problem seems to be more one of digesting and arranging the large amount of evidence actually available, although it must be admitted that much of what has been presented so far is drawn from the decades after 1760.[46]

It is all the more interesting in the light of this scholarly endeavour to discover that the rank-and-file only really figure in the Bagshawe Papers as commodities, to be recruited, drilled, managed, disposed of when worn out or reluctantly drafted into other units. There is scant justification here for Dr Sylvia Frey's wistful characterization of the regiment as a brotherhood of men.[47] The 39th's cat-of-nine-tails may well have been kept 'in terrorem' rather than for use [64], but

Bagshawe's common-sense view of the men under his command was that only those officers who treated them with severity were likely to be well served [38]. Bagshawe had shouldered a musket in Gibraltar for seven melancholy years, so we should credit him with knowing what he was talking about.

Even some of Bagshawe's non-commissioned officers seem little better than naughty children, not to be trusted out of their officers' sight [45]. One of them, Sergeant Macartney of Captain Francis Forde's company in the 39th, absconded with the company funds [64]. Other n.c.o.s were simply unfit for the trust reposed in them, although when they were reduced to the ranks it could be a ticklish business replacing them [187, 196]. As for the soldiers' families, Bagshawe lamented the fate of women and children abandoned in Cork when the 39th embarked for India [92], but not long previously the captains had agreed to suspend allowances to the wives of men serving as marines, lest they should lose money themselves by the men dying at sea.[48] Dr Paul Kopperman has suggested that there was a high stability rate in these legal or common-law unions,[49] but the prevailing view of the regiment's womenfolk seems to have been that of Captain George Symes of the 39th, who dismissed them all as 'strumpets' [56].

Such callousness must have been a product of the exigencies of wartime service, which overshadowed much of Bagshawe's career. In the absence of any centrally-organized recruiting service or depot system, successful recruiting depended on the individual officer's local connexions and huckstering ability, a situation which Bagshawe seems to have found distasteful as it frequently obliged '... the Officers to take such Advantage of Young Fellows as are contrary to their Inclinations and Disposition.'[50]

The underlying motive for many enlistments seems to have been economic, although at this period it was probably not so much the collapse of traditional employments suggested by Dr Frey that drove men to the colours as the condition of 'underemployment' analysed by Dr Glenn Steppler.[51] Other, totally unquantifiable, influences were also at work, for the pool of unemployed was invariably greater than the number of regimental vacancies, yet at no time were the units up to establishment.[52] The truth was, that going for a soldier appealed to the kind of men who wanted to liberate themselves from dull routine or escape from some intolerable domestic situation. Samuel Bagshawe's own enlistment came about as the result of some ultimately unknowable personal crisis. It was the job of the recruiting officer and his small party (a sergeant and a drummer), to buttonhole these likely lads amid the bustle of a fair, market day or a public holiday, persuade them to join up and bring their friends. This was demanding and potentially ruinous work, for the last word on the acceptability of any recruit rested with the field officers at regimental headquarters [69, 70].[53]

When competition for recruits was intense (and it never seems to have been entirely slack), officers were tempted to lower physical, and their own moral, standards. Some very inferior recruits indeed were taken during the Seven Years' War, especially from 1759 onwards. Even the high-minded field officers of Bagshawe's 93rd seem to have fallen away from the ideal [150, 196]. Such a state of affairs had a corrupting influence on the officers' attitude to the men under their command.[54]

Constant recourse to drafting added to the uncertainties of regimental life. When units already on active service were badly under strength, or when it became necessary to augment a regiment quickly as it transferred from the Irish to the British Establishment, the authorities seized control of effective men as required, regardless of the impression this made on the officers who had gone to all the trouble and expense of raising them. Samuel Bagshawe's 93rd Foot was drafted three times in this way, and on the final occasion, it was almost wiped out [189]. Young regiments were especially liable to be hit, but old corps were not exempt. For example, 200 men were drafted from the 39th and other Irish units for service in Flanders in 1744.[55] Once men were drafted, the tedious business of recruiting and basic training had to begin all over again, with no certainty as to when, or to what extent, the value of the drafts would be refunded [173].[56]

The end result of this method of managing the army's rank-and-file was one in which regiments were often chronically under strength and suffering from too high a turnover of men, at the same time having too great a proportion of recruits under arms to be considered 'fit for service'.[57] To find a unit in peak condition like the 39th in 1754 was comparatively unusual. As it was, the expedition to the East

Indies ended by destroying it as a fighting force for a considerable time.[58]

6. The Irish Dimension

In an article in the inaugural number of *The Irish Sword* (1949), Major S. H. F. Johnston called for research in public and private archives in Britain and Ireland that would help fill the massive lacuna in military studies created by the destruction of the Public Record Office in Dublin in 1922.[59] Thanks to the efforts of devoted scholars like Dr Kenneth Ferguson and Dr John Houlding, a great deal has come to light since that time,[60] but this has in no way diminished the significance of the Bagshawe Papers for an understanding of Irish military affairs in the mid-eighteenth century.[61] Samuel Bagshawe's numerous official and private connexions with the sister kingdom have already been mentioned, and many of the letters and papers which follow have been chosen to highlight the 'Irish dimension' of army life.

The two most important issues in a study of the British army in Ireland at this period are its relationship to the Roman Catholic population and its general standard of efficiency.

Although by 1760 there were powerful intimations of agrarian troubles to come,[62] rural Ireland was quiet for much of Bagshawe's lifetime, and this helped soften appearances to the extent that Dr Francis Godwin James concluded that the country did not constitute 'occupied territory'. Elsewhere however, he was compelled to admit that '... in the last analysis the Irish state in the early-eighteenth century rested upon British military power.'[63]

Samuel Bagshawe would certainly have agreed. 'The common people of this Country', he declared, 'are naturally fond of times of Confusion because they have an Oppertunity of indulging some favourite appetites among such as Thieving and Cruelty; and if it were not that they stand in Awe of a Sett of Folks in my Neighbourhood We should have had some Instance of both, but We use so little Ceremony with 'em that they do not have any Disputes [where] We are concerned.'[64]

The soldiers knew that the Protestant community outside Ulster had '... no Pretensions to any Property they may enjoy, but what they received from Military Power', and expected a fraternal reception in

Protestant settlements, which, we may be sure, they did not always get.[65] Popish influence was deplored, all the more so if it in any way touched on the interest of the army [74]. Bagshawe's experiences in the Cork riots of 1753 have a depressingly modern ring [80], and it was perhaps fortunate for the reputation of British military power that the only French attack on Ireland in the period was Commodore Thurot's small-scale raid on Carrickfergus in 1760 [152]. As an infantryman, Bagshawe would have seen rather less of Ireland's wild side than his brother-in-law Sir James Caldwell who, as captain-commandant of the 20th Light Dragoons, the 'Enniskillen Light Horse', led his Ulstermen against the 'Whiteboys' of Tipperary and the illegal distilleries of Connacht, but he would have been under no misconceptions about it other than those inseparable from his nationality, his Presbyterian heritage and the King's commission he held.[66]

During 1749–50, word reached the ears of the Duke of Cumberland, Captain General of the army, that things were far from well in some of the regiments quartered in Ireland. The stories came from a trusted subordinate, but there was little the Duke could do, for though he was all-powerful at Horse Guards he held no command in Ireland and the Secretary at War was equally powerless [57]. Ireland was the military province of the 'Lord Lieutenant General and General Governor of Ireland', and to assist him in the ordering of the 12,000 officers and men under his command he had a generously-proportioned army staff, a Chief Secretary and a Muster Office.

It was doubtless necessary for the Lord Lieutenant to enjoy a large measure of military autonomy, but this being the case, it was unfortunate that the viceroys of the period lacked military experience. Grandees and politicians that they were, they tended to keep at least one eye on English developments, and until the arrival of Major-General George, Viscount Townshend, as Lord Lieutenant in 1767, they showed little interest in the finer detail of military business other than the patronage aspect. With the notable exception of Lord George Sackville, chief secretary to his father, the Duke of Dorset, from 1750 to 1755, the chief secretaries were similarly ill-equipped. It was all the more disturbing therefore that serious doubts existed about the capabilities of the Irish staff, and about the disposal of commissions and the quartering of the troops which, it was believed, were unduly influenced by political considerations.[67]

Samuel Bagshawe's connexions with the vice-regal court were close. His career had been launched there as a young officer with an appointment as 'gentleman at large' in the household of William, 3rd Duke of Devonshire. In later years, as a field officer on the Establishment, he was often obliged to visit the capital and was on familiar terms with the Dublin Castle bureaucrats. Latterly, as a relation of the Caldwells, colonel of an Irish regiment and M.P. for an Irish borough, he occupied a place close to the centre of affairs. So, his silence (and that of his correspondents), on the 'efficiency question', though not conclusive, is somewhat reassuring for the period spanned by these letters. And, if Bagshawe's horizons seem limited to the regiments under his direct control, this was entirely in keeping with his understanding of the fundamentals of officership and professional education. With his help, John Adlercron had rebuilt the 39th during 1752–54, and he would win renown by repeating the job in 1758–59, regardless of any alleged shortcomings in the Irish high command.

I
1713–1753

'I go abroad ... with great Advantages'

The Bagshawes are '... amongst the oldest families in Derbyshire, where they have possessed property from time immemorial'.[1] The family seat of Ford Hall, near Chapel-en-le-Frith, a township '... seated in a deep valley, on the road between Manchester and Sheffield, completely surrounded by barren and lofty mountains',[2] was acquired early in the seventeenth century by William Bagshawe of Hucklow and Litton (1598–1669). He was the father of William Bagshawe, 'the Apostle of the Peak' (1628–1702), 'nobilissimus in the Bagshawe pedigree.'[3] Educated at county schools and Corpus Christi, Cambridge, this young man became a preacher of the gospel in opposition to the wishes of his family, and was partially disinherited as a result. Ordained after the Presbyterian manner at Chesterfield in 1651, he was appointed vicar of Glossop the following year. Ejected from his living as a result of the Act of Uniformity (1662), he retired to his father's home at Ford, but continued to preach '... both at his own house, and from house to house.' This Dissenting tradition was to endure for several generations; Colonel Bagshawe's eldest surviving son, Samuel (1753–1804), seems to have been the first member of his family to rejoin the Church of England.[4]

The 'Apostle of the Peak' was a '... decided though not an extreme Calvinist', and whilst hostile to '... the blasphemous fables of Romanism' was politically cautious. He ministered to several Presbyterian congregations in the area, but continued to attend the parish church at Chapel. He took advantage of James II's Declaration of Indulgence and discouraged his acquaintances from having anything to do with Monmouth's Rebellion (1685). On his death, the ownership of Ford passed to his second and only surviving son, Samuel Bagshawe (1656–1706), who had the reputation of being '... an accomplished gentleman, a good scholar, a pious Christian and a true Englishman, yet possessing a temper '... somewhat inclined to passion, but it was quickly gone and left no impression of malice ...[5]

Piety and passion were very much the distinguishing traits of Samuel's successor at Ford, his eldest son William Bagshawe (1686–1756), Colonel Bagshawe's uncle and guardian. William spent his whole life at Ford, '... surrounded by spiritual advantages of no ordinary kind' but, as his biographer reluctantly admitted, although he was '... a God-fearing man ... his temper was warm, and there is much reason to doubt whether he ever attained to that spirituality of mind which was so conspicuous in his predecessors.'[6] He was supposed to have made two promises to his father: never to borrow money from any one, nor to be a surety to any one, and never to lend that which he could not afford to give. William's interpretation of these precepts was to involve his nephew in many difficulties, but the uncle's prejudices could only have been reinforced by the behaviour of his brother, Colonel Bagshawe's father. Samuel Bagshawe (1689–1712) had the reputation of being '... a very sensible, serious young man, public spirited [and] active for God', but his disastrous losses in shipping ventures included a large sum lent by William.[7] Samuel died in 1712 leaving a widow, Frances, a daughter of John Hardwar of Bromborough Court, Cheshire and an infant daughter, Frances (c1712–c1784). His son, Samuel, was born posthumously at Bromborough Court in May 1713. The little girl was brought up by her Hardwar relations; William Bagshawe of Ford took responsibility for the boy.

The lives of William and his nephew were bound up with the fortunes of the local Whig magnates, the Cavendish family, in particular William, 3rd Duke of Devonshire (c1698–1755), and his son, William, Marquess of Hartington and 4th Duke (c1720–64). William Bagshawe was a frequent guest at the family's great house, Chatsworth, '... a palace fit for a prince, a most magnificent building'[8] and feasted his patron on venison from the deer park at Ford. He admired the Cavendishes for their part in bringing about the 'Glorious Revolution', and for their staunch support of the Hanoverian Succession, and he campaigned on their behalf against the rival Tory magnates, the Curzons. During the 1734 general election, when the county was divided between the two families, he rode to the hustings with a retinue of 800 to vote for Lord Charles Cavendish, the Duke's third son.[9] As Dr Johnson later remarked, the 3rd Duke of Devonshire

'... was not a man of superior abilities, but he was a man strictly faithful to his word. If, for instance, he had promised you an acorn, and none had grown that year in his woods, he would not have contented himself with that excuse; he would have sent to Denmark for it. So unconditional was he in keeping his word; so high as to the point of honour'.[10] He was thus unfailingly obliging to William Bagshawe, who, for a choleric man, seems to have steered a middle course between his patron's interests and the importunate demands of the gentlemen freeholders, whose spokesman he had become, with considerable skill.[11] In time, the ducal favour was to be extended to William's nephew.

That young man, meanwhile, seemed hell-bent on ruining his prospects. His uncle had sent him first to a school in Knutsford and subsequently (October 1729), to read with a Mr William Ingram of Wakefield. Here he fell into extravagant habits and, after receiving a number of reproofs, left Mr Ingram's house on the afternoon of Thursday 13 May 1731, never to return. Day after day passed in anxious suspense, until it came to light that he had enlisted as a private soldier in Colonel Philip Anstruther's regiment, the 26th Foot (the Cameronians), then based at Gibraltar. Nothing could divert him from his purpose, and he left England for what proved to be an exile of seven years.

Bagshawe made good use of his time in Gibraltar, rising to the grade of quartermaster-sergeant. Indeed, he was so useful that his captain, Adam Ferguson, was very reluctant to let him go, until the officer commanding, Major the Hon. William St. Clair, paid over the odds to transfer him into his company [4]. Bagshawe seems to have made one close friend in Gibraltar, Thomas Rothwell, a private soldier in the 26th, later a sergeant in the 39th,[12] but he hated life in the ranks and was often sick and melancholy, a common fate in that isolated garrison.[13] Protracted negotiations were required, involving his uncle, his cousin, Richard Bagshawe of Castleton in the Peak, Richard's son William Bagshawe of the Inner Temple and Sir Peter Davenport, a deputy commissary of the musters,[14] before Samuel could be redeemed from St. Clair's successor, Major William Hooke [5]. He arrived in London on 22 June 1738 and reached Ford a few days later.[15]

Bagshawe remained at Ford for two years, '... enjoying the privileges of a well-ordered home and faithful ministry of the gospel'.[16] His private journal of this period, excerpts from which were published by his biographer, sounds a note of religious exaltation: 'May it please God to create in me a clean heart and to renew a right spirit within me' … 'O Lord, enable me to bear all my afflictions in a becoming manner, they are far less than the multitude of my sins deserve', etc, sentiments very much in accordance with the spiritual legacy of the 'Apostle of the Peak.'[17] Although he remained a stickler for Sabbath day observance,[18] he professed in later life a quieter faith in 'Providence' or 'the Supreme Being'[19] and does not appear to have been offended by the saltier jests of correspondents like Lieutenant-Colonel Windus of the 93rd [164].

In January 1740, the 3rd Duke of Devonshire, in his capacity as Lord Lieutenant of Ireland, obtained for Samuel a second-lieutenant's commission in Colonel Andrew Bissett's 30th Foot on that Establishment.[20] Despite legislation barring Dissenters from public appointments, his Presbyterian affiliations did not affect the nomination in any way. He crossed to Ireland in April and, after presentation at the vice-regal court, joined his regiment in Limerick, where he began to study French.

In March 1741 the powerful interest of the Lord Lieutenant was exerted in his favour once again, when he was promoted over the heads of many other officers to a lieutenancy in the 1st Foot (the Royal Scots), commanded by the formidable Major-General the Hon. James St. Clair.[21] St. Clair was less than pleased at having the young man foisted on him. The story goes that he accosted Colonel William Degge, a Derbyshire neighbour of the Bagshawes, and demanded, 'Dee ye ken a chiel called Bawgsha? The Duke of Devonshire has put him in my reegment, and they say he has lived in law leefe'. 'I know him well,' retorted the colonel, 'and he was in low life if you consider it low life to be a private soldier,' (St. Clair himself was supposed once to have been in the ranks), 'but I can tell you he is of as good a family as any in all Scotland, and I can tell you more, he rose to be a serjeant major (or something like that), in a Scotch regiment; and an Englishman, you know, must behave tolerably well to be taken notice of in a Scotch regiment.'[22]

After narrowly escaping selection for a campaign in the West Indies [8], the office of 'gentleman at large' in the Lord Lieutenant's household was conferred on Bagshawe in November 1741. This 'place of no profitt', he informed his uncle, 'only procures a Man the liberty to appear often at Court and of improving himself.'[23] Despite his disclaimers to his aunt Mary [10], he led an active social life in Dublin, socialising with Anglican divines and society beauties alike, attending plays and recitals, lounging in fashionable haunts like Lucas's Coffee House and exercising daily in the riding house.[24]

In April 1742, Bagshawe travelled to London in search of preferment. Although large-scale augmentations were in progress, captaincies were still priced at £1,500,[25] but Devonshire intervened once more to get him a company in Colonel John Battereau's young corps (the 62nd Foot), without purchase.[26] In April 1743, the Duke arranged his transfer to an old corps on the Irish Establishment, the 39th Foot, then commanded by Colonel Samuel Whitshed.[27] Whitshed was soon afterwards succeeded by Colonel Edward Richbell. Richbell did not prove to be an ideal proprietor of a regiment, but he soon formed a high opinion of Bagshawe and did what he could to help his career. By November 1743, Bagshawe was captain of the regiment's élite grenadier company[28] and was looking forward to a spring campaign in Flanders.

Bagshawe's new regiment had endured a rather chequered history since it was first raised in 1702, and this state of affairs was to continue throughout his 17 years with it. After five years' garrison duty in Ireland, it had served in Portugal and Spain during the War of the Spanish succession, but only fought in one major action, Campo Mayor (1709), when its colonel was taken prisoner. Posted to Minorca in 1713, it had its first taste of sea-service aboard Admiral Sir George Byng's fleet at the battle of Cape Passaro (1718), returning to Ireland the following year. Shipped out once more to the Mediterranean at the beginning of 1727, it formed part of the Gibraltar garrison during the Spanish siege of that year. Its next campaign, against the insurgent negroes of Jamaica (1730–32), was a much more hazardous affair. It lost one-third of its strength in six months and only 100 rank-and-file came home to Ireland in May 1732. The regiment was to remain in that kingdom until March 1744.[29]

As it turned out, Samuel Bagshawe's baptism of fire was delayed for two years. Orders for the 39th to proceed to Ostend were countermanded, and he was so useful as regimental paymaster that his request to go north as a volunteer to fight against the Highland rebels was refused.[30] (Prince Charles Edward's army passed within a couple of miles of Ford during its retreat from Derby. William Bagshawe, who had been helping Devonshire organize the defence of the county, was obliged to bury his valuables and keep horses saddled for instant flight.)[31]

For Samuel, police actions against straggling seamen in Hampshire or the notorious Hawkhurst gang of Sussex smugglers[32] were poor substitutes for real soldiering. He began to worry about losing ground in his profession, a concern that was to recur with increasing urgency as he grew older. He also suffered the first serious check to his promotion when a scheme to purchase the 39th's majority fell through, despite the fact that the Duke of Devonshire had persuaded the reluctant William Bagshawe to part with the bulk of the asking price [16–18]. At length however, in March 1746, Richbell obtained for him an appointment as major of brigade (at ten shillings per diem), in a projected expedition against Quebec under the command of Lieutenant-General James St. Clair, his former colonel in the Royal Scots.[33]

The expedition's departure was delayed beyond the time that it was considered safe to risk ships on the coast of North America, so in order that the preparations might not be wholly useless, it was decided to launch it against the Breton port of L'Orient, arsenal of the *Compagnie des Indes*. The fleet, carrying about 8,000 troops, sailed from Plymouth on 14 September 1746 and came to anchor a few leagues from L'Orient on 19 September. Disembarkation began the following day.

On 21 September, the advance on L'Orient began. The French had been taken completely by surprise, but the peasantry and militia sniped at the British from the hedgerows and thickets lining their route, and near the village of Plomeur ('Plymieur') they succeeded in routing Richbell's and Frampton's regiments, neither of which had been under fire before. The 39th's colour was dragged out of Ensign Perrin's hands as he was trampled in the rush to escape; Lieutenant-Colonel Cotes and the remainder of the officers struggled to regain control over their men, a number of whom had fled. Major Bagshawe, who was serving as a staff officer, does not seem to have been involved in this incident, which was to have serious repercussions for the corps.

The following day, the invaders advanced to within two miles of the fortress and summoned the place to surrender. Favourable terms offered by the governor were unwisely rejected, and the British sat down to a formal siege, for which, as it soon appeared, they were ill-prepared. When their two-gun battery opened up on the morning of 25 September, the French responded with seven guns and kept up an incessant bombardment all day. Towards evening, as Samuel Bagshawe stood in an exposed position near the battery, a roundshot from the town shattered one of his legs.

By tremendous good fortune, he had been speaking with a surgeon of the Royal Artillery at the moment he was hit [24]. The surgeon immediately amputated the limb, at least seven inches above the knee, and rode for assistance. A party of grenadiers crept up in the lee of a wall, and then upon their hands and knees, and carried the major away to the church at Plomeur. He was placed on a bed near the altar, and next day was carried to the shore by a fatigue party from the 39th commanded by Corporal Kirkland (later sergeant-major of the 39th and adjutant of the 93rd).[34]

After months of pain and weakness, Bagshawe began to regain mobility, first with the aid of crutches and then with a succession of ingeniously constructed wooden legs, secured by a belt and shoulder straps, with a spring to cushion the stump.[35]

At first sight, his prospects appeared bleak. Retirement on half-pay, a commission in one of the companies of invalids or the governorship of some town or petty fortress were the usual options for the old or shattered. He felt that his future depended on being able to learn to ride again, '. . . for if I cannot serve, I do not know what will become of me, As my inclination went with my profession, another kind of life would be awkward for me.'[36] In fact, his steady recovery against the odds and the influence of Devonshire, the Marquess of Hartington and, most importantly, the Captain General, William Augustus Duke of Cumberland, secured his return to regimental duty in the summer of 1747 and tenure thereafter.[37] His patrons' interest did not extend to getting him the majority in the 39th however. When it became vacant in October 1747 the Secretary at War, Henry Fox, remarked that '. . . Bagshaw is a good man, but has lost a leg',[38] and the rank was conferred on Matthews Sewell, a half-pay captain of Marines. Sewell had served for 38 years and had held a lieutenant-colonel's commission in a short-lived regiment raised by the Duke of Bolton during the '45. He had a genuine interest in the welfare of the men under his command and he was fundamentally good-hearted.[39] Unfortunately he was also '... Infirm, of a Litigious Temper, & not liked in the Regiment.'[40] Bagshawe's correspondents reported on Sewell's ponderous pursuit of trifles with a mixture of glee and growing resentment [41, 42, 44, 47].

By this time, the 39th was a deeply unhappy regiment. An inquiry into the disgraceful events of 21 September 1746 began almost as soon as the troops were back aboard the transports.[41] In July 1747, Captain Edward Williams, Sergeant John Green and 16 private soldiers were tried for their part in the affair.[42] All were acquitted, but there was a strong feeling in the regiment that its honour had been compromised [23, 25].

This demoralization was intensified by a stint of sea service which lasted from May 1747 until the end of the War of the Austrian Succession in October 1748.[43] Service aboard the fleet was among the most gruelling tasks a regiment could be allotted. Unspectacular for the most part, (although on this occasion the 39th took part in Admiral Hawke's victory over a French squadron off Cape Finisterre on 14 October 1747),[44] it was unhealthy and potentially ruinous financially, for it was almost impossible for officers ashore to keep track of payments due to men afloat.[45] Bagshawe, based in London, was still paymaster, assisted by Lieutenant 'Archy' Grant at regimental headquarters in Portsmouth, but their joint endeavours could not solve financial problems which delayed the clearing of the regiment's accounts until April 1751,[46] by which time it had long since returned to Ireland. Bagshawe and the London agent of the 39th, Captain Thomas Levett, both lost money as a result, [59, 61–62].[47]

This unfortunate transaction could hardly have come at a worse time. At first sight, Bagshawe's position was improving rapidly. In April 1749 he had fought off a challenge from the tiresome Sewell and purchased the lieutenant-colonelcy of the 39th with the aid of a £1,000 loan from his reluctant uncle [52–58].[48] Then, in September 1750, he met Catherine ('Kitty') Caldwell, younger of two daughters of Sir John Caldwell of Castle Caldwell, Belleek, Co. Fermanagh (deceased) and sister of Sir James Caldwell, Count of Milan in the Holy Roman Empire.[49] They were married by special licence at Castle Caldwell on 25 March 1751.[50] Samuel quickly became a great favourite with his in-laws, especially Kitty's mother, the dowager Lady Ann. His first son, William, was born on 30 November 1752.[51] A second child, Samuel, his eventual heir, was born on 28 December 1753. The pleasing domestic and professional prospect was darkened however by his nagging ill-health, (Kitty's was scarcely better), and by pecuniary embarrassment, which made it all but impossible for him to maintain the dignity of a field officer [63]. William Bagshawe, whose temper had worsened with age, was thoroughly unsympathetic and threatened to cut Samuel out of his will unless interest on the loan of £1,000 which had clinched his nephew's promotion was promptly paid [72, 78–79].[52] There had been little or no improvement in this state of affairs when, on 29 January 1754, the startling news reached Dublin that the 39th was under orders to embark for the coast of Coromandel.

I

Sergeant Samuel Bagshawe to Richard Bagshawe JP of Castleton in the Peak, Derbyshire

[Copy]
Gibraltar
2 October 1734

Honoured Cousin
S.^r

The Generous Regard you was always pleased to express for me make[s] me flatter my self you will pardon the Liberty I now Assume, and that notwithstanding the late ungracious part I acted deserves the perpetuall Displeasure of You and all my Friends, my Reformation may influence them and you to Compasionate my unhappy Circumstances by Errours the Result of evill Example rather than my own depraved Inclinations. In the Inclosed to my Uncle (which I beg you will deliver with your own Hands) I have endeavoured to declare my real Sorrow for past Enormities and the Disturbance they must have occasioned him, be pleased to further my good Intentions; soften him to hearken to my Grief and accept my Penitance, lay before him my deplorable Condition almost consumed by Sickness and Melancholy and forc'd to be often Companion (against my Will) to the most desolute of Men, perswade him to remove me from a Conversation so dangerous and from which with the greatest Circumspection I find it difficult to reserve myself; yet if he doubts my Sincerity, or fears immediately to restore me to his presence from an Aprehension I may relapse prevail upon him to procure me an Employment where my publick Amendment may dissipate those Fears and make Satisfaction for publick Miscarriages. Worthy S.^r I cast my self upon your Goodness, let not my Unworthyness prevent your kind Assistance to extricate me out of the Miseries I labour under; As I clearly see my Folly so I am heartily sorry for any Offence and do sincerely promise my future Conduct shall give neither Uncle cause to repent he hearkned to You, nor You of your Undertaking ...

JRL, B2/2/789a

2

Sergeant Samuel Bagshawe to William Bagshawe of Ford Hall, Derbyshire

[Copy]   Gibraltar
21 November 1734

Honoured Sir

Your Goodness must be my Ward against this repeated trouble in a Copy which the fear of Miscarriage of a Letter I did myself the Favour to send you some time ago has caused; be pleased to Imagine a Youth who for some fancy'd Distate flings himself into the Sea, in his fall he sees his Folly, but when he views the Miseries that surround him (tho' sensible its owing to Compassion alone if he is taken in) with all his Might he strives to regain his Ship; you may easily conceive the earnest Desire I have to reposses a Happiness (the Favour of my Friends I so foolishly lost) which, the more I reflect upon the more I am Confounded and the more I covet to recover; I hope the Remembrance wont be grating that you have interpos'd in behalf of a distressed Orphan who accounts it a Felicity to be esteem'd
Worthy Sir
Your sincere and most
obedient humble servant
Saml. Bagshawe

JRL, B2/2/789

3

William Bagshawe of the Inner Temple to Sergeant Samuel Bagshawe

London
3 July 1737

... I need not inform you of the Steps which have been taken to mitigate y.ʳ Uncles Resentment, nor will I trouble you by relating his Behaviour on those Occasions; I doubt not but the reflecting on y.ʳ own folly and misconduct has been a grievous & sufficient punishment, so that I would not willingly add to it by enumerating the unhappy Consequences which have attended it, but rather congratulate you on the hopes you may now have of regaining (in some measure) y.ʳ Uncles favour for tho he continues resolutely of Opinion y.ᵗ you have justly forfeited all Right & claim to his friendship & affection, yet he is now prevailed with to promise that if I can procure y.ʳ discharge immeadiately & bring you over into Derbyshire directly he will be tender hearted, and not entirely withdraw his Compassion from you; so y.ᵗ I hope if y.ʳ Commanding Officer will be so indulgent as to grant y.ʳ discharge, it may be greatly to y.ʳ Advantage & will give a real pleasure to y.ʳ sincere Kinsman & Wellwisher,

Wᵐ Bagshawe

PS I have advanced a considerable Sum of Money for y.ʳ Ransom, but it must be kept a Secret from y.ʳ Uncle, for as his covetous disposition will think it too much, so I may reasonably doubt whether he will ever repay it; however if it be laid out for y.ʳ Advantage, I can (tho hardly) spare it, & I shall not lament the loss of such a Sum—

Cap.ᵗ Wilson[53] is so kind as to write to y.ʳ Officer[54] by the same Ship which brings [this] Letter, so I desire youll wait on him immeadiatly for if this proposal don't take effect I shall intirely despair of doing any thing for you, or ever making a Reconciliation betwixt y.ʳ Uncle & you; it must therefore be concluded speedily & you must make all possible hast into England—in the mean time I shall endeavour to engage your Uncles Affections, & don'[t] doubt of success —

JRL, B2/2/796

4

The Petition of Sergeant Samuel Bagshawe

[Draft]   Gibraltar
                                                      [1737]

To His Excellency Joseph Sabine Esqre: Lieutenn: General of all
His Britannick Majesties Land Forces and Governour and
Commander in chief of the City and Garrison of Gibraltar

The Petition of Samuel Bagshaw Serj: in Brigadier Anstruther's
Regiment

Humbly Sheweth

That some time ago your Excellency's Petitioner received a
Letter imparting the advantage of my coming home wou'd be to
me, which was little regarded by my then Captain,[55] but taken
notice off by my commanding Officer Major S: Clair, who in
Compassion to my Circumstances, and that he might have it the
more in his Power to do me a Service, paid Captain Ferguson
ten Pistoles for me, and gave him a Serj: out of his own
Company in my room, Declaring his intention in it & promising
I should have my Liberty upon Encouragement from my
Friends returning the Major ten Pistoles, and the money he
shou'd pay for a man,
    That your Petit: received a Letter from a near Relation
representing the absolute Necessity of his Appearance in England
and the vast Detriment to his Affairs and Fortune if he could not
obtain leave or a discharge: This Letter I Shewed to Major S:
Clair who confirmed his willingness to promote my Intrest as far
as his present Situation wou'd allow him; the Truth of which I
refer to the Major's Honour; and my Letters which I beg your
Excellencys condescention to favour with a Perusal,
    That as Major St Clair to whom I properly belong and who has
engaged his Honour on my Account is going to leave this place
    Your Petitioner therefore most humbly implores your Excel-
lency of your great goodness wou'd take into Consideration the

Nature of his Case and the Emergency of his Occasion to recover the time he has spent in a low Life, your Pet.^{r} procuring such Satisfaction to the commanding Officer of the Reg.^{t} he belongs to as the Case requires ...

JRL, B2/2/797

5

William Bagshawe of the Inner Temple to William Bagshawe of Ford

London
6 December 1737

...I doubt not but youll be desirous to know what steps have been taken towards obtaining y.^{r} Nephews Discharge, which I hope is now infallibly fixed (if [there] be any certainty in humane Affairs). I have not only agreed with his Major[56] but took an opportunity of having it done before a Coll. of ye Guards & some others who have an influence over him & will prevent any equivocation or shuffling. The Agreement is for twenty Pieces which must be paid before the Major goes for Gibraltar he giving me a Discharge in writing & a Promissory note for the Money in case any unforeseen Accident should happen; the Coll. and he are to spend an Evening at my Chambers about the middle of next Week & shall then appoint a time for paying the Money; of which you shall be timely advised ...

JRL, B2/2/802

6

Dr. Thomas Fletcher, Dean of Down, to William Bagshawe of Ford

Dublin Castle
17 January 1740

S.^r

His Grace intending to give your Nephew a pair of Colours, desires you will send him his Christian Name in a Letter directed to His Grace the Duke of Devonshire Ld Lieutenant of Ireland at the Castle in Dublin.

I congratulate you upon this, & am S.^r
Your most Humble Ser.^{vt}
Tho. Fletcher

JRL, B2/3/671

7

William Bagshawe of Ford to William Bagshawe of the Inner Temple

Ford
19 March 1740

Dr S.^r!

I heartily thank you for this fresh instance of Kindness to my Nephew, whom I should be willing to assist in any way that might be for his advantage, but as to the Adjutancy mentioned & the good effects thereof I am very much a stranger to Military affairs & so doubtful, as well as you are, whether it would be attended with such, but rather fear the Contrary, & my reasons are these—As his Grace of Devonsh.^r has took him into his

Protection & Advanced him further than he promised & I expected &, as you acquainted me, [has] given encouragem.^t for his higher preferm.^t I am doubtful, if this step of his own taking, may not be ill thought of, as it may seem tacitly to argue something of distrust & be looked upon as a slight, which is what I principally dread, & I make no doubt of it but his Grace will do well for him & it is but fit to leave it to him to do it in his own way & time so therefore I think he should not be too forward & seek for any office which is independent on his Grace's favour, nor can I give my consent thereto before his Grace is informed of it & his Approbation obtain'd. I have also been informed that ye Adjutants Commissarys and other Collateral Officers, when they are such, Seldom [or] never receive any further preferm.^t, Commissary Davenport[57] of Macclesfield is an Instance of this, who was in that Post, I believe, in Queen Anne's Reign, these are my present sentimnt.^s [,] but as you are so good as to promise to come here I desire you will do it, shortly, & then we may talk these matters over ...

JRL, B1/1/53

8

Lieutenant Samuel Bagshawe to William Bagshawe of Ford

Kinsale
2 October 1741

Dear Uncle
      Sir

Tuesday last I marcht for this place and the same day reced a Letter from Dean Fletcher which informed me of your kind request to him and which is a double obligation as it is agreable to what I desir'd of you, You may confide in me that I shall make a right use of your Goodness, whilst I continue in Country Quarters my pay shall be sufficient and if I get leave to go to Dublin will make no demand but what has the Dean's Approbation.

Perhaps you will not be displeased to know the Method made Use of to determine as one say[s] the Lives and Fortunes of the Officers of our Regiment for this expedition,[58] which was as follows, Those Ranks of Officers where there are only two, such as Lieutenant Colonels, Majors and Adjutants threw Dice; The Captains, Lieutenn[ts] and Ensigns drew Lotts each Rank by themselves, after this manner[.] The Names of the Officers were put into one hat, a like number of Papers were cut on which for the number of Officers to go was wrote Expedition, the rest blank, these were put into another hat and the hatts held by different persons, then two Boys were call'd and placed by each hat, and one of them drew out an Officers Name and at the same time the other Boy drew a paper out of the other hat on which was that Officers Destiny, when it came to the Lieutenants the chance was ten Officers to go for Seven to stay, it is mine to be of this last Number, when that Affair was settled the Companys that lay in Cork not to go were order'd to Kinsale by which I have left a place where I was not one day in perfect health at a time I dreaded sickness tho most lest ill natur'd people should give it an ill natur'd construction. We are yet and shall till the embarkation is over be in a tumultuous hurrying way, I dont know how to give you a better Idea of it than by comparing it to an Election Assizes or a fair[59] and the advantage people take of our Situation will bear the same comparison. A melancholy Circumstance attended this Draught; An Officers Lady big with Child whose husband drew for the Expedition being told of it abruptly fell into her pains & died in twelve hours after, This Lott has falln on almost all the Old Officers ... There is in this Regiment and in the same Company, A Captain, Lieutenant, a Serjeant and Drummer whose Ages put together exceed 340 and who have been more than 200 years in the Service. I expect to be one of the Officers order'd to recruit for the Regim[t] but cannot tell which is to be my rout. My exemption from the Expedition permitting I shall be glad to be entertain'd again with domestick occurrences ... I beg my Love and Duty to

Aunt and to be remembered to all Friends and acquaintances
and am
> Dear Uncle
> Your affectionate and dutiful
> Nephew and most hum. Servt
> > Saml. Bagshaw

JRL, B2/3/79

9

Memorandum by Lieutenant Samuel Bagshawe

[Fragment]   [1742]

... When a Capt has leave to quitt the Service & dispose of his
Comission 'tis generally done in this manner, the Lieuten.^{t}
recomended either gives him his Comission & the difference between the Comissions of a Capt & L^{tt} or a certain sum
of money in which last case the L^{tt} has the disposing of his own
Comission which if sold to an Ensign that Ensign acts in the
same way that is, gives the Lieuten.^{t} his Ensigns Comission
and the difference or else a certain Sume & sells the Colours
himself, So that the price of a Captains Comission is either a
certain Sume, or is compos'd of the difference between a Capt
and a Lieutenn^{ts} Comission, the difference between a Lieuten-
antcy & a pair of Colours & the Colours, Now suppose a
Company is dispos'd of this last way & sold for eleven hundred
pounds the Case stands thus

The Difference between the Captains & the L^{tt} Comission	} 600:	:
The Diff. between ye Lieutenancy & ye Colours	100:	:
The Colours	400:	:
	£1100: 0: 0	

JRL, B2/3/699

38

10

Lieutenant Samuel Bagshawe to Mary Bagshawe of Ford

Dublin
2 February 1742

Dear Aunt

I am very sincerely sorry to have by Uncles last Letter a confirmation of your indisposition[.] I do assure you if it was in my power, or that I could any ways contribute, you should not be long out of order. I was in hopes that by coming to Dublin in a parliament Winter, I should have been able to afford you some Amusement but the great expence prevents me having a thorough knowledge of the publick diversions, and the narrow Circle of my acquaintance of many private ones, however the Access I have to the Castle enables me to tell you what is done there and one Week gives a view of the whole. We have then every Tuesday a Levée, first the Dukes, at which appear the Men, after that the Duchesses, to which come both Men and Ladies, At Night is a Ball which opens before Nine, where are seldom fewer than two hundred Ladies a great number of which have patience and Strength to stay till one or two o'clock though the Room will be so hot I have been often ready to drop with faintness, to alleviate this when the set dances are over a Room is open'd where each calls for what Wine they please; On Friday is a Levée and at night a drawing room where they only play at Cards[,] this is soon over and seldom crowded. To divert in the City, on Mondays and Thursdays there are plays at two houses, on which occasion the Ladies are divided into parties some espousing very warmly one house and some the other, so that if a Gentleman has acquaintance on both Sides he's under a sort of necessity to take tickets the same Night from both; On Wednesday the Town has of late been entertain'd with musical performances by the celebrated M.r Handel from London,[60] Tickets to those who subscribe five Guineas are Six Shillings[,] to others half a guinea a piece for an entertainment of two hours and yet there are seldom fewer than Six hundred Auditors, On Saturday is a Ball at which are generally present from six to eight hundred persons, there are besides these musical assemblies for charitable uses and others at private houses which would be agreable enough if they did not vie with one another in expence. If from what I have observ'd I might venture to give a character I should say the Irish Ladies are of a frank generous disposition an open and easy behaviour, love Dress and gaity and are passionately fond of dancing, were they as perfect in the oeconomick duties of a Family as in doing the honours of it and appearing abroad they would be most [excellent] ...

JRL, B2/3/82

II

Captain Samuel Bagshawe to William Bagshawe of Ford

London
1 May 1742

Dear Uncle

Sir

last Thursday night at ten o'clock my Lord Duke sent for the Dean of Down (knowing {as the Dean was so kind to say} the News would give him a pleasure) to tell him, and Yesterday I had it from His Graces own mouth that I was to be appointed to one of the Companys of the new Reg^t., commanded by Colonel Battreau[61] a favour which when considered in all its Circumstances is really a surprising great [rise] for very great Interest has been made out by many who seem'd to have reason to expect Success, but His Grace was steady in his determination to serve me. I beg you will lose no time to write His Grace a Letter of thanks and in the strongest terms in which you are to [sig]nifie the little reason to expect such a favour and his great goodness to distinguish me at this time without any Application when so many have been made to him.

Dean Fletcher has given me to understand that it [will] be agreable to His Grace that I be as speedy [as possible] in raising my Men ... so I beg you will look out yourself and engage Friends to do the same for such in their Neighbourhood as may be spared and if any likely fellow comes to offer himself get him sworn, and he may enter into pay of Sixpence a day immediatly and stay at home if known and follow his employment 'till I come or may be quarter'd at Chappell, I shall return as soon as we receive our recruiting instructions. Our Companys are to consist of a hundred Men each.

I shall be oblig'd to trouble you for a further remittance hither of about thirty pounds to furnish me with some necessaries I believe I shall have occasion for. I spent part of yester afternoon with the Dean who seem'd to have a real pleasure in my good fortune and took a great deal of Pains to instruct me what behaviour would [be] agreable to my Benefactor, if you write a line to him likewise you will oblige me ...

JRL, B2/3/84

12

Dr. Thomas Fletcher, Dean of Down, to Captain Samuel Bagshawe

[London]
20 January 1743

I rec^d ye favour of yours, of ye 11th Ins^t, & am glad that your Recruiting goes on so well. But give me Leave to ask you a Question as a Friend; & that is, whether you have not Listed some Irish men? The reason of my asking this, is, because when I was last with ye Duke, his Grace told me, that he had heard that ye Officers Recruiting for Ireland had Listed a great many Irish. Upon which I was determined to write away to you & give you a Hint of that Report, that if you have been imposed upon in that way, you may do what you can towards setting things right, or at least be more cautious for the future. It being a thing which his Grace I know looks upon to be of a very [dangerous] Consequence. A word to ye Wise the Proverb says is enough; & therefore I shall say no more ...

JRL, B2/3/673

13

Captain Thomas Levett, Regimental Agent, to Captain Samuel Bagshawe

London
17 April 1744

Col^o Richbell has directed me to acquaint you that he wou'd be glad you wou'd take the Paym^t of the Regim^t upon you, wch in my letter to you at Uxbridge I gave you a little Sketch of the nature of, and shall inform you more as soon as I know what footing you are to be upon here, and I look upon the Setting out in this affair to be the most difficult the Reg^t being so dispersed and you will be under the Necessity of going round the Quarters once to fix the manner of their getting money and in Case the Collectors or the Trades men in y^t Town can't or won't furnish you for the whole the Commanding Officer at Each Quarter must try to get Money there for wch you must give y^r Bill and make a Musterly distribution, and I find all the Officers want their March^g Money, wch won't be paid [for] some Months but to serve them for the present I will Advance it, for wch if you please take a perticular and all the Constables receipts and send them to me when you find an Oppertunity of any Officer comming up and I have writ to acquaint the Major[62] and most of the other Officers that you are Paym^r and they must apply to you and I shall in a few days send you a Scheme of how you are to Pay ...

JRL, B2/2/310

14

Captain Thomas Levett, Regimental Agent, to Captain Samuel Bagshawe

London
25 April 1744

I defer'd answering yours of the 19th in hopes of being able to inform you upon what footing y.^r Regiment is to be on here wch. we dayly Expected to have settled but is not yet done, and till that is, I can only receive upon Acco.^t, nor can I or you pay otherways, So the Major must content himself whilst he is here with receiving his Pay according to the Customes of England, for you can't have Monthly Abstracts here as you have in Ireland, and as y.^r Regim.^t was paid by that Country to the last of March y.^{re} Pay in England on course Comences the first of April, and the difference between the Irish & English pay from the days of your Embarkation will be made up, a Certificate of wch. I last night received from Capt Desbrisay,[63] and I shud be glad to know whose Companys Embarqu'd Each day, and as it is the Method & Custome of Paying in England vizt 30 and 31 Days wch. generally Comences the 25th. of Each Month, I have sent you a Sketch of the Cred.^t you may at present take and draw for Accordingly, that is for the Commission & Non Commission Officers and Eighty private Men p.^r Company, and as y.^{re} Numbers increase in lieu of the draughts you must Credit them Accordingly, but if Compleat not to draw for the Warr.^t Men,[64] nor the Pay of any Absent Officer to whom I shall account here, And the Captains shall have abst^{rts} at the End of the Muster wch. is the 24th. of June, in which the Stoppage for Surgeon and Paym.^r shall be made and properly Credited, and Explained in Such a Manner as will afterwards make it Easie to you, and I was in hopes to have sent you a Coppy of the Regulation Sign'd by the King's order directing the Stoppages wch. are printed for the Use of the War Office, but at present they have none and I have disposed of all I had, but more will be printed off soon, & you shall have one as likewise the Customary Method of appropriating these Stoppages,[65] and as to the manner of your

43

drawing, to be sure [it] must be done so as is most convenient to you provided your Bills are not payable before I can receive the Money here wch is generally paid about the 25th 26th or 27th of Each Month, So the more days after date or Sight you can get the Bills at the better it will accommodate me, and I take it for granted all payments hitherto has been upon Acco^t [,] if you please to Compleat this Paym^t to the 24th of June before wch you will let me have the Distribution the Method of wch is to charge y^{r}Self wth the Bills you have drawn, and to take Cred^t for each Officers Subs^{ce} as likewise what Sum you pay Each Company on Acco^t or any other sums that you Pay, for Marches or otherways, all wch must be Separate Articles, to Shew you the Method of wch I have here sent you an Acco^t of a Paym^t to me wch will Shew you the form, and I begg you will return [it] the first Opportunity you have of any officer coming up here, and you have likewise herewith, y^{re} Abst^{ct} from Capt. Desbrisay and, I will send the other Captains theirs, and you shall have the Subalterns soon, and their Ballances where any are may go towards their Tents & Regim^{tls} ...

JRL, B2/3/312

15

Captain Samuel Bagshawe to Sir William Yonge, Secretary at War

[Copy]

Petersfield
24 February 1745

Sir

I find it almost impossible to execute His Majesties Orders to take up Straggling and Deserting Sailors the outrageous insolence of some of the Inhabitants of this place is so great, who not satisfied wth informing where my patrolls are placed and assisting them to escape (wch they own to my face they have and will do) but they insult and molest these patrolls, beat my Men in their quarters; go out in Numbers armed with Clubs and threaten to knock my peoples Brains out if they catch them in such places where it is necessary to post them to discover the Runaways, Nay they have come into my quarters armed in this manner publickly insulting me and threatning to beat the Soldiers.

There are eighteen different Waggons go backwards and forwards through this Town from Portsmouth each Week and if they are to be excused a Search, the Deserting Seamen need not be sollicitous for any other means to escape, When my people have been refused [leave] to search these Waggons (wch has only been to open the Till at each end and look in) & I have gone to countenance them, besides the Insults and abuse they have received I have been called, Scoundrell, Villain, Thief, told I should be broke like a Scoundrell, challenged to fight, threatned to have my Head broke, to be shook out of my laced Cloaths, Sticks lifted at me, & attempts made to strike me, In short if I cannot find protection from the Insults of these lawless Ruffians I must grow remiss in my Duty and His Majesties orders lye unexecuted[.]

When Mr Joliff[66] the Member is on the Spot I meet wth Redress. I have nobody else to apply to, the nearest Justice of peace to me is one Mr Brown ... at Eastmean[67] about four Miles but from an Application I have already made to him (though of another nature) I find him little disposed to assist ye Military. I beg leave also to represent to you, That when we take Sailors to Portsmouth it is rather like conveying prisoners through an Enemys Country than among people equally obliged to do the King's Duty, such numbers of Sailors assemble to attack the Guard and rescue their Comrades. I make no Application for the fatigue we undergoe, how greatly we are harrassed, what Numbers of my Men are sick, how they suffer in their Regimentals, Arms and Acoutrements but I hope our Treatment will come under your immediate consideration & That we shall meet wth immediate redress. I am with ye greatest respect Sir & c. S.B.

JRL, B2/4/31

16

Captain Samuel Bagshawe to Dr Thomas Fletcher, Bishop of Kildare

[Draft]   [Fareham]
                                                   31 May 1745

My Lord

having your Lordships permission I take the Liberty to inform you in this manner that the Sume necessary from my Uncle to purchase the Majority is eight hundred pounds for which he need not put himself to any immediate Inconvenience[.] Capt Levett who will provide it for the present, is satisfied to receive the money back at any time within the Year and I will pay the Interest for it during that time. And next Christmas will repay my Uncle one hundred pounds and one hundred every half Year after 'till the principal (& Interest he requires) is discharged. This is the substance of what I can offer to remove my Uncles apprehensions for his money. ~~I need not say anything to convince your Lordship of the Advantage of this promotion to me at this time of day when I am the Youngest Captain save one in the Reg.~~^t – – [68]

JRL, B2/3/675

17

Dr. Thomas Fletcher, Bishop of Kildare, to William Bagshawe of Ford

London
1 June 1745

Colonel Richbell, who has been so kind to your Nephew, came to me, yesterday morning & told me, that there being now an Opportunity for Capt.ⁿ Bagshaw to gain ye Rank of Major in his Reg^{mt}, which would be a very great Consequence to him, &

such another favourable Juncture, might not happen again in some Years; he wish'd the young man so well that he could not help coming to me whom he knew to be his Friend, to enquire whether he had not a Relation that would be so good to him as to assist him, upon this critical occasion, with about a Thousand Pounds for a little while; that being the Sum which is necessary to procure this Advancement for him. To which my answer was, that he had a very kind Unkle, who was, I knew, able & would, I dared to say, be willing to accommodate his nephew, in a matter of so much importance to him. The Colonel replied, that the young man in his opinion well deserved all the Encouragement that could be given him, that he had a great regard for him, & wish'd him heartily well; that he would be very glad to have him rise in his Reg^{mt}, & therefore came to talk with me on that Head. I told him that I could say nothing to it myself, but would write to you, inform you how ye Case stood, & desire an Answer soon. Upon which he observed, that ye thing must be done soon, if at all, because ye present Major could not wait long, & if your Nephew would not, or could not purchase ye Majority it might go to somebody else.

This Acc^t, S^r, I accordingly send you & with it a Letter from y^r Nephew which he sent me in answer to an Enquiry I made of him, with regard to ye whole State of ye Case, the exact sum that would be necessary, & what proposals he had to make with regard to repaying the Money, in case you should be disposed to assist him. In which letter you will observe, that he says that only £800 will be necessary for this purpose. The meaning of which is, that he has been so far a Prudent Manager, as to be able to produce ye other Two Hun^d himself, without troubling you. Which in my Opinion looks well, & deserves Encouragement. As does also that General Good Behaviour which has made Col. Richbell & Capt Levett so ready to serve him in so kind a manner, & every body that knows him to have a good opinion of him.

In short, S^r, by what ye Col said upon this Subject, & what I find by talking with other Persons who are good Judges in ye Case & real Friends both to you & your Nephew, your assisting him, in some shape or other, with ye sum mentioned, £800, will do him more Service than giving him <u>Double</u> or even <u>Treble</u> that Sum at another time ...

JRL, B2/3/676

18

Captain Samuel Bagshawe to Dr. Thomas Fletcher, Bishop of Kildare

[Draft]   Eastbourne
                                                    7 February 1746

My Lord

The Last time I did myself the favour to write to y.ʳ L.ᵈ Ship I had a prospect of being present at the Siege of Ostend; our Regim.ᵗ begun its march for that purpose but were countermanded, the Shortness of that Siege & the little knowledge [I] could have gained there with what hapned afterwᵈ to the Garrison made our return an Advantage;⁶⁹ Since that, though I earnestly sought leave to go to the North, I have the Misfortune to be of the Number of those who have done their Country no Service this War & continue ignorant of their business: The Affair of the Majority also which blossomed so well and made so fine a Shew for Fruit was blasted all of a Sudden, My Lord Duke had brought my Uncle to comply to assist me, Coz. Will Bagshaw who was in London & knew it, never thought of informing Col. Richbell, My Aunt writes a Letter to inform me which some how or other lay upon the road or in the Agents office Eleven Days, In this very space of Eleven Days the Sen.ʳ Captain⁷⁰ had borrowed Money for the purchase wᶜʰ. Effectually overturned my Scheme, & Col.º Richbell could think of no other Expedient for my succeeding unless my L.ᵈ Marquiss of Hartington would consent to speak to the Secretary at War⁷¹ in favour & procure that the Major might retire upon the difference of pay betwixt Maj.ʳ & Captain & sell his Comp.ʸ by wᶜʰ. I was to succeed & Do the Duty on Captains pay; Perswaded by the Colonel I ventured to apply to my L.ᵈ Marquiss, and stated the case truly, making use of no other Argument for myself than this, That as the Vacancy was kept open purely on my Acc.ᵗ & would otherwise have been filled by a still younger Captain, the Captain who had now raised the Money, would only be in the same Situation which (only upon my Acc.ᵗ) he must have been in; My L.ᵈ Duke of Devon. consented that [the] L.ᵈ Marquiss should appear for me & His Grace also was pleased to speak several times to Sir W.ᵐ Yonge to represent this Affair to the King, but Whether this business of State prevented or that Sir W.ᵐ Yonge from time to time forgot, he has not yet done it, and in this manner it has depended since last July. This, My Lord, is my present Situation. I am now on a Detachm.ᵗ in Sussex to destroy a Gang of Smugglers who besides divers Outrages have had the Insolence to call themselves the Southern Rebells; They immediatly dispersed upon our coming, but carry on their Smugling almost under our Noses, For as the Generality of the Country are Friends to the Trade, the Complaint being only against the manner in w.ᶜʰ of late it was carried on, so whenever we make the least Motion, the Smuglers have notice of it and escape us. I hope your Lordship will receive this Letter with your usual Goodness, I wish I had a Subject more entertaining & more worthy your Acceptance, being with true respect,

My Lord
Your Dutifull and most Obed.ᵗ
humble Servant
S.B.

JRL, B2/3/677

19

Major Samuel Bagshawe to Mary Bagshawe of Ford

London
6 May 1746

Dear Aunt

I have a fresh pleasure every time I read your last kind letter, Your Wishes for my Safety and your Blessing are so affectionate and at the same time so natural that I am sure you meant them, and if I return I hope I shall deserve your kind opinion of me, I go abroad (beside my Employment) with great Advantages; Health, Strength & Inclination, If Providence thinks fit to dispose of me otherwise than these promise, His Will be done; if I can attain to meet you in Heaven I shall have eternal reason to rejoyce at the Change. As to the nature of Expeditions they often carry more Danger in Idea than reality, and that increases in proportion to the Distance; A Man who makes a Journey from the North of England to London privatly makes his Will, he who goes to Ireland does that and take[s] leave of his Family, but to go abroad he must run through all the Ceremony of Parting: Our Expeditions to America hitherto have not been lucky,[72] that I am afraid has been chiefly owing to the manner they have been conducted, and as to particular Persons I have it from very good Authority That more have died from their own Aprehensions than the Climate, I thank God I am pretty free from those prejudices, at the same time not careless, I propose to pursue all reasonable means both for my Health and Safety & leave the rest to Providence, and to my own endeavours[.] [I] hope to have your, & the good Wishes & prayers of my Friends. I beg to be remembered to all our Neighbours ... Dear Aunt, That God Almighty may bless you, May give you Comfort in this Life and happiness in the next, is the sincere prayer of Your most affectionate Nep^w.

Sam! Bagshaw

JRL, B2/3/105

20

Major Samuel Bagshawe to Dr. Thomas Fletcher, Bishop of Kildare

[Draft]   [Portsmouth]
                                                     7 June 1746

I have in part obtained what I have long desired to be employed on Service, I own had I been at Liberty to choose I should have chosen Flanders the scene to act my part in because [it is] the place where most Improvement is to be gained, however, there is scarce any where I would not serve rather than be always idle, Your Lordship must have heard of the Expedition talked off, the Embarkation is made here & Brig.ʳ Richbells Reg.ᵗ one of the Number, The Destiny of these Troops is the Subject of much Discourse, if I knew it might be wrong in me to tell, The World have sent us to Cape Breton, Be where it will I realy think the Goodness of the Troops promise as much success as any Expedition yet undertaken, Our number is ab.ᵗ 5000 Foot & a Thousand Marines are taken on board the Men of War as a further Aid, the Whole Commanded by L.ᵗ Gen S.ᵗ Clair,

I am at last disapointed in the Majority, but not from the Justness of the pretentions of my Antagonist[.]

Brig.ʳ Richbell who goes as Brigadier upon the Expedition has been so kind to recomend me his Brigade Major by w.ᶜʰ means I shall be in the way to acquire what is to be acquir'd & I shall also have Oppertunitys to shew whether I am fitt for business or not. If any thing should happen worthy your Notice w.ᶜʰ I may relate I will transmitt it to your L.ᵈShip, I beg to recomend myself to your Remembrance & Blessing ...

JRL, B2/3/678

21

William Bagshawe of Ford to Major Samuel Bagshawe

Ford
2 November 1746

D.ʳ Nephew!

I can.ᵗ relate the Concern your L.ʳ gave us, accompanyed by the Newspaper ... no doubt but your Misery has been extream & our Sympathy not small, I ordered your case to be laid before the Almighty this day & all private prayers have not been wanting, may he hear and Answer them So as to be most for your good. I have been so hindred by one or an other coming to Enquire of you that I have no time to write more than only to Ask you a civil question, What will you say if 2 ... Old fellows should come to see you in a fortnight or 3 Weeks time M[r] Barber[73] one & the Other

Y[r] very Affect[e] Uncle
W. Bagshawe

JRL, 2 B2/3/110

22

Mary Bagshawe of Ford to Major Samuel Bagshawe

Ford
2 November 1746

My Dear Nephew

I heartally Condole you upon the lose of so usefull a member as y[t] of y[r] leg but y[t] your life is spared & y[t] there is hopes of your recovery doth somewhat aleviate that great shock y[t] yours at first gave us − I am very sensable that tis not to be expressed what you have undergone, I pray God perfect y[r] recovery is the ernest desire of y[r] very affectionate Aunt

M. Bagshawe

JRL, B2/3/110a

23

Captain David Hepburne to Major Samuel Bagshawe

Cork
5 December 1746

We are Scarce Warm in our Irish quarters[74] when we have received orders to prepare for a fresh Voyage, you knew no doubt before we did, that Genl. S[t] Clair with the Six expedition

Reg^ts. are to return to Great Brittain, & every thing is getting ready for our Embarkation. I hope you are before this time in London, & perfectly recovered, the uncertainty I was in with regard to your being able to reach London soon, after your landing in England, prevented my writing to you before & acquainting [you] of all our doings since we parted, & indeed what I had much more to heart, of opening the way to hear from you, to hear that you were well, to hear that you were like to do well after your wound, was not only my great Concern but that of every body from the Genl. downwards, & if any thing Can Make Amends for the loss you have sustained, it must be the General regret, & universal Esteem for the Sufferer, but as I hope & pray, that you are now perfectly recovered, I will say no more on the Melancholy Subject –

I send you Inclosed the distribution of our quarters, & wish I could send you as distinct an account of our other transactions but Shaddows Clouds and darkness rest upon them, a general Court Martial has [been] held ever since we came into Harbour on those Men of Framptons[75] & ours who returned to Guidell after the Affair of Septr. y^e. 21st., & 'tho there is no knowing what passes before such Courts till the Sentence is disclosed, yet by the great delay, & frequent Messages that pass between the General & them, & some Whispers, we can guess that all does not go well, I heartily wish it was over, for if both sides continue stiff in their present opinions, I will not pretend to forsee the Consequences[.] Brigad^r. Richbell is at Limerick Where he was ordered to take the Command, as neither Messrs. Offarel nor Graham[76] were here, it was against our friends Will, but he must.

You will be sorry to hear how Sickly we have all been & what we have lost since we landed, in the Six Comp^ys. of our Reg^t. we have now about 150 Sick & we have burried about a Dozen, Framptons is still Worse, Indeed we are all much alike, the Highlanders[77] best off, poor Philips of Genl. Fullers[78] one of our Voluntiers died soon after we landed, Captain Cunningham of the Royals[79] is in a bad way, & Major Fox in a Worse, I look on him to be in great danger & so say the learned, I thought proper to give you this timely Notice, that you may be prepared for what I believe will happen, & which you shall hear of as soon as it does ...

JRL, B2/2/255

24

Major Samuel Bagshawe to William Bagshawe of the Inner Temple

Gosport 'at M^rs.
Pitts, Cold Habour'
10 November 1746

***

I have been 'till now so weak that it was a pain for me to write, so that the publick has acquainted you with my Misfortune before I was fitt to do it, tho' I wrote to Uncle the Day after I was brought Ashoar but I did not recover that fatigue [for] two Days[.] I thank God I have reason to hope that I am now past danger from the loss of my Limb, Yet I can do scarce any thing without help notwithstanding this is the forty seventh day since the Chance hapned to me, Indeed I have suffered more than the consequential Misery of such a loss, I was obliged to be carryed the day after the Amputation Eleven Miles, lying on a Bolster between two poles, & Eight of these Miles in the Night through Woods that catcht hold of me every now & then & the Worst Road I think can be travelled, after this severall Days upon a Rolling Sea more distressfull than the former, My Life is next to a Miracle nay I may say A Miracle, for when I receved the Shot which took away my Leg I was talking to a Strange Gentleman I never saw before[80] who came up to me as I was waiting to see a Detachment of Men enter our Battery, in order that I might make a Report to the General, there was no person near me but this Gentleman & no likelyhood of any coming that Way as it was much exposed to the Cannon from the Town[,] this Gentleman proved to be a Surgeon, & if all the World had been Surgeons & this Gentleman not one, I must infallibly have bled

54

to Death for no other person though it had been possible for them to have seen the Accident could have arrived time enough to give me Assistance, I have been twice since in danger of bleeding to Death & twice that all our Physicians & Surgeons said it was ten to one against me, I lay one time Six hours that all my Limbs were as cold as Clay with a dead sweat upon them & I gasping one time & at another could hardly breath fast enough my Lungs were in so violent a Motion, Yet now I am reasonably hearty, can sitt up Six or eight hours a Day & eat my Breakfast & Dinner very heartily & have been able to write you this Scrawl in about an hours time & am very little weary, My Wound grows every day more easy & in a fortnights time I believe will have a Skin over all the fleshy part of it ...

JRL, B2/3/216

25
Lieutenant William Dawkin to Major Samuel Bagshawe

Shrewsbury
4 February 1747

I reced yours three posts agoe, which I sho^d have answered sooner: but one of those reasons you give me for a stop being put to our Aff^{rs} shock'd me a good deal, which is the happy situation our Regim^t is in—I remember to have heard it was a Rule wth the Duke of Marlboro', that when a Regim^t was supposed not to behave so well as it sho^d have done, he always gave them an Opportunity of clearing themselves by sending of them upon some extraordinary Service: but instead of that, our Regim^t must stand censured wthout being able to Justify themselves in one shape or the other—wth this prospect I think no man in the Regim^t can be supposed to have the Interest of the Service much at heart, but however, I think as you do that every officer sho^d Joyn in a memorial for an Enquiry to be made, & let the odium fall upon those that deserved it, & I hope the Brigad^r for the Good of the Regim.^t will put it upon some footing or other, as for my part I will Joyn wth ever so few or ever so many, & if report be true there are some in our Regim.^t who I believe wo^d not much care for such an Enquiry, but it is hard that the Innocent sho^d suffer wth the Guilty, & let Justice give every Man his Desarts—whatever steps you take I am ready to do the same—I have a great notion that instead of one hundred's applying for leave to sell there will be three times as many next year & I believe no more from want of Courage than those that are preferr'd ...

JRL, B2/2/142

26

Captain David Hepburne to Major Samuel Bagshawe

Portsmouth
24 April 1747

It would vex me to leave my bones in this vile hole after all my Escapes for I never enjoy a moments health in it, I live as temperatly & Soberly as any in this parish, yet I have not been without a violent Flux while within these Walls. Portsmouth proves to me what Hibernia does to many of our Raw Country Folks, believe me dear Bagshaw, 'tho I am not Confin'd to my Chamber, I have scarce Strength to Crawl Abroad. I must therefore Change Climate or do Worse, poor Lyons[81] is as bad even Forde[82] ails & except our tottering Major we have all of us some Complaint or other, to add to our grivious aprehensions there is an order for forty of our Men to go on board the Maidstone (Capt Keppel)[83] on a Cruise. I fear they will not stop at 40, as we are so ready at hand—but the will of our Superiours be done—

JRL, B2/2/257

27

Major Samuel Bagshawe to Mary Bagshawe of Ford

Portsmouth
1 August 1747

The few Incidents worth relating to you that have hapned to me, has been the only Cause of my Silence, My present Situation is, that I am restored to a seeming very florid State of Health and fuller of Flesh than ever I was, this last owing to the little Exercise I can take in Comparison of what I formerly used to Do; I am bless God in a pretty good State of Health, the pain that I feel in my Stump being rather a kind of a Sensation as it does not much interrupt Sleep, business or Amusem^t. Sometimes I have strong Shootings in it, but as they generally happen after I use Exercise I believe them owing to that and I have reason to hope time will rather discontinue than encrease them. I am still upon my Crutches from the tenderness of my Stump and to encrease a Shelter of Flesh to the End of the Bone which is but indifferently and will never be well defended, however as soon as I might with any Safety, I attempted to ride on Horseback and have already succeeded more than I expected in a long time, so that I could travell on a sure Horse a reasonable Days Journey, Practice this way will be my principal Exercise 'till winter when the Return of His Royal Highness the Duke I expect will determine whether I shall be thought fit to continue in the service or that I must sollicit some other Provision ...

JRL, B2/3/124

28

Major Samuel Bagshawe to Brigadier-General Edward Richbell

[Copy]   Portsmouth
                                                  13 October 1747

Dear Sir

You have before this been informed of the illness of Major Fox
which has gradually increased and is at this Ins.^t so heightened
that he is given over & not expected to live 'till Night. If his
Death happens I wish to have your Approbation & recommendation to succeed him, and if there should be no other
objection to me than the loss I have met with I hope that will be
none as I can ride sufficiently to discharge the Duty & only
expect to be continued in the Service on those Terms. I rely
upon your Friendship more than any thing I can say for myself,
to represent me in the most advantagious light and shall make it
my study to meritt the kindness you shew and the Character you
give of &c ...

JRL, B2/2/498

29

Major Samuel Bagshawe to Brigadier-General Edward Richbell

[Copy]   Portsmouth
                                                  13 October 1747

What I wrote you by this Mornings Post as likely to happen, has
hapned, Major Fox is Dead, I know Nothing that I can say, I rely
upon your Friendship & Favour &c

JRL, B2/2/498a

30

Major Samuel Bagshawe to Brigadier-General Edward Richbell

[Copy] Portsmouth
14 October 1747

I begin to fear I shall be accounted troublesome but I presume more upon the Friend than the Colonel and therefore hope the Occasion will be my apology. I am informed some people are already sett out from this place to Sollicit for the Majority, Strangers, because they were Majors in the County Regim^{ts} and as there may be other pretenders of that sort in Town I thought it my Duty as well as Interest to inform you, for the same reason Capt Townsend[84] has desir'd leave to appear before you in person. I hope your Goodness will excuse this Freedom ... Capt Williams[85] not caring to take the Comand of the Reg^t on him, I am by a C^t M^l taking an Acc^t of the Majors Effects & Settling the Funeral.

JRL, B2/2/497

31

Brigadier-General Edward Richbell to Major Samuel Bagshawe

London
25 October 1747

Dear Bagshawe

Capt Levet has just brought me y^r Lt^{re} in relation to the Complaint Mr Delangley was about making of the Raggedness of my men on board the Fleet: to wch I have this short answer to make, that I have in every respect conformed to His Maj^{ts} order for clothing them at their Quarters, & that they are ready to be given to the men as they come into Harbour [as] is Customary wth the Marines: a sort of one at present I look upon mine to be, & that I am not obligated to runn the risque of loosing my Cloaths by sending them about the world to find the men where possibly they may never arrive. As they come into Portsm. I wou'd have them cloathed except such as are obliged to be sent to Hospitals, & those to be cloathed the minute they are dismissed thence & fitt for Duty, in short I mean & intend not to put it in any mans power to say I have done him the least injustice.

Capt Keene[86] is come to Town tho' I absolutely forbid the contrary, not being well I have not yet seen him, when I do my answer will be, what I have given under my hand to the King that I dont think him Qualified for that, or indeed any other Post, but that he may make his own application, when if I am asked my reasons for objecting to him, all his failings that I have known off whilst under my comand shall be made known; And I wou'd gladly be inform'd of any others not yet reached my ears; this last of inlisting the fellow whipt out of Graham's[87] wth his knowledge I am impatient off together wth yor opinion of the rest of the Recruits he sent, because the sooner the objection (if any reasonable) is made, the better. Lord Semple[88] has left word at my house he is in Town, it is yor leave he had, not mine, or woud he, had I been there: because he never was punctual on that acco^t[,] in yor next monthly acco^t you best know how to return him, for I will have nothing to do with him.

I hope you and your Legg are by this [time] well acquainted, you allways have my warmest wishes for the success of your undertakings being very truly

Y^r most Affec^t Friend
& hum. Servant
Ed. Richbell

JRL, B2/2/501

32

Captain Thomas Levett, Regimental Agent, to Major Samuel Bagshawe

London
27 October 1747

... I am not a little concern'd that any difficulty shu'd attend your promotion which you have so Essentially merited, but nothing I find is to be doing in the Army without the consent of the Duke but when he comes home the Brig.^r design's having an Audience, and will represent your Services, and every thing Else in its proper light, and when the Duke of Devonshire comes to Town I hope he will speak to him, & I doubt not but that you have taken proper Steps for acquainting the Duke, and I shall if you think proper wait upon him or Ld Hartington if you will advise me what to say, for you may be assur'd my attention shall not be wanting in any Shape that is in my power ...

JRL, B2/2/354

33

Major Samuel Bagshawe to Lieutenant John, 12th Lord Sempill

[Draft]   [Portsmouth]
28 October 1747

My Lord

I have wondred for some time that you have stayed so much longer in London than you mentioned to me when you desird to go up & my Surprise is encreased to hear you have sent for your Baggage, I wish with all my Heart y.^r L.^dShip may succeed in what you propose to your Self but your Continuance in Town which has reached the Brigadiers Notice exposes me to his resentment at a very unseasonable time, I must therefore insist that you immediatly return to quarters or procure the Brig^{rs} Consent for your stay and approbation of the Share I have in your being away without first consulting him ...

JRL, B2/2/823

34

Major Samuel Bagshawe to Brigadier-General Edward Richbell

[Draft]   Portsmouth
                                                    28 October 1747

The part you have already acted to favour my promotion is the fullest proof of your Friendship to me, It shall always have my thankfull gratefull Acnowledgements whether successfull or otherwise, for the sake of your Regiment I hope Keene will not be the Man, I believe if the Voices of the Officers would weigh any thing with the King it would be their unanimous request, While he is under Controul he may be guarded against, but when he should Command I fear you would find it difficult to be secure against his Disposition, That All that know him believe him to be as bad a Man as ever carried a Comission would easily be proved but it may be difficult to prove the Detail of his Pranks, the Witnesses to many of them are one way or another out of the Regim^t; however there is nobody acquainted with him that doubts he robbed the Dying Officers in Jamaica beside a variety of other Rogueries in y^t place not to mention his giving Sir John Cope[89] a Bill of two hundred pounds to forward the getting his Comp^y on a person in Ireland when there was no such person in being. The 4 Days Act in favour of persons hastily enlisting[90] is supposed to owe its Birth to him, from his torturing of Men to make them list and afterwards he used to rob them, this last and Selling them pewter Buckles for Silver &c were the means of bringing him to a Court Martial in Ireland from which I believe you know how he escaped, He lyes under a strong belief of hiding himself in France in the first Engagement [91] & I believe it would be proved, he also brought liquers &c to his C^y on board[.] His behaviour at Arklow both to his Comp^y & [a] particular person in the country is not unknown to you as also his other tho' not all his Misbehaviour since you got the Reg^t, besides he is not at all qualified in point of Discipline for the Employment, and you know at Sir Philip Honeywoods[92] Review he refused to exercise the Reg^t and said he was unfitt for it on acc^t he has been run through the Body, Indeed if conversing & keeping Company with [the] lowest of people, Washing of Linnen & Dishes and cooking of Victuals are proper qualifications for a Major you cannot meet with a more compleat one in the Army. As to the Recruits they are not any of them very good Men but with respect to Size I believe may be within his Instructions, Except the best man among them is an Irishman ...

JRL, B2/2/502; 823a

35

Captain Thomas Levett, Regimental Agent, to Major Samuel Bagshawe

London
3 November 1747

It was no small concern to me to tell you that ye Majority is given to one Col. Sewell, who was a Lieu^t Col^o to the Duke of Bolton's late provincial Regim^t who has been recommended by the Gentlemen of Hampshire, and in particular by Mr Bridges,[93] one of the members for Winchester who personally ask't the King ... I hope they will think of doing some thing better for you ...

JRL, B2/2/357

36

Major Samuel Bagshawe to Mary Bagshawe of Ford

London
17 November 1747

A few days after I wrote to you last, I was informed that the Majority to which I and most who knew me thought I had so good Pretensions was given away to a Stranger (that is to an Officer who was not of our Regiment which is uncommon in the Army upon a Death) and that I was set aside for the very reason for which I believed I had so good a Title to it, The Loss of my Leg, and my earnestness to discharge my Duty has prov'd the means to deprive me of the Reward of it. Upon the News I immediatly got leave to come to Town and am determined never to return again to the Regiment, unless to settle my Accounts as Paymaster, so that I shall be obliged to enter upon quite a new Scene of Life at a Time that I am indeed under very improper Circumstances for a Change, but what will be done for me I cannot tell; The Duke of Devonshire and the Marquiss of Hartington are generously pleased to interest themselves in my Disappointment and by their means I have a prospect when my Case is represented to His Majesty to be someway provided for, as I have the Satisfaction that I cannot be reproached with any Misbehaviour ...

JRL, B2/3/125

37

Lieutenant Archibald Grant to Major Samuel Bagshawe

Portsmouth
[10 December 1747]

***

Im sory to be obliged to inform you of any thing that can be any wise disaggreable to you, but Friday last Serj^t Shearer of your

Company sent me an Acco.^t that three of your Men viz. Josh. Beains Joseph Harrison and William Ward had Deserted that morning from on board Ship, I would have acquainted you sooner of it but was willing to postpone it in hopes of having some acco.^t of them which we have not been able to do yet tho we have taken all Methods we could think of[,] they went off armed with a case of pistolls and cutlash each[.] I have not yet mentioned them to Coll. Sewell in a Return of the Deserters from the Regiment which I send him this day in order to have them advertised, because as they are on board Ship I presume youll chuse to continue y.^m Effective till they are disembarked, but if you chuse to have them advertised [I] shall send you a Description of them in my next ...

JRL, B2/2/197

38

Major Samuel Bagshawe to Lieutenant Archibald Grant

[Copy] London
15 December 1747

I can hardly perswade myself that those three Men are gone off and am in hopes tis some drinking Scheme they are upon, for I should as soon suspect the Desertion of the whole Company as of those Men[,] however please to send me their Discriptions and I will tell the Brigadier what has hapned and satisfie Sewell for your not reporting them directly to him, though if you think it necessary that he should receive the information from you pray do it. There is not one of those Men but have particular Obligations to me, one would be near moved never to do a kind thing to a Soldier, Those that treat them with the greatest Severity are best served by them ...[94]

JRL, B2/2/199

39

Lieutenant Archibald Grant to Major Samuel Bagshawe

Portsmouth
27 January 1748

As the money I had in my hands is very near Exhausted and Several Demands Making, I have taken the Liberty to draw this day on Captain Levett for Two hundred pounds for the use of the Regiment payable to M^r M^{c}naught on Order at Six days Sight, which I hope will be duly honoured. I deferr'd it in hopes of having the pleasure of hearing from you, as long as I could, but I hope my taking the Liberty to draw will make no difference. Munday last we embarked Ninety men & two Subs. on board the Invincible, there was to have been a Captain[.] Adml. Stewart[95] intended to have had Hepburn & the same party that disembarked from the S^t. George, but Coll. Sewell insisted that they had done their tour of duty and that he would send the next on Command, wherefore Stuart only demanded two Subs. who are L^d. Sempill & Wray[96] & deferr'd the Captain till Sr Peter Warren arrives who tis thought will insist on having Hepburn[97]. We have glorious doings here, Our Commander not only works those under his Command, but the Admiralty, Admiral & fleet, the extent of whose Authority he will soon let them know ...

JRL, B2/2/211

40

Major Samuel Bagshawe to Lieutenant Archibald Grant

[Copy]
London
29 January 1748

I have been very uneasy since I received your favour of the 27th. as you there take no notice of two Bills of a hundred pounds each which I sent you last Saturday[98], and this morning I have been forced to hurt my own Creditt by ordering whatever Bills appear at the Office in my name to be Stopped; if you have received them I beg you will immediatly put me out of pain[,] as I have not heard of the Portsmouth Mail being robbed, I have charged my Servant with neglecting to put the Letter into the Post Office, therefore if you have received those Bills please to let me know the Day they arrived and the date of the London mark, that I may acquitt my Servant or discover how I am to trust him for the future. I shall take care that proper Honour is paid to your Bills for two hundred pounds and I have on the other Side sent you Bills for the same Sume, of the receipt of which I beg you will advise me for I had rather pay postage of Fifty Letters, than suffer what I now do on Acc^t of these two Bills. I am afraid I give you too much trouble to that you have from another quarter, if I do I beg you will be so frank to tell me so. I desire you will not give yourself any more than to receive and pay, and refer to me the Settling of all kind of Acc^{ts}: indeed a very little time must now determine whether that will not also cease on my side ...

JRL, B2/2/212

41

Lieutenant Archibald Grant to Major Samuel Bagshawe

Portsmouth
1 February 1748

Dr Major

I had the favour of yours of January 29th yesterday, which I should have Acknowledged but did not Receive it till after Church when it was too late for the post, Im very sorry to find that my having omitted Acknowledging the Receipt of yours of January 23rd. with the Inclosed bills has occasioned you so much uneasiness, You may be assured that for the future I shall be very punctual in Acknowledging the Receipt of your favours to prevent your being any further uneasy on that Account, it was intirely owing to forgetfullness, for believe me Dear Major, I am keept so constantly imployed sometimes about business, but much oftener about nothing by our Commander that I cannot promise myself an hour in the day, When ever he has a letter to write which you know happens pretty frequently, I must sit by till tis done, then read, give my opinion And afterwards Copy into a great book, And I have two or three letters from him every morning generally before Nine O'clock, but from all this dont imagine that your business gives me any trouble[,] I give you my word of honour that it does not the least, but if it did ten times more, I should think myself an ungratefull monster if I did not perform it with the greatest Chearfullness, for nothing can ever give me an opportunity of suitably acknowledging how sincerely I am

> Dr Sir
> Your very much obliged and most
> obed.^t Servt
> Arch. Grant

I now have 4 Bills by me for £100 each

JRL, B2/2/213

42

Captain David Hepburne to Major Samuel Bagshawe

Portsmouth
8 February 1748

My Dear Major

My being a Lazy fellow, & having almost forgot the use of pen ink & paper, will not be a sufficient excuse for not having wrote to you sooner, but besides the above no reason, an Affair, little in itself, but like to prove Otherways in its Consequences, has taken up all my time, & very much Imployed my Mind — I beg leave to lay the Case before you for you[r] own Satisfaction only, & mine, with regard to your Sentiments of me.

You know that ever since we returned to Spithead (on account of Sr Pr Warren's Illness), I still flattered myself (especially as I had S^r peter's promise for it) that I should serve under him the next Cruise he made[,] you know likeways that we were continued on board the St. George some months, waiting till the Invinsible was Commissioned, where S^r. peter was to hoist his flag. On the 17th Jan^{ry} last we were landed by Admiral Stewart's orders not as dismissed from the Service (as he said) but to refresh the Men for about a Week or 14 days, before we reimbarked on Board the Invincible. Col^o Sewell opposed this as Irregular & insisted, that when any part of the Reg^t was landed, they were absolutely disingaged from any farther Service at Sea, & were then from under the Command of the Admiral who, if he wanted a party for the fleet, must have a fresh one, we having already done our tour of Duty. The Admiral persisted in his first oppinion & said, that had he thought any objection would have been made to it, he never would have landed the party from the St George, but transfer'd them to the Invinsible. While this contest lasted, (Incertain who was in the Right or who would get the better) I spoke to Capt Loyd^{d99} of the Invinsible, I told him Col^o Sewell opposed our going on board his Ship, & without entering into the Merits of the Cause, left it to him to act as he thought proper — the day following Adm^l Steward, either Convinced by Col^o Sewell's Reasons, or to avoid farther Contest, yielded to the Col^o all Claim or design of sending the same party again on Service, & only required that a Certain Number of Officers & Soldiers of Brigad^r Richbells Reg^t should be sent on board the Invincible. On the first notice I had of Mr Stewart's giving up the point, I waited on Col^o Sewell, I told him what I had done at the beginning of the Contest betwixt the Adm^l & him, I said that it was not my business to enter into a dispute that could only be decided by our great Superiors, that whilst the Admiral maintained an Argument in which his Authority & powers was concerned, I was in some Measure to be on his side of the question that I might not appear as if I were indifferent to the Service, or think lightly of the Honour S^r peter

Warren did me in Choosing me to serve under him — But now that M.ʳ Stewart had given up the point I was determined to take no step that might be deemed Irregular, or do any thing that would give him (Col.º Sewell) Offence, that I should neither speak, write, nor act any farther in the Case, but rest satisfyed with what should be done by my Supperiors.

Another party & other officers were ordered on board the Invincible & Imbarked, & thus things stood when S.ʳ. Peter Warren came here. I avoided going near him till Col.º Sewell had seen him, what passed betwixt them is nothing to the present purpose, but a day or two after, I was ordered, together with Me.ˢˢʳˢ. Tobell[100] & Perrin,[101] to Command the party of the Invincible which with regard to the private men & low officers stood as first appointed. I could easily perceive Col.º Sewell was displeased, & indeed he told me so, & said he would not have done as I did for £500. This surprized me — Conscious of having never intended to offend him or any body in what I did, I endeavoured to explain myself and satisfy him as to my Intentions, I offered to go to S.ʳ peter & request him to lay aside the Honour he designed me that I might neither be obnoxious to my Commanding Officer nor ill looked on by my Brethren as officious in going where I was thought to have no right, but I was told that it was now too late & better let things rest as they were — I thought so too, & believed all was over, but every day produces something new to find fault with, with regard to my proceedings & I have reason to believe I stand very ill with Col.º Sewell, diffident of myself I have askt the oppinion of my friends here, who all agree that if I have erred, it was in mistaking the extent of Adm.ˡ Stewarts power, & that I have acted by Col.º Sewell in a manner to have even a greater Mistake excused, do me the favour to let me know your Sentiments en Army, for I will always Act by the advice of my friends, especially One of whom I have had such constant and signal proofs of good will, pardon this long and wild epistle, I am a good deal Uneasie but constantly say I mean no Offence — I am

Dear Major
your ever oblidged
& most faithfull Humble Serv.[t]
David Hepburne

for the truth of what I have said about I appeal to all the gentlemen here, one would make bad worse, by palliating & disguising any part of a fact, which I think unworthy a gentleman, as I write this only to satisfy you D.[r] S.[r] unless my Name be mentioned in this Affair give yourself no trouble about me, but if you hear an old Friend blamed, if you think the reasons I have given above, any way sufficient for my Conduct be assured they are all true.

JRL, B2/2/261

43
Lieutenant-Colonel Matthews Sewell to Major Samuel Bagshawe

Portsmouth
13 February 1748

Sir

As the Accounts of Our Companys require very great Exactness during the time of our having any Men on Board the Fleet, and many Companys are now without any Officer [,] Captains Hepburne, Williams, Forde and I have agreed to allow L.[t] Grant a Mans pay p.[r] D.[m] each, to keep the Accounts of the respective Companys, As He will be allways on Shore, & he is extremely capable of it, and the many minute artickles necessary to be regularly inserted as soon as known, will give him no small trouble & the Security of the Captains from being loosers, which they may otherwise easily be; makes us imagine, That The Brigadier, to whom Our Compliments, will aprove of it. We shall be obliged to you, if you likewise aprove of it, to recomend

it to L: Col° Cotes and the rest of the Captains who are absent. I
have wrote this post to Captains Lovett & Symes.

> I am Sir
> Your most humble Servant
> M. Sewell

JRL, B2/2/521

44

Captain David Hepburne to Major Samuel Bagshawe

Invincible
28 February 1748

After many difficulties & Objections I am at last on Board his
Majesties Ship the Invincible, we are to sail tomorrow to join S:
Peter Warren. I shall not trouble you any more about the
opposition made to my going this Cruise, but only Acquaint you
that I can perceive a Settled Rancour in the Mind of a certain
Person with regard to me, notwithstanding all my Endeavours
not to justifie my self, but rather to excuse my self for what had
passed. When nothing else would do I was ordered on board in a
Hurry, with threats of a Complaint to the Admiralty, & an
Actual Application to Adm! Stewart for that purpose, & Many
Cautions about my behaviour, as I should Answer for at my
Landing Again. It is impossible to tell you all in the Compass of
a letter, Equally so, for you to believe all, without having seen
most of our late transactions. I say no more on this head till time,
& opportunity, shall produce things in their true light.

The many proofs I have already received of your sincere
goodness & friendship, would make me almost ingratefull not to
try that friendship again. I must therefore beg you to inform
yourself if an Exchange to any of the Reg:s at Gibraltar or Minorca
might easily be brought about for me, I mean in an old Reg:. This
does not so much proceed from any uneasiness as I am, but rather
in my desire to be in a Situation which you know is so greatly my
Inclination. I could wish either to be in the way of doing

something, or out of the Way of doing anything, but you know my temper as well as I do myself, if a peace issues, I could be Satisfyed to return to the quiet of Ireland, 'tho I believe either of the above mentioned Climates would agree better with my age & Constitution, which I find declining daily. I would therefore willingly settle in any honest way but marriage, which Service, I really find myself the most unfit for.

I have left with Archy Grant a power to receive my prize Money, it will be paid soon & 'tis said will amount to £60 or 70. I once intended to have applied to you for a little Indulgence for this Sum which if you had been pleased I design'd for Lyons to help his promotion but not without your leave, as I believe it now too late, I hope you will dispose of that Money as is most agreable, either to pay the debt I owe you or to serve Lyons if you can forbear me a little longer, I have no Occasion for it Myself ...

JRL, B2/2/260

45

Captain Verney Lovett to Major Samuel Bagshawe

Peterborough
1 March 1748

... It woud take up too much of y.^r. time to give you an acc.^t. of how I have been used, by some of my noncommissioned officers, Serj.^t. Streett lost the money I gave him (when I went to London) to carry on the recruiting service at Cards, Corp.^l. Parker his proportion spent at the ale House & some other extravagances that has oblidged me to draw for £40 since I left London. When I imagined [the] Serj^{ts}. had money to inlist men I find for many weeks they had not a Shilling. When they heard I was likely to leave the Regiment, they went to the shopkeeper for money on whom I had given y.^m. Creditt, & w.^d. have large sums but he finding the Cash going, & no Recruits luckily refused them, or else I know not how far Streett w.^d. have run me. I cannot change them by reason of the Regiment's lyeing at so great a Distance, nor bringing y^m. to a Court Martial here is impossible, I must be on my Guard as much as possible, for any help from y^m. I can't expect. I'll do my own endeavour as far as lyes in my pow'r, but I think their proceedings in some measure account for the ill success I have met with. I had a fine recruit to whom I gave £3 claim'd as a Deserter from the Welsh Fuzileers.[102] These putt together I shall make a Glorious Voyage of it ...

JRL, B2/2/414

46

Major Samuel Bagshawe to Lieutenant William Dawkin

[Draft]   Ford
                                                          31 March 1748

Dear Dawkin

This will inform you that I am in the Peak, for I found my abode in London answered but one purpose to impoverish me, I believe your Opinion of me is that I am not over ready to flatter myself with Success, but the assurances I had of it came from such Hands that I dare say one less credulous might have given heed to them as I did and have waited as long, and indeed the Farce if it was a Farce was carried on to the last, for when I had received certain Notice that His R.H. was to go for Holland and that the Vacancies were filling up, (this was Monday morning and the Duke went Wednesday Morn) I waited on my Patron who immediately went to the Secretary at War[103] and by him was told that my name was to be given in to the Duke that very Night, on the Wednesday I attended at the Warr Office but the Secretary had no Levée, on Friday I attended again, The Secretary was there & took me into his Room [,] told Me he was very sorry I was disappointed but that it was impossible to resist

the Interest made in favour of Forrester[104], that H.R.H. expressed so great concern on my Account that he did not doubt I
should very soon be taken care of; I went from him to my patron,
spoke my mind pretty freely and desired He would procure me
leave to go into the Country, which he asked & was readily
granted me. My Patron I am fully convinced was so greatly
concerned at my Disapointment that it really gave me as much
pain as the Disapointment gave me Chagrin. I have left the
Affair in his Hands for I only expected to be provided for
through his influence & Interest, Maimed Soldiers seems to be
regarded like old Horses, not worth their Meat, however I think
I can justly comfort myself with the reflection That they cannot
reproach me with any Misbehaviour ...

JRL, B2/2/822

47
Lieutenant William Dawkin to Major Samuel Bagshawe

Portsmouth
16 June 1748

Dear major

The Results of my Regard & Friendship will follow you to the
Devils A–e[105] but pray why so Secret to one whom I hope you
think to be a wellwisher of yours? Whatever you may imagine of
it I do assure you I am most Sincerely so, let not your Solitary
hours forget me: In faith I love you & wish I c.^{d} say more, but let
the Will go for the Deed. Now for our Noble Major & I, in April
last I reced his orders to repair to the Regim.^{t} & as at that time I
really had business to do, & as I knew there was not much to do
here I apply'd to him for leave to stay some little time which he
refus'd, I then applied to the Brigad.^{r} & got Col.^{o} Weld[106] to back
(this Gentlem.^{n} was Lt Coll to the Regim.^{t} Richbell was first Capt
too). Richbell I took for granted w.^{d} not deny him & he never

75

answered either of our letters, while in this Suspense I was Seiz'd w^(th) a Violent Fever & as soon as ever I was able to get on Horseback I came here which was last Sunday Night & I am now in the Cribb by the Majors Orders, he is himself at Winchester where his family lives. Cotes is gone to Sherburne.[107] I have wrote to Richbell, but he is such a Man that he won't trouble himself about me, confinement is what I have not been much used too therefore can brook it but badly, & if I am not released soon, I will have a General Court Martial if I can, & by the Eternal God if Sewel carries himself tow^(ds) me in any other manner than that of a Gentlem^(n) I'll cut his throat or he shall cut mine, but let things turn out as they will, if I can, I'll quit rather than be in such a Corps as ours is now, I think that I never saw any thing so altered for the Worse ...

JRL, B2/2/144

48

Lieutenant Archibald Grant to Major Samuel Bagshawe

Portsmouth
28 June 1748

In my last I sent you a Copy of the Distribution of money to Aprile last, with an Account of the Payments made to the Officers to the 25th of Febry according to your Desire, both of which I hope you received, tho' I have not had the pleasure of hearing from you since, I have likewise sent you a Distribution to June 25^(th) a Copy of which I have this day sent to the Agent, in the last Distribution he was Surprised to find that the payments made to some of the Companys exceeded the Subsistance of the whole Company for the Muster, which I afterwards explained to him by sending the particulars of the payments made to each Comp^(y) whereby he saw that severall of the men had been cleard off their whole Sea Pay on their Landing, by Coll. Sewells orders, if there is any thing either in this or the former

Distribution that is not right, or that you would Chuse to have explain'd be so good as to let me know and I shall indeavour to Rectify it, or give you a Satisfactory reason for it being so, for I keep the Vouchers for every Article by me.

Im Affraid when the Regiment comes to be landed I shall be difficulted a good deal in Settling their Accounts, as we shall have such a Number of different Accounts, come all at once, and I am so little acquainted with those things, that would require a more Capable hand, but in that and every thing else in my power, be assured that I shall always with the greatest pleasure and willingness, do the best as far as I am capable to do any thing that can be of the least service to you or show my gratitude for the many obligations Im under to you

***

Reports here are various with regard to our fate upon the Conclusion of a Peace, One day we are to be sent back to Ireland, another, we are to be made Marines, and all the present Marine Regiments broke, and some say there are eight old Regiments to be broke, in which event tis easy to tell our fates, but this a little time only can determine. The Brigad.^r Im told lives at his Countrey house and gives himself very little trouble about us, Coll. Cotes was here two nights last month[,] Coll. Sewell has been at Winchester these 3 weeks past ... As for Town News we are all as dull as possible, we have lost all our gayety, The Ladys never are seen by us, Our Assemblys are dropt for want of Company ...

JRL, B2/2/227

49
Lieutenant William Dawkin to Major Samuel Bagshawe

Portsmouth
17 July 1748

... Here we are in the most disagreable way I ever was in since I knew the Regim^t[.] Grant, Lewis[108] & I live together in the best manner we can, as for the rest of those here they are not worth associating wth, & it is uncertain when the Fleet will return, an Express being gone but the other day to give Warren an Acc^t of the Preliminaries being sign'd by Spain. Sewell & I are as great as can be now but I do think he is one the most trifling Fellows I ever saw or ever met wth. Richbell and he between them kept me in Arrest for 15 or 16 days & [I] never co^d receive an Answer from either till at last by my frequent writing to the Brigad^r he at last vouchsafed me an Answ^r wth an Appology for his being much out of order & not able to transact any business, & he likewise wrote a very kind letter to Sewel in my behalf, which I heard off by Accident & Sewel who came here to sign the Returns released me & afterwards made great many fine Speeches which my Matrimoniall Situation oblig'd me to Acquiess wth in hopes of gaining some indulgence soon, which I intend to Sollicit as soon as the Regim^t Lands & our destiny known, for I want to go home my poor wife being so much out of order & is vastly uneasy at my Absence, which thro' her prudence she endeavours to conceal from me: but upon the whole I find I shall be under a necessity of quitting or suffer one of the most Affectionate & tenderest of Women to lead a Miserable Life, & while this is the case, I shall leave no stone unturn'd to contribute towards the Peace and Tranquility of her whom I ought in gratitude as well as Affection to Esteem and Regard, & another thing I am most heartily tired of my Subalternship ...

I must needs tell you how Sewel has like to have drawn himself into a scrape, he came here on the last day of June to Sign the Returns, & went back to Winchester that same day, as he lives there now entirely: but the next day, being the day for signing & sending off the Returns, one Dumond a Capt. of the Invalids here[109] finding Sewel was gone look'd upon himself as Commanding Officer & accordingly sent for all the Returns of the Garrison in order to sign & send off, but Grant told him Sewel had done it, the old man wth much difficulty was prevail'd upon not to send other Returns, alledging that Mr Sewel was not upon the Spott the day they ought to be sign'd, therefore it was his duty & if I co^d have brought the thing about, it sho^d have been so ...

50

Captain Thomas Levett, Regimental Agent, to Major Samuel Bagshawe

London
11 October 1748

... I am Extreamly glad to hear that you and the family at Forde are well. I hope before this time you have received mine of the 6th, in wch I gave you the last Acco.^t I could of all our affairs here, and till this day had heard nothing from ye Regim.^t or of any Occurance remarkable otherways, but have just now had a Letter from the Brigad.^r who tells me that he has found a good deal of disatisfaction amongst the Men of the Reg.^t in regard to Sea Stoppages, such as Beds &c,¹¹⁰ and that the disputes & uneasiness's that is amongst them can't be sett right till their whole Acco.^{ts} are Adjusted, wch he aprehends cant be done without your Assistance, as grant has not Settled anything but paid them on Acco.^t and therefore the Brig.^r has desired me to let you know that he thinks your presents is absolutely necessary, and that he shall take it Extreamly kind of you, if your private affairs would not Suffer greatly by it, that you wou'd joyn the Regim.^t for he can't Stir from it till he see the whole adjusted and Settled, in order for which I propose Sending by next Post open Acco.^{ts} for all the Captains, with an Acco.^t of all Charges that have occur'd thro me, but that I fear without y^{re} Assistance will not make things clear to them, and the Conduct of y.^r wrong headed Major will no Ways add to it, and therefore if y.^r Affairs will permitt you to come soon, it will be of infinite Service, and give both the Brigad.^r & me great Satisfaction & pleasure and if you make this your way, I can give you a Bed, as I am now alone having left my family in Staffordshire, and what I think will make your presents with the Regiment the much more necessary is, that I aprehend a reduction will be very soon, for the Duke had order'd that all the Men of the Aditional Comp.^s belonging to the Regim.^{ts} in Flanders, sh'd March to Colchester and be there review'd by a General Officer & the best of them be sent over to Flanders, but the General apointed for the Service was last night countermanded, and I am told orders are preparing for Reducing them and that the Peace will come in a few days ...

JRL, B2/2/363

51

Captain Thomas Levett, Regimental Agent, to Major Samuel Bagshawe

London
8 November 1748

I hope this will find you safe & well at Portsm.^{h} and all things there to your Satisfaction, & shall be glad to know the day fix't for y.^{r} Reduction, at wch I hope the Brigad.^{r} will be, having acquainted him that it was Expected, and I thought absolutely necessary; and I am told that part of the Reg.^{t} that is not Reduc'd will continue upon English Pay to the 24th. of Decr notwithstanding they shu'd Embarque sooner, & I hope the officers that are to be Reduced will have there pay to that time, but that I am not certain of, but will inform you as soon as I can ...

Last Post brought me a Letter from a Gentleman in Staffordshire to desire that I wo.^{d} (if it could conveniently be done) get a discharge at this Reduction for one Thos Robinson of y.^{r} Company, whose Father he says works with him & has an old Wife, to both which the young Man might be of use to if he came home, but I don't find he proposes giving any Money, and as I have no obligation to the Gentleman, if the parting with this Man will be any sort of inconveniency to you, don't do it out of a Complym.^{t} but if you don't keep him y.^{r}Self I could wish he might be discharged rather than drafted. So you will do in it as is convenient & agreable.

I have likewise an application from Major Sawyer[111] for the discharge of one Robt Thomas who is one of Lt Lewis's last Recruits, listed at Hereford, and whose Father is a Tennant of the Major's and is willing to pay any Listing Charges as far as five pounds, wc.^{h} I beg you will mention to the Brigad.^{r} if he comes or to Col. Cotes, & I hope they will be so kind as to comply with the Maj^{rs} request, for the Man is but a Recruit that has just joyn'd the Regim^t ...

JRL, B2/2/364

52

Lieutenant Archibald Grant to Major Samuel Bagshawe

Bristol
29 December 1748

This morning Capt Keenes Lovetts Williams & Symes Company embarked on board the Duke Transport, on which Occasion Lieut. Supple[112] took it into his head to behave very indecently & impudently to Coll. Sewell As you may be more fully informed by the Brigadeer to whom he has this day Reported him in Confinm^t[,] As he has likewise done to the Secretary at War & desired it to be laid before his Majesty, In his Letter to whom viz. the Secret^y at War he has wrote the following paragraph, of which I thought it necessary to acquaint you, that in case there are any Steps still necessary to be taken, to prevent any bad Consequences from such application you may be prepared therefore as early as possible, The paragraph is as follows,

"It is Reported that Capt Bagshaw third Captain in this Regiment is to purchase the Lt Coll^{os} Commission, As his Majesty has Already honourd me with the Rank of Lt Coll., And as I have been 40 years an Officer, And am now as fitt to Serve as ever, it is worth his while to give a great deal more money for it than me, but I am willing to purchase the Difference of pay between Major and Lieut. Colonell, And humbly hope that you will be so good as not to Recommend any one to my Prejudice

He has wrote to the same purpose to the Brigad^r of which he can inform you more fully.

I thought proper to give you this hint though I hope the Steps you have already taken are Sufficient to Render any application of his useless. But as you cannot be too well prepared ag^t such Attempts, I hope youll pardon my giving you this trouble ...

P.S. As I picked the above paragraph by Stealth let it be entre nous till you hear of it from another quarter, Dawkins Hepburne & all the brethren greet you, Poor Billy is in a very indifferent State of health.

JRL, B2/2/238

53

Lieutenant Archibald Grant to Major Samuel Bagshawe

Bristol
2 January 1749

... This forenoon C. S–l hearing that I had rec^d a Letter asked me from whom it was I told him from you, he asked me what news, I told him, none, but that you desired me to draw for 30 days Subs^{te} for the Reg^t he then asked is there nothing else, Yes I told him that you was affraid that you should meet with some Rubs in your Affair, that the Old Gentleman your Uncle did not care for Depositing so much money, Says he, If Im not mistaken he will find some more than that, for I have wrote Lord Harrington,[113] the Secretary at War & Coll. Cotes to let them know I am willing to purchase the Difference of pay, Or to be Lieutt Coll. upon Majors pay & let Coll. Cotes go out on his full pay during Life some of which proposals I fancy will put a Stop to his affair, he then showed me a Letter he Rec^d today from the Secretary at War in Answer to that I mentioned in my last, in which he tells him, "As to Capt. Bagshaw's Affair I can say nothing to it but referr you to the Lord Lieutenant or Lords Justices of Ireland since now the Regiment is on that Establishment it must be done through them – in consequence of which

he has this day wrote to Lord Harrington & to the Lords
Justices of Ireland, Reporting Lt Supple in Arrest and I presume
mentioning the other affair but I could not see their Letters, he
afterwards said I fancy either one or other of the two Schemes I
mentiond will take place or we shall have a half pay Lt. Coll. put
in upon us by paying Cotes the Difference for the whole pay &
giving him up his half pay –

Thus, Dr Major you have all the Intelligence I can pick up,
And hope that you will be able to Countermine all his Schemes
as Im pretty well convinced theyre done rather to dissappoint
you than from any hopes of his Own Success ...

I need not Caution you to let the above be Entre nous

I burn'd yours this morning after Reading least it should by
some Accident fall in worse hands.

JRL, B2/2/240

54
Lieutenant-Colonel James Cotes to Major Samuel Bagshawe

Coleshall
4 January 1749

... I think you have no reason to be alarmed about any
proceedings of Colonel Sewells; I acquainted him of my intention of disposing of my Commission when I was at Portsmouth,
& there made him an offer of it on ye same terms, that I had
purchas'd; he desired to consult with his friends in London;
which he acquainted me he had done, and was advised against
buying; I don't know whether I have kept his letter, but I declare
this is fact and shall certainly mention it when I make my
application to My Lord Harrington; and tho' the affair will not
come before the Secretary at War, I shall certainly acquaint him
of the truth of this matter. I have been informed of some of M^r
Sewell's late transactions, & will not approve of some alterations, that he has made, he seems to endeavour to make people

unhappy, & himself hated for which he may some time or other meet a due reward ...

JRL, B2/2/122

55
Lieutenant-Colonel James Cotes to Major Samuel Bagshawe

Woodcote
14 January 1749

... I don't doubt Sewell will give you all the trouble he possibly can, as to any proposals, that he shall make to me, I do assure you that I shall answer none of them. I am advised by my particular friends who will be chiefly concerned in the transaction of our affair, not to appear in town 'till I hear of the Regiment's being settled in Ireland, when I have advice of that, I shall set out for Town, and nothing shall be wanting on my part toward a conclusion. I think you should take care to fix your Successour, or it may occasion delay; for before I give in my Memorial to my Lord Harrington, the whole Money must be secured to me, and in the same terms too, on which I purchased from Col? Savage.[114] I believe you are acquainted with them, however I shall briefly mention them; I am to receive £3360, & to have my personal account, & the non effective account of my Company made up to the day you succeed me, I am to give the Company Compleat, & if you will take my Tent, & field bed on y? same terms, that I bought them. My Trunk containing two Suits of Regimental Cloaths, Linnen &c are all at your Service ...

JRL, B2/2/123

56

Captain George Symes to Captain Thomas Levett, Regimental Agent

Dublin
31 January 1749

I received a Letter from Capt Bagshaw by Brig^{dr.} Richbells orders, to send Anth^{oy} Thomas of my Comp^y who died aboard the fleet his account, in order that his wife may get the ballance, this Woman or one of his wifes, was at Bristol and apply'd to Col.^o Sewell upon which he ordered a Court Martial to inspect into ye deceased mans accounts, and the ballance paid her whose receipt I here Enclose you, as also the acon.^t[,] it is very hard that an officer must be Eternally plagued with such Strumpets ...

JRL, B2/2/722

57

Lieutenant Archibald Grant to Major Samuel Bagshawe

Dublin
7 March 1749

***

Now as to News—you must know that our Commander has made no small eclat since his Arrivall in Dublin, poor Supples affair of which every body knew the Circumstances before he came to Town established his Character before he made his appearance & his name was as well known in Lucases as in Moll Smiths Coffee house, he had severall applications made him by Supples friends & from the Speaker (who showd himself very Strenuously in Supple's interest) to pass from the prosecution and Accept of a Submission, which he at first seemed very averse to, alledgeing that as he had reported him to the Duke, the Secretary at War, Lord Harrington & the Lords Justices it was out of his power to forgive it to which he was Answered that neither the Duke nor the Secretary at War had any business with it, the Regiment was on this Establishment and he had no business to Report it any where else, he said as the Duke was General of the Army it was his Duty to Report it to him, & upon his mentioning the Duke on Several occasions, in that affair, The Speaker gave him to understand that he had better drop that, that the Duke had no Command here, And that the Lords Justices were quite independent of him, Sewell then agreed to accept of a Submission provided that Supple would ask his pardon at the head of the Regiment, for which he likewise got a sort of Cheque & was told that his Acknowledging his fault & asking pardon by Letter was sufficient Recompense for his Crime & that he must accept of that, which was done and Supple Released accordingly.

When he came to Town the other Lieu.[t] Coll.[os] here viz.[t] Warburton of Lord Molesworths[115] and Pearce of Irvines[116] were Determind to Dispute his Rank with him, & Warburton who commanded in the barracks applyd to L.[d] Molesworth[117] that he must command only as Major as he imagined that his Commission in the Provincial Reg.[t] gave him no Rank, as he had no half pay for it upon which L.[d] Molesworth desired Warburton to acquaint him that it was his orders that he should Assume no Command, only as Major till the Affair was decided, As he did not know whether or not or how it had been determind on the other side of the Water, Whereupon Sewell drew up a Memorial & Caryd it with his Commission & L.[d] Molesworth's order to the L.[ds] Justices who upon Reading his Commission & some queries in regard to that, that had been Stated & answered at the raising of those Regiments decided in his favour and appointed him to Command as L.[t] Coll. immediately on which he removed from his Lodgeings & went into the Barracks & assumed the Command there, where I assure you he does COMMAND—

JRL, B2/2/245

58

Lieutenant Archibald Grant to Lieutenant-Colonel Samuel Bagshawe

Dublin
4 May 1749

Dear Col?

I received the favour of yours of Aprile 25th with the greatest pleasure & do most sincerely Congratulate not only you but the whole Corps upon your Affairs being at last done as Im sure it has given much the greatest part of it the utmost joy both on their own and your Account, we had the Accounts of its being to be done some time before the Commissions were Signd by the Notifications being sent over to the War Office here, but Coll. Sewell was certain notwithstanding of that, that they would not be done & affirmd it to some of his Acquaintances, but seemd very much surprised and disappointed when he heard they were Signd.

***

We all long much to have the pleasure of seeing you with us being pretty well tired of the present administration ...

JRL, B2/2/246

59

Lieutenant-Colonel Samuel Bagshawe to Captain Thomas Levett, Regimental Agent

Dublin
20 June 1749

[Copy]

I have imparted to the Brig.^r and to the Captains of the Regiment that part of your Letter of the 6th Instant which mentions the Overhaul threatened by the Secretary at War and they are preparing Contingent Accounts, but in the mean time to prevent a Proceeding which must give very much trouble to the Secretary at War & will hurt them they desire you will represent to him the many great and unavoidable Expences we were put to for the three last Years we were on the English Establishm^t. In the year 1746 We had compleated our Companys in April, at which time We were ordered on board for the Canada Expedit^n. When we got to Portsmouth in order to embark We were obliged to compleat again; for as our Destination had been known a Month before the Embarkation, our loss by Desertion, feigned sickness (which Men we were forced to part with & take others in their Room) and Men discharged Who would have served some years at home but whom We did not think sufficient for this Service, I say our Loss on this Occasion upon an Average amounted to fourteen Men a Company, At the same time We were obliged to pay a Shilling a day for Quarters for all our sick both feigned and real all the time we lay at Spithead & the same at Plymouth y^t Article amounted to above a hundred Pounds during the Expedition, And we have been under a continued large Expence ever since that time having always been quarter'd at Portsmouth and in the Service of the Fleet, our Sick having scarse ever been fewer than Fifty and sometimes a hundred, A hundred & Fifty & two hundred at a time[.] We have lost great sums by Deaths, Desertions &c for whenever the Fleet demanded a party We were forced to furnish them with all Sea Necessarys[118] & our Loss was particularly great in the October Engagement in 1747 which hapned on the 14th of the Month[119] and a great part of our Men were only put on board the beginning of the Month, I could enumerate many other Charges we have been put to, but I hope there will be sufficient to incline the Secretary at War to consider our Sufferings, and not make us a presid^t. or distinguish us from the rest of the Army, I Do assure you that in my own Company the Roll of it amounts to above two hundred since we come to England in 1743 beside all other Charges[,] I dare say the rest of the Regiment bear a Proportion.

JRL, B2/2/371

60

Lieutenant-Colonel Samuel Bagshawe to
Dr. Thomas Fletcher, Bishop of Kildare

[Draft]   Dublin
[10 August] 1749

... If your L.ᵈShip has heard nothing of me since I saw you
last, it will be news to you that I am a Lieu.ᵗᵗ Col. on this
Establishment but none by what means it was brought about.
When I last waited on y.ʳ Lordship I was preparing to go
into the Country and indeed I went thither with a Disposition
to remain there if so it had pleased my Uncle, but notwithstanding he met with [an] unusual & violent attack against
his Health insomuch that he himself thought his Life in
Danger he was no ways inclined to put any Power in my
hands, though I proposed no other Share of it than the
trouble, therefore I was not sorry for an order which requird
my joining my Regim.ᵗ. in order to settle the Acc.ᵗˢ of it; the
Reg.ᵗ was afterwards reduced & sent to this Country, Cotes
our L.ᵗᵗ Col. had Affairs in England which required his constant Attendance & desired to quitt the Service, I acquainted
Lord Hartington with this who wrote to my Lord Duke & His
Grace at length prevailed with my Uncle to furnish a thousand
pounds towards the purchase Money ~~which I was to pay for it
over & above my Company~~, My friend Cap.ᵗ Levett furnished
the rest that I might not be disapointed, & I am now acting the
L.ᵗᵗ Colonel as well as I can & I hope in a manner as shall meet
with y.ʳ Lordships Approbation ...

JRL, B2/3/682

61

Lieutenant-Colonel Samuel Bagshawe to Captain Thomas Levett, Regimental Agent

[Draft]   [Dublin]
                                                        28 November 1749

The order that came from the War Office to the other Reg^{ts} came last to ours, only with this Difference, That the Returns required from other Reg^{ts} are to comence from the 25th June 1747 wheras ours are required from the 25th December 1746. I am sorry We are obliged to give you so much trouble but I am convinced a great deal depends upon it & the Manner in wch you appear for us. We desire that you will plead strongly that the Returns & Accounts may not be required further back from Us than is required from other Regiments, for the following Reason, That We should not be distinguished from others since We hope it will appear We took equall Pains to keep up the Strength of our Companys; that the Regiment having been seperated part being in Ireland & part in England the Returns were not made regularly & We cannot come to a true State of the Companys; & That this Seperation with the frequent landing & Embarkations was the Occasion of great Expence to the Captains on their own private Acc^{ts} as well as on Acc^{t} of their Companys which became very sickly & many Men were left behind in different parts of both Kingdoms for whom they were obliged to hire lodgings & provide Nurses & Necessarys, and for these & many other reasons they were paid the greatest part of their Non Effective Acc^{t} to the 25th of June 1747 ... There was likewise a change among the Officers, one Capt vizt Major Fox is dead, one vizt Col. Cotes retired & a third in the Country for his Health[120] & so ill that he is not able to form an Acc^{t} nor has he left any papers or Acc^{ts} behind by which to form one, however lest the Secretary at War should insist to have a Return & an Acc^{t} from the 25th Decr to the 24th June—I have sent one made up from what Meterials we could find, though I know it is very deficient, for Instance—Col. Cotes Comp^{y} Contingent Acc^{t} I dare say is Thirty or Forty Pounds short &

many of wch charges are cash for as we never imagined there would be a Retrospeck, it was common to pay a Contingent Acc^t when it hapned and take no further Notice of it & very often a Capt paid it out of his own Subsistance because he expected it would be made up again in the Non Effective Accounts. We must desire you to urge the great Charge We were at in the Draughts which you will be able to Compute from the Return I sent you of the State of Reg^t at the time We were ordered on the Expedition & the Number of Draughts we took afterwards, and [it] may not be amiss to mention the great Expence the Captains were put to Who by the Order of the General Commanding in chief laid in stores for an Expedition to Canada a great part of which were lost or Wasted[.] Your Arguments for the great Contingent Charges in the Acc^t from the 25th June 1747 to the time of the Reductions will arise from the nature of the Articles themselves and the long time [and] the kind of Service the Reg^t was upon on board the Fleet for from August 1747 to Novr 1748 the time of the Reduction We had from Fifty to one hundred and Fifty Men in Sick Quarters at a time for whom We were obliged to furnish Nurses, Fire Candle &c—Please to observe also that when a Man was sent on board the Fleet he was to be immediatly furnished with a Sufficient Stock of Sea Necessarys to near the amount of forty Shillings which if any accident hapned to him soon after his being put on board became a certain loss to the Captain and this was our Case in the Engagement with the French Fleet which hapned within fourteen days after the 2^d Embarkation, beside the Service itself tore our Regiment to Pieces, for the best Men generally suffered most, as they were more ready upon all Occasions so that with respect to the Return of the Reg^t at the Reduction, We must desire you to urge what the Strength of the Reg^t would have been, were it not for the many Casualties which hapned from March the usual time of being Compleat to the time of the Reduction & that will appear to you by the Return I sent you lately & you will be also enabled by it to give a State to the Secretary at War if he will see it.

Please to let your Books be examined for the Contingent Charges you have paid & order them to be added to the general

Acc.[t], I beg you will also order a State to be made out of Subsistance paid to Recruits charged in your Office for I am of Opinion that the Charge I have sent falls greatly Short, being taken from Return[s] which according to our Situation could not avoid being erroneous for sometimes the Remains of a Company left on Shoar was not only without any of their own Off.[rs] but even without a Serjeant and this Charge that I have sent contains both What we imagine was paid in your Office & also what has been paid & charged at Quarters without being included in the Acc.[ts] sent to you ...

JRL, B2/2/375

62

Captain Thomas Levett, Regimental Agent, to Lieutenant-Colonel Samuel Bagshawe

London
December 1749

Dear Sir

I have received y.[r] favour of the 28.th pas't with the Several Returns, which I show'd M.[r] Sherwin[121] and consulted him upon, and he tells me that your first request, w.[ch] is not to go back so far as the 25.th of Dec.[r] 1746 can by no means be Comply'd with, your Reg.[t] being Muster'd no farther then that time, the Secretary Expects such an Acco.[t] from that time that he can be able to answer to allow a Warrant for shu'd the Parliament Enter into an Examination, and he says the same is expected from Framptons, and all other Regim.[ts] and as to the representations you desire me to make [it] will be of little (if any Consequence) as most of the grievances you represent are answer'd for by the allowance of 3 Conting.[t] Men to the Reg.[ts] that are 70 y.[e] Comp.[y] & four to y.[rs] that was 100, for you are Expected to Acc.[ot] for only 100 y.[e] Comp rank and file, and that the other 4 with the Casualtys that may have happen'd in Each

Month is thought Sufficient to answer all y.ᵣ Conting.ᵗ Charges,[122] and therefore the most regular method that occurs to me is to take from the Monthly returns the Non effectives that are Wanting to Complete the Reg.ᵗ to 1000 Rank and File, in w.ᶜʰ. Method Jordans[123] & Some other Regim.ᵗˢ have sent their Noneffective Acc.ᵒᵗ and is aprov'd off, and in that Shape I have made a State of yours in the most correct Manner I can from the Returns you Sent me, and you will observe that I begin the first Month with the Number you return for Jan.ʳʸ and to proceed Supposing them to Stand so at the last of each Month, and I have added to Each Month's Effectives those that you put down at the bottom as Casualtys w.ᶜʰ. makes them appear so much more complete, and consequently the Noneffectives so many less, So you will see at one View the amount of the whole Noneffectives to answer which I Cred.ᵗ the whole Number of Recruits that you mention having raised in that time at £5 y.ᵉ Man, but I don't take any notice of the two Warr.ᵗ Men, but if they shu'd Expect them to be brought into the Acco.ᵗ it may be done here, but that will Enlarge the Ballance Considerably, to answer which there may be a Charge under the head you mention of Subsisting the Recruits from the time of Listing till they joyn'd their respective Comp.ˢ but the Several other Conting.ᵗ Articles that you mention must by no means be taken Notice off, as the 4 Men y.ᵉ Comp. are Expected to answer all them and you must be Cautious not to make y.ᵣ Noneffective ballance apear too Small, for fear they Shu'd Scrutinize more Nicely, and I am apt to believe the most favor you can Expect will be the taking of £5 a Man for what was wanting at the time of Reduction ... And I must desire you will lose no time in Settling this Acc.ᵒᵗ and returning it to me, and you will Sign it at the bottom, & lett me have full instructions, and if I find any alterations Necessary I shall acquaint you.

I must desire you will let me know the Names of all the Officers that belong to the four Comp.ˢ that went first to Ireland, that in Case the Governm.ᵗ do's think proper to allow them English pay from the 25 of Dec.ᵣ to the time of their landing I may know how to account with them, and I shall be glad to know when the Party landed in Ireland that was left at Ports.ᵐ to take care of the Sick, for if any difference of pay can be got on that Acc.[t] I'le try for it in the Conting.[t] Bill, w.[ch] was not thought proper to be given in till the going off the Establishment was absolutly fix'd, and if you think of any thing necessary to represent as to y.[e] Expedition, or Accidents that attended the Officers & Reg.[t] in the Several Embarkations, It must be done by a Memorial to the Secretary at War, for my Speaking from y.[r] Letters will be of no Consequence, but you may be assured that nothing shall be wanting that is in the power

of Dear Col.[o]
your very faithful and
Obed.[t] hum.[ble] Serv.[t]

Tho. Levett

JRL, B2/2/376

63

Lieutenant-Colonel Samuel Bagshawe to William Bagshawe of Ford

[Draft]

[Dublin]
[May 1750]
Irish Money

	£ s d
My yearly Income as Lieuten.[t] Colonel or Subsistance paid me being Money I may depend on is	229: 2:11
My Arrears for a Year, (the Payment of them uncertain) is	51:14: 2
51:08:10 true Arrears	£280:17: 1

Payments to be discharged by the above Income

Interest of £1000 at 5p^{r}C^t being £50 English is in Irish Money	£54: 3: 4	
D^o of £350 D^o 17:10 is D^o.	18:19: 2	
Allowance to my Sister[124] 30 is	32:10: 0	105:12: 6

The Keeping of two Horses Shoeing etc upon an Average of 3s
   a day is   54:15: 0

Whenever I am in Dublin I am obliged to keep two Servants on
Account of my Horses, in the Country I only keep one. Their
Wages, Board Wages & Cloaths upon an Average is   34:12: 6

Lodging when in Dublin (wch as the Government are generally
attended by one Field Officer of a Reg^t I suppose half the
Year) at a Pistole that is 18s:3d a Week   is   23:14: 6

Coach & Chair hire when in Dublin at a Pistole a Week   23:14: 6

Coals and Candles about   4:10: 0

A New Cane for my Leg every Year four Guineas is   4:11: 0   145:17: 6

                        £251:10: 0

Supposing the Arrears paid there remains for my own Diet
   Cloaths and other Expences   29: 7: 1

The Method of an Officers Diet in general is, Breakfast at his own
lodging, Dinner and Supper at a Tavern, I will suppose the Breakfast
Sixpence, Dinner Thirteen Pence, (no Officer dines cheaper in any
part of the Kingdom) Supper and different kinds of Drinkables one
Day with another two Shillings & Sixpence

The Diet of one Day will be 4s: 1d wch for a year is	£ 74:10: 5
A Suit of Regimentals a year about	20: 0: 0
A Frock Suit with Several Pairs of Breeches as I wear them out fast occasioned by the Cane of my Stump Leg	13:10: 0
Five Shirts Coarse & fine Stocks	6: 0: 0
Four pairs of Stockens	2:11: 5½
Two pairs of Shoes	10:10
Washing & mending my Linnen	6:10: 0
Books, Pen, Ink, Paper & other Trifling Articles	10: 0: 0
	£133:12: 8½
Expences exceed the Income	104: 5: 7½

The above State will enable you to form an Idea of my Situation, in what manner I live and What Payments I am able to make. At the same time beside the Interest I owe to you I am indebted about Six hundred Pounds english of which I pay Interest for £350.

There is but one Means that I depend on to raise Money to Pay my Debts and this is, The Royal Favour, We have so good, so gratious a K. & one that considers the Sufferings of his Servants with so much Tenderness that I shall not sollicit his favour in Vain, but I cannot expect any thing considerable at this time sufficient to answer my Purpose, but if I forbear to ask anything 'till such time as my service in the Rank I am in gives me Pretensions to ask a favour of Consequence to me, I have good Reason to hope I shall succeed, and that thereby I shall be enabled to discharge all my Debts. I lay it down as a fundamental Principle, that it is not my Interest to do anything against yours or to disoblige you. My Dependance is on you and you have it in your Power to shew me a great kindness, Therefore if I could lose myself so far as to forget what you have done for me, and to be incapable of Gratitude, Affection & Duty, Yet if I am allowed common Sense, I cannot be supposed to be wanting to my own Interest, and so it may be granted I should be carefull how I offend you; On the other hand, from the kindness you have shewn me, from that you have profest to me, and from my Relation to you, I have Reason to hope you will always continue my first and best Friend. And the favour I now desire of you provided you can contrive it so as not to hurt any Scheme you have forward, is, That you would not desire me to pay you any Interest 'till by the Bounty of the Government I am enabled to do it, If you will grant me this Favour I will imploy all the Management I am capable of to pay the Six hundred Pounds I now owe & when I have done that although I should not have received any favour from the Government I will pay you all the Money I can save, if I had the Money now I would pay you as readily as you could desire it. I hope therefore you will be pleased to consider and Weigh this Matter with your wonted goodness and Affection to me and the Desire you have always shewn to promote ...[125]

JRL, B2/3/148

64

Lieutenant-Colonel Matthews Sewell to Lieutenant-Colonel Samuel Bagshawe

Belfast
23 July 1750

I troubled you with some Letters lately, but imagine you was not then arrived at Ballyshannon to which Place I have directed them.

Evans of my Company has wrote to buy his Discharge. I have told him, if he will bring a Young Lad of 5^{ft} 8^{in} without Shoes, & in every Respect a good Man, but on no other terms it can be granted which I hope you will aprove of ... I have ordered a Cat of nine Tails to be bought, in terrorem, but hope we shall have no Occasion to use them, The Expence 7^d ½ a Company, which I aprehend must be stopt out of the Drum Maj^{rs} allowances. On Thursday last Serj^t Macartney of Capt Forde's Company Deserted, I have wrote to The Agent to desire he would mention it to Weller[126] or any of our Officers in Dublin, That They might have him secured by Means of Irwin's Reg^t who all know him well, I have wrote to the same purpose to Lt Col^o Pierce to desire he would give Orders for his being Secured if their People can meet him, & desired them to write to You, & wait on the Brigd^r for what was to be done with him.

Serj^t Macartney was pay Serj^t to Capt Fordes Company[,] he borrowed £1:15:8 of Shields & his Wife in the Presence of Serj^t Thomas & others, likewise 3 pounds 13^s of the wive of James Grant of the s^d Comp. this Day returned from Plymouth. He alledged to them it was for Sub^{ce} to pay the Company the Capt. being out of Town & daily expected; Macartney called Serj^t Shields to witness he had borrowed the £3:13^s of M^{rs}s Grant for to subsist the Company.

Had Macartney come to me, I should readily have given him Money as They did, upon such an Occasion.

Cap^{t}n Forde says he will not pay them, That Macartney never had Power from him to borrow money, & that he had paid Serj^t Macartney all Pay whatsoever for his Company for the 27th Ins^t.

As they have complained to me, I am obliged to acquaint you with it, besides I believe you will think it hard the Poor People should loose so much money, lent upon such an Occasion; In Case Capt Forde is not to pay it, [I] can think of no other Way, but that by Order of a Court Martial & your approbation, The new Serj^t to live on Corporal's Pay & the Corporal on Private Man's Pay 'till these Demands are all Satisfyed. Every One here joins with me in Compliments to you & all friends ...

JRL, B2/2/549

65

Lieutenant-Colonel Matthews Sewell to Lieutenant-Colonel Samuel Bagshawe

Belfast
25 July 1750

Capt Forde desires me to make his Compliments to you & proposes that with your aprobation The money due from Serj^t Macartney be raised by A Vacancy of a Man & that Sturgeon be Serj^t on Corporal's pay, Drew Corporal upon private Pay untill Serj^t Shields is repaid $£1:15^s:8^d$

(The youngest Serj^t	Grant	3:13
& Corp^{ll} on the same	Sturgeon	3:10
footing 'till p^d		$£8:18:8$

Which at 4^s a Week will be repaid in 45 weeks. That being the complete Difference between Serj^t & Private man.

That the Vacant pay of the Man goes to raise another & then to be continued as long as you shall think proper to repay Capt Forde 20$£$ about which sum he says, Macartney is in Debt. We imagine seven Guineas of that may be recovered, for Capt Forde has found among Macartneys Papers Lt Walsh's note for that sum. Capt Forde further proposes that in Case Walsh's note for the 7 Guineas is paid the 1st of next Septr as due, he will then

pay Shields & Grant their Demands out of it, You will be so
good to let me have your orders about it[.] It is not quite clear
to me, how this Scheme can be executed without Leave from
the Governm.^t or a Court Martial, of which you will give
Direction ...

JRL, B2/2/550

66
Lieutenant-Colonel Samuel Bagshawe to Lieutenant-Colonel Matthews Sewell

[Draft]   Ballyshannon
                                            7 September 1750

This comes to acknowledge your Several Favours to the 28.th
Aug.st & the proceedings of the Reg.^t Court Martial upon the
Demands made against McCartney[127], I think the Distribution
which the Court has made of the Note & Effects of McCartney
is a very fair [and] a just one; & I believe that the Several
demands of the Claimants are true, but the more I consider the
pretence for borrowing & the belief or Credulity of the lenders,
The more I am against making them any sort of Allowance that
it is my power to prevent, I hold it to be a very bad President and
of a very bad tendency[.] If all those who are entrusted with the
paying of Money to a C.^y are to be believed when they say they
borrow Money for the Use of the Comp.^y it will be in the power
of every pay Serjeant at any time to injure his Captains
Reputation & to make his hands weak for the Soldiers will have
but an indifferent opinion of[,] at least they will consider with
less respect[,] an Officer who they believe makes Use of their
Money & they will think that the reason for [the] borrowing [of
the] Money. And therefore Such a Practise cannot be too much
nor too soon discouraged, & it never will be discouraged so
effectually as by letting those people who will part with their
Money on such a pretence, See, that they must lose it. As the
present Sufferers have had hopes that they shall be paid back

their Money, I will this time consent That the Succeeding Serjeant shall pay them, but I also promise I never will suffer such a thing for the future where I have any Power to hinder it.

I think the Stoppage of four shillings a Week from the succeeding Serjeant too great a Stoppage, I have computed that three shillings a week for Fifty Seven Weeks from the beginning of Sep.^t with the difference between a Serj.^t & private Mans pay from the Desertion to that time will make up the Several Demands as now fixed, therefore whoever is apointed to Succeed must agree before hand to submitt to that & to avoid a Complication of Acc^ts, I will have it fixed upon this Vacancy & to remain there till the Money is paid ...

JRL, B2/2/559

67
Lieutenant-Colonel Samuel Bagshawe to Captain Francis Forde

[Draft]   Ballyshannon
                                         25 September 1750

I send this to thank you for complying with my desire to oblige Mr Gore[128] in making Huggins a Serjeant, And I am sorry that this is not the only Subject of business of my Letter, but a paragraph in [a] letter of yours to Co.^l Sewell wherein you claim a Right to the Pay of the Serj.^t during the Vacancy makes it necessary that I should reason with you on that subject for I cannot with Self Approbation speak as a Commanding Officer upon an Occasion wherein I think myself obliged to you, for the Service did not require me to make use of the Authority I have to appoint Non Commission Officers & I hope I shall never make use of it on any other Pretence. You seem to think that you have a right to the Pay of any Non Commission Officer, which becomes vacant in your Company during the vacancy, that is that it is your Property. If I had thought you desired to have the Difference in Question I believe I should not have opposed it, &

indeed it would not have been much matter when I consented to a thing to have strained a little farther, but with regard to your having a property in the Vacant Pay it is a new Doctrine & what I never heard of before. As I only write to you in friendship I will tell you how that matter appears to me[.] You have too much reason to make Opposition if you are convinced & on the other hand I promise to acknowledge my Conviction if you can make it appear to me from Reason, the Nature of Discipline & Practise of the Army that you have the Property you Claim. I have often known that a Capt has enjoyed the Vacant Pay, but I never heard that he enjoyed it by any other right than connivance or applying and obtaining for certain reasons the consent of the Commanding Officer of the Reg.^t; I have frequently known a Vacancy that has been open for some time filled up & the Person preferred ordered to receive the Pay from the time of ye Vacancy[.] I have known Vacancys sometimes immediately filled up at other times kept open a considerable time & the Pay disposed off by order of the Commanding Officer of the Reg.^t & I never yet heard it disputed that he had not a Power to do both the one and the other; he is to take care that he can be answerable to the Service for what he does. No doubt a Captain of a Company has his Priviledges for beside the natural Weight he must have in a Reg.^t he is not accountable to a brother Captain (unless he should be the Commanding Officer of the Reg.^t) for the private transactions of his Company, but it is a Contradiction to military Common Sense that he should be independ.^t of a Field Officer in particular a Field Officer commanding the Reg.^t & entirely destroy that order & subordination without which an Army could not subsist, And the fresh Instances which we have all experienced are sufficient to convince us both that Captains and Field Officers are accountable for every Penny of Money they received.

If therefore a Commanding Officer of a Reg.^t can fill up the Vacancy of a Non Commission Officer when he pleases, & does dispose of Vacant Pay as he thinks he can answer to the Service, & if a Captain can do nothing relating to the Affairs of a Regiment or his own Comp.^y where the Service is concerned independent of his Commanding Officer, and if a Captain is

answerable when called upon for all the Money he has received
on account of his Company, I think I may conclude that a Capt
can have no Property in the Pay of any Vacant Non commission
Officers in his Comp^y ...

JRL, B2/2/186

68

Lieutenant-Colonel Samuel Bagshawe to Miss Catherine Caldwell

[Draft]   Ballyshannon
                                                    2 January 1751

Dear Miss Kitty

I cannot express my concern that I must not be of the Party to
Belleek[129] tomorrow, but both my Horses are so ill that they
cannot be taken out of the Stable without great danger. I never
so sensibly felt the Loss of my Leg till now. I wish you all the
Pleasure such an Excursion can afford but I fear for your Health
from the Inclemency of the Weather. To tell you the Truth
beside the want of my Horses I am not well—a heaviness every
now & then seizes my Spirits in a manner that I cannot account
for & that I never felt before, I am really an object of Pity and an
Expression of Pity from Miss Kitty Caldwell would restore me
to better health than the Advice of Ten Physicians ...

P.S. It is a Saying that none but old Wives & Children or Fools
relate Dreams but I had one lately [which] was so lively & so
circumstantial & remained so fresh on my Memory that I cannot
resist the Temptation to tell it you, & upon my Honour &
Veracity I tell it to you directly as it hapned. I fancied that I was
in a plain and all of a Sudden there appeared in the Air two
beautiful Majestick Female Personages with each of them a
Troop of young Ladies under her Direction, Something told me
that the one was the Goddess of Wisdom & the other the

Goddess of ~~Wantonness~~[130] Pleasure & that I must choose a Wife out of one of those two Troops, no sooner was this said than the two Troops intermixed & danced through each other with surprising Swiftness & besides were at such a Distance from me that though I could see they were all pretty yet I could not clearly distinguish their Faces or dresses with any Certainty, My Inclination led me to choose from the Troop conducted by Wisdom but the Motion of the Ladies was so quick & the Distance so great I was afraid I should pitch on one belonging to the Troop under the Goddess of ~~Wantonness~~[131] Pleasure, I for this reason acted with Caution & delayed greatly to make my choice till I was told I must make my choice directly, at last I fixed my Eye upon one whose modest Dress engaged my Attention & I cryed out "I fix there"; In an Instant the Ladies all stood Still and I heard a rejoicing from Invisibles all around me who cried out he has chosen from the Troop of the Goddess of Wisdom, & immediatly the other Troop vanished away; I was then led up to the Goddess of Wisdom Whom I entreated to tell me what Lady I was to marry; The Goddess turned & shewed me a Couch on which was a ~~plumpish~~[132] Young Lady reclined upon her Side, I aproached her all trembling & as I aproached She sunk with her Face to the Couch, & when I endeavoured to see her Face held herself [covered] with both her Arms, I flew in the greatest Agitation imaginable & stooped down & whispered in her Ear, Is it my Kitty? I thought I had whispered so low as not to be heard, but instantly the other Ladies who had followed me & now surrounded the Couch all burst out in a loud Titter Which I found was because I had betrayed my Inclination. This threw me into so great Confusion & my Spiritts were in so great a flutter that I awakened, but as I awakened I thought I heard one say—It is She. Perhaps you will think [this] a fiction but I repeat again upon my Honour & Veracity that it Was plain and directly as I have related it[.]

JRL, B2/3/2

69

Captain Archibald Grant to Lieutenant-Colonel
Samuel Bagshawe

Leeds
22 December 1751

On Friday the 13th Ins.^t my Party arrived at this place and next day being Mercat day we beat up, when I inlisted a very pretty boy of 16 years of age, 5 feet 7 inches high but had only time to have him Dressd & made a little clean, when as he was turning out to go about with the Serj.^t a man came up & Challenged him as his Apprentice who he said had run away from him two days before from Sheffield, And upon examining the boy and being Shown his Indentures which he acknowledged, I was oblig'd to let him go, and last Tuesday being Mercat day I inlisted four very good Recruits in my opinion all Shoemakers in this Town, they came together in a body and told me that if I would take them all they would Enlist but they were determined not to separate, they cost me £2:17:6 each but I was determined not to lose them, As there were four more Recruiting Officers in this place, either of whom would have been happy to have got them, besides Im hopefull they will be of Service to me in getting more men before the Hollidays are over, the talest is 5 feet 8 Inches high and twenty four years of age born in the Parish of Keighley & county of York his name is Thomas Scot, Another's Name is James Freeman aged 21 years, 5 feet 7¾ high born in this Town, the Third is John Booth aged 22 years, 5 feet 7½ high born in Hallifax in Yorkshire [,] And the last is James Bullen aged 18 years, 5 feet 6¾ high, born in the Parish of Preston in Lancashire a very pretty boy, Im hopefull that tho' I have presumed upon takeing some of them at a little under the Size prescribed by my Instructions I shall be so happy as to meet with your approbation in it as in my opinion they are all Exceeding good men, And if I had not immediately Accepted of them they knew there were others here that would, And besides it is fixing a sort of Interest in the place that may be of service to me, I propose keeping them till after the Holydays in which time Im hopefull and they give me great Assurances of bringing some of their Companions. I had this day a letter from Lieu.[t] Abbot[133] at Pontefract, who says he has not yet met with any Success, Nor had Mr Powell[134] at Hallifax better success [two] days ago when I heard from him, tho' Im Assured by both, that they neither have nor will leave any thing in their power untryd, but they say that as almost all over the Countrey there are Recruiting Officers, most of whom can take men of a Lower Size than we, those lower men whom they take induce others whom we could take to go to the Officers with whom they are ingag'd, which makes us find it more difficult to get good men than otherwise we should, but Im hopefull that before the Hollidays are over we shall be able among us to get a Sufficient number to send off ...

JRL, B2/2/249

70

Captain Archibald Grant to Lieutenant-Colonel Samuel Bagshawe

Halifax
9 February 1752

I had the favour of yours by Serj.[t] Carver and I am heartily sorry that the Recruits I sent by him did not prove aggreable, I hope you'll do me the justice to believe that my only motive in taking them was the good of the Service and not any self interest, And if I err'd that it was in judgement only, As you desire I have Examn.[d] my Standard and believe it was rather short, but upon honour Freeman whom you rejected measured by the Standards of 4 Recruiting Officers from different Regiments, at Leeds 5 feet 7 inches and a quarter, and his age I could have Attested by the parish Clerk of Leeds to be but 22, but as he did not prove aggreable to you Im very well Satisfyed, Only in case I should be so unlucky as [to] send any more that should not meet with your Approbation, I shall be obliged to you to Discharge them there, as Freeman cost me not only 3 weeks pay & his passage money, but likewise 5 Sh[s] too for a pair of shoes which the Serj[t] was obliged to buy for him ...

JRL, B2/2/252

71

Colonel John Adlercron to Lieutenant-Colonel Samuel Bagshawe

Dublin
18 April 1752

Sir

I should have answer'd the favour of your Letter sooner, but could neither find Lord George[135] or Capt. Desbrisay till yesterday: I am sorry I could not prevail on his Lordship to consent to Colonel Sewell's selling to Cap[t] Lovet, tho' I represented to him the Colonel's long service abroad, the wounds he had rec[d] which render'd him incapable of doing his Duty, & that Cap[t] Lovet had at times acted as Major & by what you had wrote to me was very well qualified for it: Finding his Lordship averse to this; I mention'd the Scheme you proposed of the Colonel's selling his Company & retiring on his Major's Pay, but this was also rejected, saying that as the Colonel had not bought the Company His Majesty would not approve of it.

I read Cap[t] Desbrisay & Col[o] Ladeveze that part of your Letter relating to the Non-effective & contingent Account, which I make no doubt but they'll settle in a proper manner. All expences attending taking up or sending for Deserters etc should, I think, be charged in the general recruiting Acc[t]. I have one thing to propose, which I hope will be agreable to the Captains, that is the Expence of recruiting may for the future be equally charged among the Captains.

Captain Grant & Ensign Powel have brought over 4 Recruits which I believe you'll not approve of, however as a few were wanting to complete the Regiment, I am glad they came before the Review; their names are, Richd Yates, John Garrish, Jerem.^y Deacon & Will. Brierly; be pleased to let Capt Desbrisay know imediately to what Companies they are allotted to.

I am very well pleased at your having sent Brigadier Richbell a Copy of the Return you had made me of the several Deficiencies; I saw the Brig.^r yesterday & told him that at my return from Quarters, I should let him know whatever things were wanting & that I did not doubt but that we should then settle them to both our satisfactions.

I shall set out for Limerick the 25.th Instant, that I may be at Quarters in time to sign the next Monthly Return, which I suppose will not be sent till the Post-day after the first of May.

I shall bring down the Rout for the Regiment's marching; four Companies begin their March for Kinsale the 25.th May, two for Clonkilty the 28.th & four for Bandon the 30.th.

Mrs Adlercron[136] desires her Compliments to you, & your Lady, she'll be very glad of the pleasure of her acquaintance when she comes to Town; I desire the favour you'd make mine acceptable to her. I am

> Sir
> Your most obidient
> humble Servant
> Jno Adlercron

JRL, B2/2/4

72

Lieutenant-Colonel Samuel Bagshawe to William Bagshawe of Ford

[Draft]   Bandon
                                                9 June 1752

Dr Uncle

I have received a letter from Mr Evatt[137] wherein he says you desire me to pay you the Balance of an Acc.^t between us which I shall most readily Comply with when I am able, but you are no Stranger to the State of my Affairs the Difficulties I labour under, the Expences I am exposed to & wch I cannot avoid & the Debts I owe which to my great grief are increased above two hundred Pounds by my last years Journey to England my living in Dublin this Winter my Wifes ill State of Health & buying a few household Necessaries, and I have been obliged by the duty of my Post to move from Place to place since I left Dublin till this Week; I am now a little more fixed and am upon the most likely Method I can think of to save Money and as I do have it will pay my Debts[,] if it was in my Power to pay you and [I] did not you would have just cause to be offended but I hope you will forgive what is my Misfortune not my Fault, My Wifes Relations will consent her Fortune shall be put in your hands provided you will give Security for it to her Trustees, this is the only present Method I can imagine to pay you, by this means you will have your Interest in your own hands and you was pleased to say you would be satisfied if you received the Interest but if you will bear with me I own I had rather her Money remained in the hands of her own Relations.

My Wife desires to join me in her most affectionate respects & Duty to you and Aunt, She still labours under a Complaint wch the Physitians have not been able to remove, As for myself the small Progress I make with all my care and endeavours in the World, & the small share I have in your Affections (Notwithstanding a Conduct which has gained me the good Opinion & Confidence of All else with whom I have been concerned) is so discouraging to me that my Spirits sink under the load of it, & if I could pass out of this World without Offence to my Maker or Injury to my Fellow Creature I should be glad to be removed [from] a Life attended with so many Vexations and so little Tranquility. I most Sincerly wish you & my Aunt health & Comfort while you remain in this World & Everlasting Felicity when you leave it,

> I am Hon^d S^r
> Your affectionate & most
> obliged Nep^w & Servt
> S.B.

JRL, B2/3/160

73

Colonel Anthony Ladeveze, Regimental Agent, to Lieutenant-Colonel Samuel Bagshawe

Dublin
11 July 1752

It appearing by the Return sent to Colonel Adlercron that the following particulars are wanting in his Regiment Viz:

Colonel's company		1 Halberd
D.º D.º		1 Firelock
D.º Comp.ʸ 1, Majors 2 Capt Lovetts	1	4 Bayonets
Cap.ᵗ Lovetts 1, Cap.ᵗ Townsend's	1	2 Belts
Cap.ᵗ Townsends Comp.ʸ		3 Slings
Major's Comp.ʸ 1, Cap.ᵗ Wemys's[138]	1	2 Drums

I am directed by him to desire you to inquire into the Cause of it and to know from the Captains Concerned in those Deficiencies what they can object to the 4ᵗʰ Article of War Section 13ᵗʰ for not providing the above particulars wanting in their respective Companies, when you have their answer you'll please to send it to the Colonel ...

JRL, B2/2/298

74

Lieutenant-Colonel Matthews Sewell to Lieutenant-Colonel Samuel Bagshawe

Kinsale
7 August 1752

Enclosed are Copys of Papers delivered to me by the Sovereign of this Town as Commanding Officer of the Garrison. On the 4ᵗʰ Insᵗ he gave me the Petition and on a morsel of Papers the

Names of five or Six Men who worked in Town, as were alledged to him & the Grand Jury amongst which Names Serj:ᵗ Shields was mentioned the only one of Col.º Adlercron's Reg.ᵗ, Yesterday he gave me another Paper of Names more particular of which you have likewise a Copy. I have desired him, to give in the Complaint to the Commanding Officers of the respective Regiments before he made any application to me as Commanding the Garrison, but as that was declined, I sent Copys of the whole to Col.º Munro[139] and Maj:ʳ Gisborne[140][.] Shields never worked but employed Frazer for my Company only[.] Frazer of my Company had hired a small Place for which he paid 5 pence a Week to work in, but he assures me he never worked for any but my Company, however I made him quit his hired Room and give him leave to work in the Barracks for Soldiers only. This the Town can not hinder, and believe the Consequence of their Complaint will greatly prejudice The Interest of the Inhabitants for I believe neither Officer nor Soldier will buy any One thing in the Town, which they can get out of it.

I am well informed Two of the Grand Jury were Roman Catholicks. I left the Act of Parliament and Articles of War for 1752 with the Sovereign, and desired him to call his Council & Town Clark, & the Complainants, and be pleased to shew me wherein The Soldiers had offended that they might be tryed & punished if Guilty. He returned me the Book yesterday saying he could find none, & gave me that Paper of which you have a Copy after the Petition.

I then told him, it was the first Complaint of this kind I ever heard of since I have been in the army, That I had been quartered in many Towns in England of Trade infinitely superior to this Place, and never Once heard any sort of Objection to a Soldier working, from an Inhabitant[141]. That the Grand Jury had certifyed their belief of what they could not know to be true having never examined one Soldier about it, but that They aserted was absolutely false, as he had now confessed They could find no breach of the Act of Parl.ᵗ or Articles of War and if Roman Catholicks were permitted to be on Grand Jurys, They would present the whole English army as a Nusance; and as a Complaint was threatened in their Petition, desired it might not be delayed ...

B2/2/639

75
Colonel John Adlercron to Lieutenant-Colonel Samuel Bagshawe

Dublin
8 August 1752

... Cap.t Desbrisay told me this morning that Brig.r Richbell made difficulties for providing the Regiment with several Deficiencies, which the Brigadier thinks the Captains are to make good; one Article he objected to was the black Pouches, to which I made answer that the Captains could not answer for them as they were worn out by long service, as likewise the Arms etc. mentioned in your Return, & tho' Captain Desbrisay shewed him the objections the Captains made for not providing others, he still remains in the same opinion that they are to answer for them: As to the Swords, when I last saw the Brigadier, I understood he was to allow me whatever they cost, accordingly I bespoke them at 5.s each, but now he says he will pay but 4.s:6.d; as to that particular it is not worth disputing, but I told Cap.t Desbrisay that when I examin'd the several Accoutrements, I might have taken notice of some Defficiencies w.ch I over looked, particularly the Grenadiers swords, the Gripes or handles of which were so short, that the Men had not room to grasp them, & I beg the favour you would report them in your next as you find them. As it's likely there will be shortly a Board of General Officers to determine this Affair between the Brigadier, the Captains & me make them more particular as to the number of each wanting with the several reasons, as I must be an Advocate for the Captains at this Board ...

JRL, B2/2/8

76

Lieutenant-Colonel Samuel Bagshawe to Colonel John Adlercron

[Draft]   [Bandon]
                                              18 August 1752

I take the liberty to send the inclosed Reasons for the Deficiencies in the several Companies in behalf of the Captains who are greatly obliged to you for appearing for them. I have examined the Granadier Hangers and they are all except about seven faulty in one respect or another some are too Short in the Gripe and others the mounting presses upon the Hand, indeed I think the mounting of the whole ill contrived and unfitt for real Service but these hangers were provided by Colonel Whitshead[142] not Brig.[r] Richbell. I am sorry there is like to be any dispute with Brig.[r] Richbell, the Brig.[r] has been my very good Friend and I have a sincere regard & respect for him and it would give me great Uneasiness to appear in any shape in a Contest with him, I hope matters will appear to him in a different light when better considered, for as far as my understanding will serve me, I do believe the Demand made on him is reasonable and that the Reasons assigned by the Captains for all the Deficiencies are true ...

JRL, B2/2/9

77

Lieutenant-Colonel Samuel Bagshawe to Brigadier-General Edward Richbell

[Draft]   Bandon
                                              18 August 1752

It gives me very great Concern to think there should be any Dispute betwixt you and your old Officers and Friends[.] I hear you are of Opinion the Captains are accountable for such

Deficiencies as are reported to be in the Arms and Accoutrements and that there [is] some likelyhood you intend to bring the Matter to a publick hearing. The publick hearing would encrease my concern[,] I must of course be a principal Actor in it & even oppose [you] who have ever since I had the happiness to be acquainted with you been my true & Good Friend for whom I ever had & always shall have the sincerest respect and affection ... As you have always allowed me to speak freely to you 'tis for this Reason I take the liberty to write to you now and hope you will suffer Friends to arbitrate between you & your old Reg.[t] whether with respect to the Col. or Captains ...[143]

JRL, B2/2/9a

78

Dr Joseph Clegg to Lieutenant-Colonel Samuel Bagshawe

[Ford]
10 October 1752

... A few days ago [your Uncle] sent to desire my company at Ford, he had some way heard that I had lately had a letter from you, and he desired to know if you had said any thing in it in relation to him; I told him you desird me to assure Him & your Aunt of your most affectionate and unfeigned Respects & Duty that you should be happy if he could think of you with confidence & affection, that he might have comfort in you, and that you might live in that friendship that ought to subsist betwixt such near Relations, that you very solemnly declared your selfe disposed to do every thing in your power to convince him of your gratitude and duty, & to contribute to make him pass the remainder of his days in ease and with satisfaction to himselfe—

To which he answered—The onely way to do all that was to

pay him ye Interest due for the moneys he had advanc'd for you, til he does that, he said, I shall never think him a man of Honour or Honesty; pray, said he, write to him again and assure him from me, that if he does not do that, the £1000 that he has had shall be all that he ever shall have of what is mine—I said I did not doubt in the least but you fully intended to pay it, and was sure you would do it as soon as your circumstances enabled you—He then produced a letter of yours in which you gave him the fullest assurance that that interest should be duely paid, I said I did not question that it would, if you had not met with many disappointments which could not then be foreseen—in short I said all I could in your favour during a long conversation when no other was present, but he still insisted on the payment of the Interest, and very often repeated the protestation that if that was not done you should never have more from him; he said he had determined shortly to alter his will, or to make a new one[.] I desired him not to do that in hast or in a passion, and asked him if he could think of any other Relation more likely to keep up the credit & honour of the family than you, he said he would rather leave the whole to pious & charitable uses than to one who would not do him Justice—in short I find there is no other way to regain & secure his favour but sending him moneys—and if I was in your case I would speedily remit him an hundred pounds whatever shift I made to procure it; I believe he has lately met with some vexatious disappointments & that he has more than usual occasions for moneys which may be the reason of his insisting so much on the payment of this now ...

JRL, B2/3/575

79

Lieutenant-Colonel Samuel Bagshawe to William Bagshawe of Ford

[Draft]
Bandon
31 October 1752

Hon^d Sir

I have received Doct^r Cleggs Letter written to me at your Instance, wherein he relates what you desired him of the Conversation which passed between you and him on my Account, among other things he says you produced a Letter of mine in which was the strongest Assurances that I would punctually pay you Interest for the thousand Pounds you lett me have toward the Purchase of my Lt Colonels Commission, I intended to pay you punctually, A Variety of unforseen Events (but of which I always gave you a faithfull Account) have hapned to thwart my Design, I had some reason to think you accepted these Representations, as after them you did not say you must have your Interest notwithstanding any reasons I could alledge. And when I was at Ford and made an Apology to you for not having paid your Interest and begged of you to allow me to pay off my other Creditors, I remember you said you ought, at least, to have your Interest, but the manner in which you expressed yourself had to me the Appearance that you would have Patience with me and I was the more confirmed in this Belief as I had pointed out to you the Probability that in a few Years (if it pleased God to spare my Life) I should have it in my Power to pay you, but besides all this You have had it in your Power to pay yourself, have I not many times offered to put my Wifes Fortune into your hands? and to convince you of my readiness, I did (upon the Receipt of a Letter from you that you should have Occasion for Money for a Purchase you were about to make) lodge Eight hundred Pounds in a Bank in Dublin to be ready for your draught, which Money I took from as good Security as the three Kingdoms could afford me, & by which I lose (unless you please to allow it me in your Accounts) the Interest for that sum from the 25th of March or 1st of Aprill to the 1st of September, how then can I deserve the severe Imputation of want of honour and honesty. I own I relied on the Relation between Us, that you would allow me to discharge the Debts I owed to People whose only Motive to lend me Money was their Opinion of my having those Principles you are pleased not to allow me[144], you know the State of my Affairs & my Incapacity to pay you & them off at the same time, however since these Reasons have no Influence with you, I must cast myself upon their humanity, I shall never presume to trouble you again on this Subject, but will punctually pay every future Years Interest, betwen the time you have made it due in February and the 25th of March and I will discharge the Arrear as I am able, I really cannot send you any Money just now, for although I have saved something every Month since I came here, I have paid it away as fast as it came into my hands.

Dr Clegg further tells me that if I do not pay your Interest, the Thousand Pounds I have had will be all I shall ever have of yours[.] From the Disposition you seem to be in towards me it is likely it will be more, I am afraid you have a mind to quarrell with me, alack a day, if you are determined you may easily find occasion, the Poor and the Unfortunate are always giving Offence, but setting aside my Poverty what do I do to offend you? When I am with you I shew you all the respect in my Power, and at all times am ready to serve you all I can. I behave with Reputation & discharge the Duty of the Post I am in with Applause, and among my Acquaintance and in my Profession I am esteemed a man of Probity, honour and honesty. I should be glad if I could please you, and I think I have several Qualities which a Person who has augmented his Fortune by his own Application would chuse to have in his Successor, but if you are disposed otherwise, Gods will be done, he can either provide elsewhere for me, or enable me to bear in a becoming manner any Affliction he shall think fitt to lay upon me, it is my daily prayer to him That, what he sees fittest may befal me. I never was very sanguine in my Expectation of your Fortune, and will endeavour to prepare myself for whatever may happen. I hope for your own sake you will not change your Will in Passion, it will not be long before both you and I must appear before a

Being where we shall be judged according to the Tenor of our Actions not the impulse of our Passions, While here, it shall be my endeavour to behave to you and Aunt as becomes
>Your affectionate and dutiful
>Nephew and humble Servant
>Samuel Bagshawe

JRL, B2/3/163

80

Lieutenant-Colonel Samuel Bagshawe to Thomas Waite, Secretary to the Lords Justices of Ireland

[Draft]   Cork
                                                29 July 1753

I do myself the honour to represent to you an Affair which I believe it may be proper to lay before their Excie[s] the Lords Justices. I am afraid there is a Spirit of Mischief broke out among the Mob of Cork against the Soldiers which if some Method more effectual or lasting than any at present put in practice is not found out[,] may prove fatal to many of both Parties. The Mob has frequently attacked the Centinals posted at the North Gate ... by pelting them with Stones[.] On Sunday the 22[d] ab[t] two o'clock in the Morning a party from the Main Guard sent to the Assistance of those Centinals took one of the Rioters armed with a Hanger, they have taken pretence from this to grow more outragious, for on Friday the 27th about the same time in the Morning, they fell upon the Two Serjeants of the Main Guard who were Walking backward and forwards within Fifty yards of the Guard house. The Mob left both of them on the Ground & robbed one of them of his Silver mounted sword, One of the Serjeants has received ten or eleven Wounds in the head besides Contusions on his Arm & Body, the other besides Bruises is cut through the Bridge of his Nose &

the wound has pierced into the hollow of the head and both are very ill[.] Before the Officer of the Guard whose Room is about Twenty or Thirty Yards from that of the Men had intelligence of what had hapned, the Soldiers on Guard alarmed with the Noise had rushed out & finding the two Serjeants on the ground, without waiting for orders or minding any thing but their Resentment pursued the Robbers & Mob and fired some Shots after them, by which at too great a Distance from the Guard to be justified a Man was killed, The Reports of him are various, Some say he had a Sword in his hand when he was Shott, others that he came out of his house to perswade two of his Sons in the Riot to come home with him, this is agreed on by all that he was formerly a great Rioter & his two Sons are now notorious Rioters, Nor is it certain that he was killed by the Soldiers for it is said by some that the Mob fired at the Soldiers as well as the Soldiers at the Mob[.] The Officer of the Guard informed me that seeing the Serjeants bleeding on the ground & in such a condition & not then knowing the Men had pursued the Mob made it his first business to take care of the Serj[ts] & see them drest after which he called the Roll of the Guard & all the Men were present[,] but the killing of the Man is by the Mob charged to the Soldiers & has raised them to such a Pitch of Fury that I am informed they [intend] to hough and destroy every Soldier [that] shall fall in their Way & that the Sons of the Deceased have taken an Oath to have Blood for Blood[.] The Mayor has been indefatigable in his Endeavours staying out sometimes the whole night & has had all the assistance he required from the Troops but his Endeavours have not answered his Intentions for when he has gone home the Mob have begun their Outrages & Insults which makes it probable they have someone [who] attends his Motions & informs them when he returns [home]. I have thought, a patrol from the time of Tattoe to Revellie in the Morning might be a check on the Mob: but if the Centries at the Gates of the Town had orders to stop in the Night time all persons carrying Fire Arms[,] Swords, Cutlasses, Bloodgeons, [and] large sticks who had not the Appearance of Gentlemen & qualified by Law to carry such Weapons till they gave an Acc[t] of themselves to a civil Magistrate, this might prevent Riots hapning at least within the Garrison but upon my mentioning this Method to the Commanding Officers of Corps they were doubtful whether the Military Commanding Officer can give such an Order as the last, and [are] of opinion that a Patrol with only his Authority would be a Mark for the Mob to insult with Impunity at every corner of a Street. So that the Military Power [is not] sufficient to put stop to these Disorders even within the Garrison without further Authority from the Government, nor is the civil Power able to prevent them without military assistance ...[145]

JRL, B2/2/731

81

Lieutenant-Colonel Samuel Bagshawe to William, third Duke of Devonshire

[Draft]   Cork
                                                                            4 December 1753

My L^d D.

It has always been my Situation to receive favours from Y^r G. for which there could be no other Motive but Y^r Graces Generosity and although I may never have it in my Power to make any sort of Return that does not hinder[,] but I may have a warm and if I may presume to use the Expression an affectionate Sense of y^r G. Goodness toward me, and an Inclination to serve Your G. if it was in my Power, As I have not much Correspondence with Derbyshire I know not how the ensueing Elections are proposed to be carried on, whether an Opposition is or is not expected, I have a Vote which y^r G. [will] please to dispose of, and if necessary [I will] come over to give it or to [be otherwise] useful, I am pretty well beloved among my [neighbours] & though I cannot promise much Service I would spare neither Pains nor

time to convince Your Grace that I am with the [greatest]
Gratitude Sincerity & Respect

> My Lord D
> Y.^r Graces
> Most Dutifull
> most faithfull
> & most Obedient
> humble Servant
> S.B.

JRL, B15/1/19

2
1754–1758

'I want to obtain a few Thousand pounds ...'

The orders designating the 39th for active service in India reached
Bagshawe at Cork on 1 February 1754. By the same post came news of
the death, by apoplectic seizure, of his aunt Mary at Ford on 15
January.[1] Great was the consternation of his family and friends at this
double calamity. William Bagshawe was particularly badly affected, a
state of affairs that Kitty was able to take some advantage of during
what proved to be a long stay at Ford [93]. Samuel's brother-in-law,
Sir James Caldwell, tried to persuade him to exchange commissions
with another officer, and there was even a possibility that he would be
offered the governorship of Kinsale, but he believed that his character
would suffer if he entertained any such proposals and he indignantly
rejected them [89]. As it was, he was carried aboard the *Britannia*
Indiaman on 25 March in a high fever and at risk of his life.[2] This was
an ominous beginning to the great adventure, for although the coast of
Coromandel was reckoned to be a healthier station than Calcutta or
Bombay, malaria, the enteric or 'putrid' fever and dysentery were daily
companions. There were, moreover, periodic outbreaks of smallpox
and cholera, and the ever-present threat of death by rabies or
snakebite. It was common for middle-aged arrivals at Madras, the East
India Company's principal settlement on the coast, to die within a year;
younger visitors fared little better.[3]

There are, however, plenty of indications that, despite the known
risk to his health, Bagshawe relished his mission. He hoped for
an independent command that would win him reputation (cheaply
purchased against an inferior enemy) and, equally important, the 'few
Thousand pounds' that he and his family needed so urgently [113].
Among his papers he kept a regulation of prize-money, drawn up by
Admiral Boscawen in 1748 before the abortive attack on the
French settlement of Pondicherry and given to him by Major John

Mompesson who had served with the independent companies of foot on that expedition.[4] In the event, illness denied him the chance of sharing in the distribution of loot after Plassey (23 June 1757), which netted his old comrade Archy Grant £11,250 sterling, besides several unregistered donatives.[5]

The 39th was in much finer fettle in January 1754 than it had been at the time of its dismal return to Ireland five years earlier. Much of this improvement seems to have been owing to the influence of its colonel since March 1752, John Adlercron, an experienced officer of Huguenot descent.[6] Adlercron's performance in India has attracted highly critical comment,[7] which is all the more reason for putting his good points on record. As he proudly informed the Duke of Cumberland in February 1754, he had spared neither trouble nor expense in putting the regiment in order, and had supplied it with many things previously neglected by Richbell.[8] He had the measure of his officers too, in particular Sewell, who was by now so afflicted with the gout that he could hardly put foot to ground.[9] It was typical of Sewell that he was still thinking of going to India, where his commission as lieutenant-colonel would have given him seniority over Bagshawe in any independent command [86]. As for Bagshawe, Adlercron described him as '... a very careful & good Officer, & one I greatly depended on.'[10] His conference with the Duke was followed by a number of speedy retirements from the regiment, including Sewell, who moved on to command a company of invalids at Pendennis Castle, Falmouth.[11] As Colonel Adlercron conferred with the great officers of state, the 39th was being brought up to combat strength of 30 sergeants, 30 corporals, 20 drummers and 700 private men by incorporating 403 draftees from 10 regiments on the Irish Establishment.[12]

Given the fact that Adlercron was clearly no fool, it was all the more unfortunate that in his role as officer 'Commanding in Chief the Land Forces to be employed in the East Indies', including '... the Command of all the Forces belonging to the [East India] Company, on the Coast of Coromandel', he totally failed to appreciate the complex situation facing the Company's servants at Madras.[13] This may be attributable in part to his relatively advanced age. He was over 60 when he sailed for India, and the younger Bagshawe proved much better able to come to terms with the realities of power at Fort St. George, but none of the King's officers had been at all well briefed for their expedition [97].

At this period, the East India Company was being forced to shift its attention away from matters of commerce to the weightier issues of war and empire. The effects of the inexorable disintegration of Moghul power, the ravages of Maratha bands, the rivalries of local potentates and the ambitions of the French governor of Pondicherry, Joseph Dupleix, were felt with full force at Madras. In the opening stages of the War of the Austrian Succession, officials of the French and English India companies had tried to neutralise the area, but after the formal declaration of war between the two powers in 1744, the French had gone on the offensive, taking Madras in September 1746. The return of Madras to the English in 1748 did not restore peace to India, for Dupleix now embarked on a plan to bring the whole southern part of the sub-continent under French control by means of military aid to puppet native rulers. The early campaigns of Robert Clive and Stringer Lawrence restored the situation somewhat (Dupleix was shortly to be relieved in disgrace), but the English remained in awe of their French neighbours. The walls of Fort St George were extensively remodelled in brick, and help was requested from home.[14] From September to December 1754, ships carrying detachments of the 39th, the first royal regiment to serve in India, came to anchor off Fort St. David, Cuddalore, in response to that plea.[15] Samuel Bagshawe, his health temporarily regained, arrived aboard the *Britannia* on 1 September, three weeks ahead of his colonel, and disembarked four days later. The five-month voyage from Cork had been healthy; only 10 men were lost in the whole of the fleet [100].[16]

The arrival of the 39th in India coincided with a dampening down of hostilities on both sides. The aggressive Dupleix was superseded, and a suspension of arms agreed on 11 October was followed on 26 October by a three-month truce. At the end of December, a provisonal peace treaty was drawn up, and the region remained in a state of relative calm until a marked rise in tension during the summer of 1756. This sudden outbreak of peace, about which Adlercron, to his immense chagrin, had not been consulted, meant that for the time being at least, the regiment's services were not required. Moreover, the Company's servants at Madras, who quarrelled amongst themselves as a matter of course and kept the officers of their own army on a very tight reign, were suddenly harassed by a prophetic anticipation of a time when their government would pass into Imperial hands, personified at this juncture by the 39th and its commander. Adlercron, with his constant references to 'the King my Master' and insistence on the full dignity attached to his commission, fast became an impossible man to do business with, especially as instructions received from the East India Company's Court of Directors in London merely described him as commander-in-chief of the King's land forces, and made no reference to any authority over the Company's troops and garrisons.[17]

With the monsoon season approaching, Adlercron was unwilling to leave his command for any length of time, so he despatched Bagshawe to Madras, '... with as full power as I think necessary'[18] to sort the mess out and persuade the Company to improve the allowances it proposed for the King's troops.

Even though his first encounter with Fort St George politics was a thoroughly mystifying one [95–96], Bagshawe soon understood that the Company possessed much more influence on the spot, and even at home, than the King's colonel, and repeatedly advised him to moderate his demands. He also managed to maintain good relations with the Company's servants throughout his time in India [117], although in private he deplored their treatment of himself, the regiment and the native population and their rulers. 'Seriously my Lord', he informed the Duke of Devonshire, 'however these transactions may be to the advantage of the English Nation, they are such that if the common Rights of Mankind deserve Consideration, both the English and French deserve to be driven off the Coast.'[19]

Unfortunately, when it came to the point of drawing up a local convention between the Company and Adlercron that would have enabled business to be carried on in a spirit of harmony, as the colonel's instructions from home explicitly stated, Adlercron felt that his subordinate was taking a much too compliant view of the merchants' pretensions. This led to an immediate and serious breakdown in their relationship [103–6]. Bagshawe was denied an independent command, and his authority within the regiment was called into question [109–11]. It could hardly have been of much satisfaction to him to hear, at length, that Adlercron had received a rebuke from home for the way in which he had conducted himself.[20]

Shunned by his commanding officer and neglected by the Company,

Bagshawe was for long periods in a state of considerable mental agitation [113,115]. He was also chronically ill, suffering from fevers, bowel complaints and headaches that resulted in the near-total loss of sight in his left eye during December 1755.[21] The following year he was threatened with complete blindness and was obliged to beg for permission to return home. Whatever his other faults, Adlercron appreciated the potentially fatal effects of the Indian climate and was very sympathetic to requests of this type.[22] On 22 October 1756, Bagshawe went aboard the *Chesterfield* Indiaman, just as a strong detachment from his regiment was setting out on its momentous (and lucrative) expedition to Bengal.[23]

Bagshawe landed in Ireland at the beginning of June 1757 after a homeward voyage so painful that he considered himself lucky to have survived it.[24] In financial terms he could hardly have been pleased with the outcome of his India tour. He had left his personal pay for the use of his family, hoping to more than make do with '... the Appointments my Rank & Command receive from the Country',[25] and he had been able to remit funds to Kitty as well as to purchase Indian muslins and pearls. But by his own reckoning, he would have needed nearly another year in India to clear his debt to his uncle,[26] and the Company charged him £100 for his passage home [124]. Adlercron and the other officers of the 39th were confronted by similar outrageous demands when their turn came to return home in November 1757.[27]

Fortunately, however, by this time Bagshawe's domestic situation had been completely transformed.

It is doubtful whether William Bagshawe ever got over the double blow of his wife's death and his nephew's exile, though latterly his temper was much softened. Kitty's brother, Captain John Caldwell of the 7th Foot, reported that he spent much of the day in prayer and 'old story telling' and unless interrupted in these pursuits was always in good humour.[28] In the late autumn of 1756 he sank into a coma and, '... after a long & lingering Decay of Nature' expired at nine o'clock on the evening of 26 November. Samuel was left in possession of the Ford estate, valued at about £500 per annum, and '... cash upon Securities about £9,000.' Included in the latter sum however was money '... devised by the late Mʳˢ Bagshawe [Samuel's aunt Mary] to her Nephews being £4,000 which is in dispute at this time.'[29] After a vexatious and expensive suit in Chancery, the main litigant, Mr Robert

Newton, obtained judgement against Bagshawe—a disastrous outcome for Kitty and the children, as no small portion of the principal had been lost by bad debts, while the interest, which Newton also recovered, had been spent year by year as part of the family income [205].[30]

For the moment, however, Bagshawe resolved to make the best of country life and contemplated retirement from the army. 'I am here playing the part of the good Farmer', he reported in April 1758, 'ploughing & planting & almost unconcerned whether I am ever drawn from this Obscurity[.] I ever had a Relish for the Country and it grows upon me.'[31] From now until his death four years later, the military element in his correspondence was off-set by the wider concerns of the country gentleman: repairs to the hall and estate buildings, the up-keep of the local turnpike, the suppression of poaching, an outbreak of fish poisoning, crop-management, horticulture and livestock, which included the Ford bull, who specialized in demolishing the wall of the deer park with his horns.[32]

But as Bagshawe's health revived, assisted by excursions to nearby Buxton Spa, so did hopes of advancement in his profession. Although he had been advised not to appear at court before his regiment arrived from India,[33] he bombarded the Secretary at War, his patrons and military contacts with requests to be allowed to go on active service once more, for the colonelcy of an old corps, or for the command of one of the many new regiments then being raised, the Seven Years' War having broken out in 1756.

Despite fair words from the army agent and military oracle John Calcraft, the continuing support of the Cavendish family, now headed by William 4th Duke of Devonshire,[34] a visit to London and even a memorial to the King [140], Bagshawe was to remain unemployed until the return of the 39th to Ireland in late October 1758. Over 450 men and a number of officers (including Major Francis Forde the paymaster), had enlisted in the Company's service and a mere 14 sergeants, 14 drummers and 61 sickly rank-and-file desembarked at Cork.[35] Forde had long since neglected to send accounts home, and as a result the regiment's finances were in a state of confusion [143]. Not for the first time, the rumour circulated that the 39th was to be disbanded.[36] In May 1759, Samuel Bagshawe arrived at regimental headquarters in Galway to superintend the task of rebuilding the shattered unit. Over 600 men were needed, and he was unable to report to Adlercron that the corps was 'fit for service' until November.[37] By that time, he was already deeply engaged in a new scheme to obtain the colonelcy he so ardently desired.

82

Colonel Anthony Ladeveze, Regimental Agent, to Lieutenant-Colonel Samuel Bagshawe

Dublin
29 January 1754

It is with Concern that I am to acquaint you that this day before twelve o'clock an Express arrived from My Lord Holderness[38] who brought orders for Colonel Adlercron and his Regiment to be in readiness to Embarque forthwith for the East Indies.

Colonel Adlercron is so busy that he cannot write to you this Post, but sends his Compliments and desires you will write to all the absent officers & Recruiters with their Partys to Join the Regiment at Cork without loss of time.

You are to be Compleated to seventy p^r Comp^y by drafts from the Regim^{ts} in this Kingdom, & to be put on the English Establishment, The Ships are to come from Plymouth to Cork to take in your Regiment, and you are to saile directly from Cork to the place of your Destination.

This is all the particulars I am able to inform you of at present. The Colonel leaves it to your discretion to manage this sudden News so as to prevent Desertion as much as you can ...

JRL, B2/5/1

83

Lieutenant-Colonel James Murray to Sir James Caldwell, Bart.

Dublin
31 January 1754

I did myself the honour to call upon you yesterday but did not find you at home. My Business was to desire you would acquaint your Brother in law Lieu^t Col^o Bagshawe that I would for the consideration of three hundred Guineas exchange Commissions with him. I should not have given you this trouble were not this a Subject too delicate for a common acquaintance to write to the Col? about, therefore if you think proper to inform the Col? of my proposals & if he agrees to them there is no time to be lost in our endeavours to get his Majesties consent ...

JRL, B2/5/5

84

Ann, Dowager Lady Caldwell to Lieutenant-Colonel Samuel Bagshawe

[Dublin]
31 January 1754

My Dr Col:

The account I have this day had of your being commanded abroad desstracts me so, that I know not in what maner to adress myself to you, only to beg & entreat you if possable, you will except of ye proposall Col. Murry sent Jemmy this day, which I hope he has communicated to you by this post. I need not make use of many arguments, in regard to your Wife and her infants, to soften a heart so succeptable of tenderness as I know yours to be, my only consolation at present is, that it will be in your power to except of this offer, which providence seems to have trown in your way, but every thing must be summitted to your better judgment, & [I] hope God will derect you for ye best. I hope poor Kitty has not been aquinted with this afair, it might have a very bad efect on her in ye low condition she is at present in. I beg you may let me know how she does, & what measures you intend to take, as soon as possible ...[39]

JRL, B2/3/268

85

Sir James Caldwell, Bart. to Lieutenant-Colonel Samuel Bagshawe

Dublin
31 January 1754

I have not words to Express the Concern and affliction we are all in on hearing that your Regment is ordered to fort St George in the East Indies. I must Intreat that you would be so kind as to lett me know by the very Return of the Post what are yours & My Sisters Sentiments on the Ocation. If there [be] any Scheme that you can think of to Decline this Voyage I beg you may lett me know that I may do all in my Power and make all the Interest I can to Assiste you in geting it Accomplished ...

JRL, B2/3/385

86

Lieutenant-Colonel Samuel Bagshawe to William, third Duke of Devonshire

[Draft]   [Cork]
1 February 1754

May it please your Grace

Though I have not the least pretence to Sollicit further favours from your Grace, but the Friendship y.^r Grace has always been pleased to shew me encourages me to hope you will excuse me giving you trouble when I am interested in so particular a Manner as on the present Occasion[.] Colonel Adlercrons Reg.^t is ordered to the East Indies, I have not nor ever had Objection to serve His Majesty in any part of the World, but without y.^r Graces Assistance I must go abroad under very disadvantageous Circumstances; I was obliged to borrow Money to compleat the Purchase of my Lt Col. Comission, & What contributed to lay me under these Difficulties was the Majority of the Reg.^t vacant by Death and for wch I believe y.^r Grace thought I had good Pretensions to Ask was given to another Person who though only Major to the Reg.^t is an older Lieut. Colonel by Comission which will give pretence to command me on Service & to apply for any preferment wch might fall to me as Lt Colonel—I am so far from desiring to be excused going abroad that I am only sorry I am not better able to serve & shall gladly seize upon every Oppertunity to shew my Disposition to serve his Majesty & my Country, I have all my Life time made my business my Study & believe I have been at least 18 y.^{rs} in 22 at my Post & flatter myself if my Life is spared Your Grace will not have Cause to be ashamed of the Countenance you have been pleased to Shew me. In Aprill I have been five years a Lieutenant Colonel[,] I presume to ask your Graces Favour with His Majesty, there is a vacant Reg.^t on this Establishment, That His M. Would be pleased to give this Reg.^t to Colonel Adlercron & the Reg.^t going abroad to me; or if I have not yet deserved such an Instance of His Majestys favour that I may have the Rank of Colonel to preserve to me the Command which of right belongs to me as Lieu.^t Colonel of the Regiment ...

JRL, B2/5/6

87

Ann, Dowager Lady Caldwell to Lieutenant-Colonel Samuel Bagshawe

[Dublin]
2 February 1754

As ye post is just going out, I have only time to let my Dr Col. know, that not with standing Col. Murrys desire of exchange with you, which he gave under his hand to Jemmy, he is now intirely off all thoughts of it, which you may be sure increaces my destress, if timely application cud be made by you to ye Duke of Devenshir, or my Ld Hartington, perhaps ye might strike out something for your advantage to prevent your taking this so much dreaded voige[.] I hardly know what I am saying or doing, & can only pray to God to protect & prosper my D.ʳ friend in whatever he undertakes ...⁴⁰

JRL, B2/3/269

88

Sir James Caldwell, Bart. to Lieutenant-Colonel Samuel Bagshawe

Dublin
2 February 1754

Yesterday Col. Aldercrown sent me a Letter that he received from Col. Murry the purport of which was that he would not on any Account treat with you for your Comition in as much as he was informed that the Regiment was to be Commanded and imployed by the East India Company. But this day about 7 a Clock he Came to the Tavern where I hapned to dine with Lord George and Some of his Sett and sent for me twice over before I would go [,] he said that the Reason he wrote Col. Aldercrown that Letter yesterday was because he heard that he had reported his having an Inclination to Change and that he did not know but he Might be fixed as L. Col. in England by the Means of Co. Aldercrown without your Knoledge and without his having any Chance of having any Consideration from you in Exchange[,] he told me that he ment that Letter only as a means of preventing those inconveniencys and that he still remains in the same disposition of Exchanging with you ... Every Body in this town are Interested in your favour, the Governm.ᵗ of Kinseal⁴¹ has been Mentioned for you by Col. Ponsonby⁴² & by me to the Duke of Dorset⁴³ but that is Disposd of[,] his Grace and my Lord George promise to do Every thing in their power for you ...

JRL, B2/3/386

89

Lieutenant-Colonel Samuel Bagshawe to Sir James Caldwell, Bart.

Cork
3 February 1754

I think and I hope I see here and there something in the Manner of your Letter as if you should be sorry I could prove the Man you have suffered yourself to be perswaded to recomend me to be. I receive Col. Murrays Proposal as it deserves, I have a Letter to the same purpose from himself. You cannot think how I am mortified by it, I did not think any Soldier who had known me could have thought of me in so contemptable a manner, And if that Gentleman will recollect he has as little reason as any body to believe I would accept his Offer: but to quit this for a more interesting and a more agreeable Subject, My dear, dear Girl, my Kitty, your Sister, is an Angel and worthy to be the Daughter of any Family or the[Wife] of any Man in the World, and can be pleased that I [may] happen to prove a man of Spirit and deserve the Choice she has made of me; At present she seems determined to go with me, not from a Romantick Flight, or fitt of sudden Grief, but from calm reasoning and cool Deliberation; If when we are better acquainted with the Nature of the Expedition, We find we can take Women with Us, and that I can obtain a decent Accomodation for her, She goes with me; if not she will submit to what is proper and best ...

JRL, B2/3/387

90

John Calcraft, Regimental Agent, To Lieutenant-Colonel Samuel Bagshawe

London
9 February 1754

Colonel Adlercron having done me the honour to appoint me his Agent, I take the liberty of informing You of it, and offering my best Services to you, & all the Officers in his Corps, who on all occasions shall find me ready to execute any commands they favour me with & I will use my utmost Endeavours to make myself agreable to them.

I have receiv'd Colonel Adlercron's directions to recomend in his Name, to you & the other Captains of his Regiment, Captain Ford to be Paymaster, whom he thinks thoroughly qualified for the very great Trust, that will be repos'd in him on this Occasion, & he hopes you Gentlemen will be of his Opinion. I enclose a proper Instrument to be sign'd by the Officers which you will please to return me.

***

The Colonel directs me to say the Ships will be so full, & provision so very precious for such a Voyage that no Women will be allow'd to go with you, which he thinks You will like to know in time.

I cannott omitt mentioning the very great Reputation Your Corps has among all degrees of People here, that H.R.H. spoke very handsomely of You to y.^r Colonel this morning & that you are much envied by the Officers, who all long to be employed in the Service You are order'd for, which I heartily wish may prove an agreable & fortunate one.

Your Coll. has been presented to His Majesty, who was uncommonly gracious to him, & when he saw the Duke, H.R.H. was not less so.

I hope Sir, one day or other to have the honour of being better acquainted with You; If at Present I can be the least usefull I hope You'l lay y.^r commands on me as freely as though I were now so, You will please to say the same for me to Your Brother Officers, telling them too that if during their absence I can transact any Affairs for them, they'l give me great Pleasure in employing me ...

JRL, B2/5/13

91

Ann, Dowager Lady Caldwell to Lieutenant-Colonel Samuel Bagshawe

[Dublin]
9 February 1754

Your resolutions being fixt, I must now acquiess as I mentioned
to you I woud to your better judgment. I was greatly rejoyced to
hear from experiencᵈ Offesers that exchanges were frequently
made on thoes accations without detrement either to honer or
Duty, which was my enducement to mention that scoame to you,
in hopes it might meet with your aprobation. I knew I might
communicate my thoughts with freedom as you woud make
allowences for yᵉ tenderness of a suffering parent without being
enfluenced contrary to your judgment, from my own way of
thinking I dreded your determination, I own I honour your
sentiments not withstanding what I feel, its true thousands goe
abroad but have not your way of engaging yᵉ frinds yᵉ leave
behind which dubles our destress, but no more of that, we will
hope [for] yᵉ best & depend upon providence who preserves us
in dangers & enables us to support ourselves under trials ...⁴⁴

JRL, B2/3/270

92

Lieutenant-Colonel Samuel Bagshawe to [Lord George Sackville]

[Cork]
[Draft]   [February] 1754

My Lord⁴⁵

I beg your Lᵈ Ship will have the Goodness to pardon the
Boldness of this Letter wᶜʰ Compassion move[s] me to trouble
you wᵗʰ, there is no part of the Expedition I so much dread as

the parting of the Soldiers from their Wives and Children, nor is there any thing more discouraging to the Men than their Cries and Lamentations and as the greatest part of them have it not in their Power to subsist otherwise than from hand to Mouth, they will be [at] the Day of the Embarkation in real distress, perhaps w.th out a Morsell of [Bread] ...

JRL, B2/5/11

93

Mrs Catherine Bagshawe to William Bagshawe of Ford

[Cork]
6 April 1754

Dear & Hon.^d Uncle

Though I did myself the pleasure of writing to you last post, (which letter I hope you have by this time got) yet it shant prevent me from again enquiring after you, & letting you know how extremely obleg'd to you I am, for ye two letters you were so good as to write me, & how happy it has made me to hear from you, I cant tell Dear Sir how much Im indebted to you for ye great Anxiety you express about my Dear Coll. Bagshaw, This I can assure you y.^t theres no one, can have a more greatfull sense of your goodness than he has, nor is there anything he wou'd not do to shew it, but he said, before he went, y.^t he was sure you wou'd not be against anything y.^t wou'd turn out for his Honour & Advantage as he & we all hope this Expedition will, you may believe all my Relations & Friends (particularly my Mother) were vastly uneasy at his going so long a Voyage, but he coud not think of Disposing of his Commission, as he thought it might possibly be a Reflection upon his Honour, ye Duke of Cumberland has a very great opinion of Coll. Bagshaw, & mention'd him in a most favourable manner to Colonel Aldercroun, ye Duke said sure it wou'd be cruel to let poor

Bagshaw go, upon which Col. Aldercron said very generously y.^{t} he could not go without him nor answer for ye success of ye Expedition without Coll. Bagshaw went with him, but this I wou'd not have spoke of very publickly, indeed every body y.^{t} knows Coll. Bagshaw loves him greatly, & without any partiallity I must say there cant be a more deserving man than he is, ye Duke assur'd Coll. Aldercron y.^{t} they wou'd not be above two years abroad, which is a very great Comfort to us, & I Trust in God he'll return in safety to us, we every Day experience ye goodness of Providence, we are not to Judge for ourselves, and though appearances may sometimes be against us, yet what ever is is best, sure I may say so, for in my Dear Coll. Bagshaw's illness when I thought my Distress ye greatest it was then Providence was most kind to me, in throwing of a Disorder which had it seiz'd him in another Climate might have been of bad Consequence to him, Coll. Aldercron & Coll. Bagshaw go in East India Ships, they chuse it as the Victualing & Accomadations are much better than in ye Men of War, Fort St George where they are going is recon'd a very fine Climate so y.^{t} we have nothing to do, but to comfort ourselves & pray to God who has every thing in his power for my Dear Coll. Bagshaws Health & safe return, you'll forgive my being so particular as I know how much your intrest'd in his happiness, & welfare, as Im sure we both are, Dear Sir for yours, & as I said before theres nothing I wont do both from Duty & inclination to be a Comfort & satisfaction to you, I take little Billy with me, who is now a year and a half old, as he's very good humour'd, I hope he'll be some Amusement to you, but if he be the least troublesome I can have him board'd out till he be older, I bring a maid to take care of him and work for us, She's a very Honest good Woman & neither Saucy nor Conceit'd as I never keep any such, She works extremely well, & will do any-thing in her power for us, I've not heard yet whether the Coll. will give my Brother [John] leave to be Absent at ye Review, if he does I shall certainly wait upon you imediately, but as leave is seldom to be procur'd at y.^{t} time, I fear he wont get it, if y.^{t} be ye case I cant be with you till ye latter end of May or beginning of June at which time please God I shall also bring the Money with me, indeed I am very impatient to be with you as my whole study

shall be to please & do everthing to convince you with w.^{t}
Respect & Regard I am,

> Dear & Hon'd Uncle
> your Dutyful Affn.^{t} & oblig'd Niece
> Cath. Bagshaw

JRL, B1/1/68

94

Lieutenant-Colonel Samuel Bagshawe to Richard Starke, Deputy Governor of Fort St. David, Cuddalore

[Draft]   [Fort St David, Cuddalore]
                                          [6 September 1754]

Agreable to your desire to me this day to from a State of Such Conveniencys as I find necessary for the Accomodation of His Majesties Troops at Cuddalore as a hint to you or foundation on wch. to make a Representation to the Honbl.^{e} the Presid.^{t} and Council at Fort St George, I take the liberty to give you this trouble, and begin with the Quarters wch. for the Officer[s] are in general very bad nor are there a sufficient Number sett forth and of those first apointed for the Soldiers several have since been cut off by Enclosures and the Rooms of others shutt up, I have forbid any of them to be forced open or the Enclosures pulled down till I Knew by whose Orders these Encroachments were made, As this requires so I hope it will meet with a speedy remedy and that you let me be acquainted with the names of the persons entrusted with executing your Orders both with regard to the Quarters and other Provision to be made for the Troops & that they shall be directed to attend me when I shall have Occasion to send for them on future Encroachments or Deficiencies. I beg leave also to acquaint you that neither Matts nor [Utensils] are yet provided; and I beg leave you will please to represent to the Honbl.^{e} the Presid.^{t} & Council at Fort St George that I think it absolutely for the Service of the East India

Company that the Kings Troops should be furnished with
Provisions after the Manner of the Companys Troops when in
the Field for at least fourteen Days after their Arrival, that they
may have time to make themselves acquainted & how to procure
it from the Country and with some of their Customs and I desire
the Presid.t & Council may be informed that in the Allowance
appointed for the Troops is left out two Drams of Arrack which
was always delivered each day to the Troops under Admiral
Boscawen,[46] it is so in the Memorandums I brought from
Europe ... The Honbl.e the Presid.t & Council of Fort S.t George
have in their Letter to you expressed with great Kindness as well
as Wisdom that to preserve the harmony I hope will always
continue between the K.s & Cy.s Forces & to encourage those of
the Kings they desire they may find an agreable Reception and
Accomodation [and] to this Purpose & that this Salutary End
may be answered I beg you will be pleased to order Fuel
Candles and some household Furniture to be provided for the
Officers in proportion to their Rank, all of which they have been
accustomed to receive in the Barracks in Ireland, are absolutely
necessary & hardly to be procured without the assistance of the
Company, please also to move an Allowance of Cotts at least to
the Field Officers and Captains, The Adjutant will want a
Horse, the Major a Horse, Palankine[47], Punes[48] and an allowance for his Table in proportion to his Rank. The Honbl.e the
Presid.t[49] & Council will please to consider what Apointments
they judge will be suitable to the Rank I hold, and the Command
I may & must have by the Date of my Commission as Lieu.t
Colonel agreeable to the Kings Commission on this Occasion, I
am the Second in Command L.t Col. Lawrence[50] not excepted and
in the Absence of Coll. Adlercron or anything hapning to him the
whole Command devolves upon me[.] I rely upon the honour of
the Governors of the East India Company that nothing will be
offered unworthy them or unworthy me[.] The Weak State I was in
when I embarked was sufficient to be an excuse for my Stay at
home, [but] I chose to run the Hazard of such a Voyage [and] it has
pleased God to restore me to health[.] I am disposed to serve the
Comp.y & I hope to be able to serve them, I shall just mention that
my want of a Leg Makes the providing me imediatly with a Horse

absolutely necessary ... I also have imediate Occasion for a Palankine, & Punes. I submit to your Opinion who are acquainted with my Situation ... what Quarters shall be assigned me, & what Table & other Apointments shall be allowed me.

I beg your pardon for observing that though you have described Col. Adlercrons Command in Stronger Terms than what the Honbl^e the Pres^t & Council at Fort St George seem to aprehend Yet I think they will bear a Stronger Discription, as his Commission on this Occasion is as full as Admiral Boscawens and as absolute over all the Forces of the East India C^y on the Coast of Coromondal, He has the power of Life & Death[,] the Disposal of Commissions at Pleasure, & is to be consulted & is intitled to sit with the Gl. Council of the East India C^y apointed on this Occasion on all the Plans of Operations wch shall be formed for the Service of the Comp^y. ...

JRL, B2/5/57

95

Lieutenant-Colonel Samuel Bagshawe to Colonel John Adlercron

[Copy]   Fort St George, Madras
                                           12 October 1754

I do myself the honor to acquaint you I arrived in Madrass Road the 10th Ins^t in the Evening and landed yesterday near Noon, but have not as yet transacted anything with the General Council; the President Mr Saunders has done me very great Honor and I am so fortunate to be agreed with him in opinion it will be better he and I should talk over all Matters contained in my Instructions before they are brought to a publick hearing, because many things may be said in a private Conversation to explain or reconcile Differences which a Meeting in Council will not permit, The President seems greatly desirous Harmony should subsist between the Kings and Companys Troops, & that the former should have no real Grievances to complain of, and

he will do great Injustice to a good Character, an honest
Countenance and as genuine Appearances as I ever saw, if his
Actions do not correspond with his Expressions.

The Second Article of your Instructions[51], but the first of
business ... has given some trouble, the King's Instructions
seeming to clash a good deal with those of the Court of
Directors and the Powers they have given to the Companys
Governors, for which they plead His Majesty's Charter; The
Presidents Observation on these Contradictions is this, That
where two Parties may each insist on the Orders they receive,
They both ought to recede something to promote Harmony and
the Common good: The President is satisfied you ought on all
Occasions to receive the Title you require agreable to His
Majesty's Instructions, and that you should Command the
Companys as well as the Kings Troops in the Field, but thinks
you should not have the same Power in the Garrisons that are
Settlements, I have said I was perswaded you had no Intention
to intermeddle with the Garrisons that are Settlements no
further than was indispensibly necessary to inform you of their
State, and what Troops they could spare for the Field, unless
the Interest of the Company's Affairs required you to introduce
the Kings Troops for their Defence, and I could not see how
(consistent with His Majesty's Instructions) you had it in your
Power to say, you would not on any occasion assume a power
in the Companys Garrison Settlements. The President then
agreed you should have your Title as I have mentioned, that
your Power should be acknowledged over the Companys as well
as the Kings Troops, and that nothing should be said on either
side with respect to the Garrisons which are Settlements, In all
other Garrisons your Authority is acknowledged the same as in
the Field, and you will also receive Returns of the Settlement
Garrisons when you shall find it for the Service to require
them, and Reinforcements from them when they can be spared.
If I may presume to give my Opinion, I think you may without dishonour make this Concession. The President is of
Opinion That the General Council may assume to themselves a
power of entring into pacifick Engagements without opposing
His Majesties Instructions but they will treat you with the

Complaisance due to the Kings Commission and inform you of their Conclusions and such Matters as may be related with Safety, and do every other thing [that] may tend to promote a good Understanding and Confidence between the Kings and the Companys Troops: If you aprove of this Expedient and this Disposition I hope every other Matter contained in my Instructions will be greatly facilitated. It is agreed you shall have your Allowance to yourself, and some Provision will be thought of for me and the Major, and I fancy you will be allowed a Horse and Palankine without any limitation of time: and I think the President kindly enough disposed to make an Allowance more to the Satisfaction of the Subaltern Officers and Cadetts.

I beg to receive your Commands as soon as possible and if I am so happy to meet with your Approbation, it will afford me pleasure [and] will make ample Amends for any trouble I may suffer . . .[52]

JRL, B2/5/99

96

Lieutenant-Colonel Samuel Bagshawe to Colonel John Adlercron

[Draft]   Fort St George, Madras
                                         13 October 1754

I Yesterday wrote you a very long Letter giving you an Acc^t of my Arrival & favourable Reception and the hopes I had Matters would be adjusted in a manner at least tolerable to all Parties, I am afraid I am a dupe to my own Credulity, this much I have to say in my Justification, that the Design of my coming hither being to promote Peace & harmony & a good Understanding, one of more Discernment might be deceived with the plausible Apearances I have met with, As every one who knows the Character of the President must be sensible of his Weight and Influence in all the Councils of the Company, I therefore thought it a prudent Measure to desire he and I to talk over

Matters before [they] were offered to the Genl. Council because
many things may be said in a private Conversation to explain or
reconcile Difficulties wch a meeting in Council would not
permit, & the President came into the proposal so heartily
& appeared so sincere & proposed expedients so rational,
acknowledged Errors comitted wth so much frankness & was
so ready to point out [ways] to remove them that I began to
aplaud my good fortune and hoped every thing would be
put upon such a footing that the Service would be carried
on with chearfulness & to every ones Content, I should be
glad to find this still the Case but my hopes by the Presid^{ts}
behaviour are a good deal lowered—Your Title was long
debated between us, he was willing to allow it & your power
over all the Cy^s Troops in the Field but thought the Garrisons
wch are Settlements could not be implyed, however at last
he agreed you should have your Title, & your Authority
should be acknowledged, You was to have Returns of the
State of the Garrisons whenever you thought the Service
required & what Troops could be spared were to be sent you,
& you was on all Occasions to be treated with the Complaisance
due to your Command, acquainted with all transactions though
of a pacifick Nature that could be communicated with safety &
every thing was to be done that could tend to harmony. While
I was writing you an Acc^t of these things I receive[d] a
Message desiring me to defer a while what related to the Title
as some of the Council differed in Opinion, when I had
finished my Letter I went to him to shew it him, that he might
see there was no more in it than was agreed on between him &
me, he very smoothly went over the Objections made by others
wch he said were none to him, but to justify himself intended
to take all the Councils Opinions separately wch was to be
done this Morning, upon this I consented to defer sending your
Letter 'till now; At Noon I wrote for an Answer[,] it is Seven
o'Clock & none come. It is a great Misfortune that I can apply
[to] no one to Inform me w^{ht} is the Presid^{ts} real Disposition,
however I shall begin to be on my Guard, & write nothing but
what is agreed beyond Revocation. I am convinced Colonel
Lawrences Silence is Design, I hear he is to come from

Camp & Col. Heron[53] to go thither & both I presume without consulting you in the least, whether you will suffer such a manifest Attack against your Authority is an affair[,] to use the Presid[ts]. Expressions[,] to be maturely weighed ...

JRL, B2/5/105

97

'Observations' by Lieutenant-Colonel Samuel Bagshawe

[Draft]   [Fort S[t] George, Madras]
                                           [October] 1754

Persons suffered to go backwards & forwards from Trichinopoly &c without Colonel Adlercron's Permission or his being first Acquainted
   Kept a Stranger to all Transactions
   Ought to be acquainted with the first occasion why Europeans were called to the Assistance of the Natives, who first offered Assistance or were first guilty of Hostilities, What has been the Consequence of those Hostilities, What Losses or Acquisitions made by either Party, What Alliances have been formed, what Treaties made[,] What Diparted from & Why? What Alliances We have now? What they can bring into the Field & when, What Force we can bring into the Field & when, What Necessary for their Subsistance and how provided; What are the Enemys Alliances[,] What they can furnish & what the Enemy can now bring into the Field and when, Intelligence of their Motions & loss or Gain of Europeans,
What the present Designs and Interest of the Company

Plans Offensive —	Defensive
Cy[s]	Enemy
State of the Troops — Europeans	Who is their Commanding
Seapoys, Horse, Morattoes[54]	Off[r] [,] what kind of

144

Country & Power to be offended   Man, how he employs
Magazines & where   his time
                                        how the Officers
                                        employ theirs

JRL, B2/5/113

98

Lieutenant-Colonel Samuel Bagshawe to Colonel John Adlercron

[Copy]   Fort St George, Madras
                                        1 November 1754

I have the honour of your favour of the 29th October[55] & the
enclosed is a Copy of the Convention I have entred into on your
Behalf; I hope it will appear to you agreeable to the Concessions
you have made, & that I have not exceeded the Limits of your
Instructions; & however the conduct of the Gentlemen here
may be censured & disaproved of at home for requiring such
Concession (tho' I must do them the justice to say they can
produce Orders and Instructions from the Court of Directors
which seem to require them to act as they have done in
opposition to your Authority) Yet as all Business & the Service
must have been suspended without these Concessions, I hope
the Part you have acted & the Moderation you have shewn will
meet with its deserved approbation.

I cannot, nor do I desire to clear Myself of an Intention from
the beginning to procure a more comfortable Provision for the
Officers than was at first apointed, & to make the Captains
advantages bear a nearer proportion to those of the Company's
Captains: but I can, & ever will, of being influenced by my own
Interest; for the Allowance now made me was offered me before
I wrote my first Letter to You; & I think there are more Traces
of Resentment than Influence in that Letter; Perhaps it was
offered as a Bait, but I have no reason to think so, & that
given for it, was a Consideration of my being the Second in

Command. I always insisted of dispatching in the first Place the Articles of your Instructions, which concerns your Title, & though I have sent you a Copy of the Regulation (because I had it by me) before the Copy of the Convention (which is left on the Council Board) yet the Regulation was not entered upon 'till the Convention was finished ...

NAM, 8707–48–1 p.84

99

Proposed Convention between the President and Council, Fort St. George, and Colonel John Adlercron

[Copy]   [Fort St. George, Madras]
                                          [1 November 1754]

It being represented to Colonel Adlercron that it would be greatly detrimental to the Reputation & to the established method of governing the Company's Settlements if the Powers granted to Him by His Majesty were exercised in their full Extent by him in the Companys Garrisons that are Settlements: He Colonel Adlercron intent on preserving the Harmony recomended to him purposes to make these Powers subservient to those Orders of His Majesty which require him to use his utmost endeavours to assist the Company in their Affairs & to promote their Interest, until His Majesty's Pleasure be further known.

The following Regulations are therefore agreed for this purpose.

His Majesty's Commander in Chief not to exercise any Authority in the Settlement Garrisons of Fort St George, St David, or any other Settlement the Company's President & Council may think necessary, nor over the Troops & Seapoys quartered by them or employed within the Bounds of the said Settlements. If at any time it shall be necessary to take any of their Troops in to Custody for Misdemeanours, they shall be sent to the Company's Guard; or the Commanding

Officer for the Company acquainted that he may send for them.

2^{d}

The Commander in Chief will allow Regimental Courts Martial to be held without applying on every occasion to him & the Sentence to be aproved of & carried into Execution.

3^{d}

The President, Governors &c for the Company will on all Occasions of Intercourse with Colonel Adlercron or the Commander in Chief for the time being, give him the Title in the Preamble of his Instructions, vizt Commanding in Chief the Land Forces to be employed in the East Indies.

4th

The President, Governors &c for the Company shall on every Representation from the Commander in Chief, or by his Direction against Persons under their Authority for Misconduct, or ill Treatment of His Majesty's Troops, cause a speedy Enquiry to be made, & ample Satisfaction given to the Person or Persons injured.

5th

And the President & Governors &c for the Company will send the Commander in Chief when he shall require it, Returns of the State of the Settlement Garrisons; & give him every other Advice necessary to promoting the Service, & give him all the Assistance which shall be consistent with the safety of these Settlement Garrisons.

6th

In every other Matter both Parties shall exert themselves to promote the good Harmony, Understanding, & Friendship which ought to subsist between them; & which is so necessary to the Common Good.

In Witness whereof this Paper is interchangeably signed by
. . .

JRL, B2/5/133; NAM, 8707–48–1 p.85

100

Lieutenant-Colonel Samuel Bagshawe to Sir James Caldwell, Bart.

[Draft]   Fort St George, Madras
                                           5 November 1754

The Satisfaction I know you will receive in hearing from me
makes me wish I had less trifling Matter to entertain you with.
So few and so much alike are the Occurences that happen in a
Voyage to the East Indies that I might refer you to any printed
a hundred years agoe, You are only to suppose the Ship the
Britannia and the Author your Brother, You may there find We
took our Departure from Cape Clear, had a rough Sea in the
Bay of Biscay; We pass by the Madeiras and saw some of the
Canary Islands, and as the time of the Year did not allow us to
put in at the Cape of Good hope, we sailed on to Madagascar
and made no other Stop till we got to India. In our passage We
see a great many Sharks and catch now and then one of them,
they are an ugly Monster, some of them very large with several
Rows of Teeth and make as few Morsels of a Man as Gulliver of
a Sheep in Lilliput, At the Tropick We see the Tropick Bird,
chiefly remarkable for being only found in that Latitude, his Tail
consisting of only two long Feathers and the Difficulty of getting
one. We also see such Shoals of flying Fish as when related is
sufficient to destroy the credit of them, As we approach the
Equinoctical Line we find a suffocating faint deadly heat, which
sure is not equalled in any except that Place we are threatened
with to deter us from Evil, to relieve us from this Calamity We
have Thunder loud enough to destroy hearing[,] flashes of
Lightning to take away the Sight and Showers of Rain that
exhibit a lively Representation of those which fell at the time of
the Deluge: on crossing the Line we undergoe the Ceremony of
a ducking or pay our Forfeit of a Bottle and a Pound[56], on the
other side of the Line we have sometimes fair, sometimes cross
Winds and amuse ourselves with catching Pintado Birds and
Albetrosses, the first so called because it looks as if it was
painted black and white, they are both very silly birds: We

sometimes meet with a black little Bird whose true Name I forget, but is well known among the Seamen by that of one of Mother Carys Chickens and then according to the marine Superstition we expect foul and hard Weather, and indeed it rarely happens otherwise (A Wonderful Instance of the Care of Providence over every part of this Creation that having framed this Bird to be nourished in such a Confusion of Elements directs it where to see its Prey & furnishes it with sufficient means for subsisting)[.] Off the Cape we see the Cape Hen or the Gannett Birds the first never the other Seldom seen anywhere else & are as sure a Mark that we are in soundings as if we saw land, and the Colour of the Sand at the bottom tells us on what Part & furnishes us with a new Departure; but I have passed over a Curiousity which affords Us a fine Opertunity to shew the greatness of our Travells & sufficient matter for Triumph over all the Sign Painters in great Britain and Ireland; we can call them Blockheads and Ignoramus's to paint a Dolphin crooked and with a great head as big as a Codfish, the true Dolphin is no more like a Dolphin on a Sign than the Moon is like green Cheese and if a Painter or anyone else doubts what I say, he needs go no further than the Latitude of twenty seven Degrees south & not above 10,000 Miles thither and home again to be convinced of this truth, he will find a Dolphin a delicate fine strait Fish, not crooked nor round but flatt, and its Colors more beautiful than those in the Rainbow; and after gratifying his Sight he may please his Palate, it will be very good eating provided he brings sawce enough to eat with it, the Man who will not come so little a way for so much knowledge must have sure little Curiosity; I must carry you now to Madagascar where the Beef is as fat and cheaper than in Ireland, the Milk is as dear as in London; the island produces many other good things and some fine Fruits, but not any I could find preferred to a Potatoe, and I am much mistaken if a Gentleman who has visited this Island and afterwards can have a Residence in Ireland will ever return to seek for one in Madagascar: I have only to make one Remark more to finish a Relation which only your Partiality for the written [word] can excuse, the Blacks of Madagascar and the blacks of India both differ from those of Guinea, they are much handsomer and of a better Temper and Disposition, the Blacks of Madagascar are a bold Warlike People, those of India except one or two Casts or Tribes the most effeminate Creatures on earth, no white Lady has a finer Finger for any kind of nice Work, they are also surpisingly supple and for Feats of Dexterity and Equilibre, the famous Slight of hand Man, the Turk with the hard name and the neat limb'd Mr Maddox are meer Bunglers: And to end as I begun the Blacks of both Countries go always quite naked which in these Climates is as great a Wonder as for a European to put on his great Coat when it snows and freezes on the Derry Mountains the Highlands of Scotland, Pentland Hills and Pennan mosses.

I come now to a part of our Voyage for which I am thankful as I am Serious, Providence has been pleased to distinguish it by a remarkable health, two of our Ships arrived without the loss of a Man, the whole landed only ten men fewer than they embarked and of y.^t Number two fell over board and were drowned, Since our landing Providence has been pleased to take away Capt Lewis[57], he was a very worthy Man, and the loss is heavy to me as he was a particular Friend; a few of our Men have died, more owing to a wilful obstinate Intemperance than the Country. The two maimed Ships[58] or others in their Place are still absent, but as the time of year is past for their coming on this Coast, We imagine they are at Bombay and will be with us in January. Our present situation is of the peaceable kind, a Cessation of Arms has been agreed on for three Months, comencing the 11.th October, and both Parties are preparing the Conditions on which they will accept Peace, which with a less remarkable Nation perhaps would be concluded, it is true Mr Dupleix the greatest Obstacle to it, is sent home, but for what is yet agreed on, his Schemes and the ambitious Views of his Nation remain behind ...

JRL, B2/5/138

101

Colonel John Adlercron to Lieutenant-Colonel Samuel Bagshawe

[Copy]   Cuddalore
                                        7 November1754

I received your Letter of the 1ˢᵗ of November with a Copy of the Convention you have entred into on my behalf : I wish I had explained Myself fuller in my Letters to You, for I never meant to make such Concessions as would lessen my Power to a Degree that I think I could not answer for to His Majesty : My Intentions were, & still are, to go as far as I possibly can towards contributing to Harmony, but not to Sign a Convention that would clip my Authority, & leave me little more than the Name of Commander in Chief. In my Letter to you of the 17ᵗʰ of October,[59] I promise the Company not to interfere in their Settlement Garrisons, except the Service requires it, & that I will agree to all Concessions that may put things on a better footing, provided they do not evidently tend to lessen the Authority His Majesty has been pleased to give me: And in one of the 24ᵗʰ[60] I accept the Title in the Preamble of my Instructions; as it seems to me to signify the same as that mentioned in my Instructions to you. These are all the Concessions I have made; & which appear to me far short of those in the Convention. My Opinion on each of the Articles I will give you separately.

In the first it is mentioned that I am not to exercise any Authority not only in Fort Sᵗ George & Fort Sᵗ David but any other Settlement the Company's President & Council may think necessary; nor over their Troops quartered, or employed within their Bounds & Settlements: Is there any thing can be stronger worded than this, to take all power as Commander in Chief out of my hands? I think not; & can not agree to any part of that Article: But as I have already said, will not meddle with their Settlement Garrisons, such as Fort Sᵗ George & Fort Sᵗ David; except the Service requires it.

I agree to the 2ᵈ, 3ᵈ & 4ᵗʰ As to 5ᵗʰ I shall require Monthly Returns of all their Troops.

My Sentiments in regard to the 6th & last Article, ought by this time to be well known: It was from the first my firm resolution to promote Harmony, Friendship, & a good Understanding; I still continue of the same mind; & hope neither my past, or future Actions, will ever contradict my present Assertion. These are my thoughts concerning the Articles of the Convention; & I cannot sign any paper but what is agreeable thereto.

Please make my Compliments to the President & the Gentlemen of the Council: If the Weather & my Health permits, I will do Myself the pleasure to wait on them in December ...

NAM, 8707–48–1 p.86

102

Lieutenant-Colonel Samuel Bagshawe to Colonel John Adlercron

[Draft]   Fort St George, Madras
                                                 14 November 1754

I should be greatly concerned & as much surprised as Col. Lawrence apears to be at your seeming Disaprobation of the Convention I have entred into on your behalf, if I did not imagine it must be owing to my not having been particular enough in an Explanation of the extent of the 1st Article of the Convention. By this 1st Article you Suspend the Authority you seem to have in your Instructions in the Settlement Garisons of Fort St George, Fort St David or any other Settlement Garison, by a Settlement Garison is meant when the Company have an established Govern^t & carry on Manufactures, they have no other Settlement Garison on this coast except at Vizagapatam & Bombay, neither of wch Places I Aprehend you will ever see except in the Map. If you was to publickly exercise an Authority in Fort St George, or Fort St David, the newness of the thing at this time the C^{ys} Servants aprehend would alarm all the Black Inhabitants, might make them imagine a new Form of

Government was going to be established & if it did not drive them out of the Settlement, it would weaken the Hands of the Governor & lessen or destroy his Influence among them [and] you will please to consider whether such a proceeding as would hurt instead of promoting the Companys Affairs does not contradict H. M.ys Intentions and your own profession, beside as the Instructions sent to the Presid.t & Council are founded upon the Power the Directors believe they have from their Charter (in which let them be never so wrong) their Servants apear to be obliged to observe their Orders under Penalty of being dismissed from their Employm.ts and as they do not in many instances tally with yours If each of you are determined to abide by the Letters of your Powers what can follow but Confusion and endless Opposition, instead of Harmony Discord, Jarring for a good Understanding and Enmity for Friendship. Wheras by the Concessions you have made, you seem to have all the Authority you can want for the common good without lessening their Reputation in their Settlem.ts[,] they furnish what you desire[,] will let you have all the Troops they can spare, you may command returns of the State of their Garisons as oft as you please[,] more than once a Month if you think it necessary ... The Companys Servants very readily allow an open exercise of power in any of the Garisons that are not Settlements, and your power will be as unlimited as you desire the moment you take the Field[.] I hope you will [be pleased] to consider this Matter in a different light, the Gentlemen here seem greatly pleased with your Moderation and Attachment to their Interest & there apears in them a great Disposition to Harmony & friendship [and] if you oppose the Concession or Convention We shall return to our former disagreements nay worse as a wound which breaks out again before it is well healed is more difficult to cure than a fresh one. Beside Who can do business for you if for All the Pains they take you rather chuse to find fault than aprove, I have acted for you to the best of my power & Capacity[,] what I am sure will be aproved of at home & agreable to my Conception of your meaning & C. Lawrence understood you in the same manner when he was at Cuddalore ... Mr Orme[61] Assures me Lord Holderness told him your Power was not intended to extend to any of their Garisons and if I am not mistaken I have heard you say Col. Napier[62] told you as much ...

JRL, B2/5/160

103
Lieutenant-Colonel Samuel Bagshawe to Colonel John Adlercron

[Copy]   Fort S! George, Madras
                                          20 November 1754

As I hope my last Letter has explained the true Intent of the first Article of the Convention ... I take the Liberty to send your part of the Convention to be signed, or if you do not chuse to sign, allow me to sign it; I am willing to incur all the Displeasure it shall occasion at home; where I have heard enough since I came here to convince me it will be approved, & that if it is not complyed with, all the Miscariages [that] shall happen in the Indies will be charged to the Kings Troops; & I am afraid the East India Company have sufficient Interest to be believed: Representations do not always gain Credit from their Veracity; Truth finds no bad support from Influence, & Falshood with it has too often passed for Truth: But in this I should be obliged to support the Company's Servants, as they have given me sufficient Reason to think they only want to save Appearances, & to keep up an external Reputation; & that your Complyance will rather strengthen than weaken your Authority. I will presume to point out as appears to me the Conveniencies that will flow from your signing, & the Inconveniencies if you do not: If you sign the Convention you give them a plain proof of the Sincerity of the professions you have made to promote Harmony, & to serve them; & in Return, for parting with a Nominal, you will get a Real Power; & the King's Service benefitted & not hurt, & every Proposal you make will be heard with Partiality: If you do not sign, you will be thwarted in all your Actions, & yet the blame of

all Miscarriages to lie at your Door, & they have it in their power
to do this many ways without appearing to do it; You will
hurt the King's Troops especially the Officers as a stop will
imediately be put to the late Regulation, & you will shut up the
Source to any advantage to yourself; the old Confusions will
return, & Colonel Lawrence has swore to me he will imediately
leave the Country & Service: the Credit he has, & the Regard I
must aknowledge he has shewn for the honour of the King's
Troops, will give great weight to what he shall assert; & however,
I think, I have been slighted, & unkindly treated, I will continue
to act the part I have hitherto done & inform you; Matters are
upon a ticklish footing; & in Case of a Miscarriage the ensueing
Year, every one will be glad to throw the blame off himself ...

NAM, 8707-48-1 p.94

104
Council of War

[Copy]   Cuddalore
                                            25 November 1754

On a Letter dated the 14th. November from Lieutenant Colonel
Bagshaw to Colo. Adlercron; it appears that Colonel Adlercron's
not agreeing to the first Article of a Convention enter'd into by
Lieutenant Colonel Bagshaw on his Behalf, is likely to interrupt
that Harmony recommended by His Majesty; He, Colonel
Adlercron, therefore thinks the Convention a Matter of that
Consequence as to require the consideration of a Council of
War: And accordingly Lieut. Colonel Bagshaw being absent at
Madrass, he has called in Captain Forde (His eldest Captain) in
his place. Captain Campbell[63] as Comandg Officer of fort St.
David, was summoned in the room of Colonel Lawrence (who is
likewise at Madrass) He attended the Council; but beg'd
Colonel Adlercron would excuse him from the honour of
assisting thereat as he had not directions on that head from the
Presidency, which the Colonel granted, not being willing to
exert his Power.

At a Council of War held at Cuddalore the 25th of November 1754

Present { John Adlercron Colonel, President
Verney Lovett Major
Francis Forde Captain

Was taken into Consideration the ... Convention sent by Lieutenant Colonel Bagshaw to Colonel Adlercron ...

Which being read the following Amendment to the first Article was proposed.

His Majesty's Commander in Chief not to exercise any Authority in the Settlement Garrisons of Fort St George, St David, Vizacapatam, except the Service evidently requires it: But expects wherever he is in Person with any part of his Regiment to act as Commander in Chief; at the same time [he] will allow the Governour to give the Parole. As to the Second Paragraph of the first Article, it never was the Colonel's intention to meddle with their Troops for Misdemeanours that would not subject them to a General Court Martial; & that what was done in regard to the Seapoy tried by his Orders, was only to show the Governour his Power; as he had reason at that time so to do; & therefore he consents to it.

It is the Opinion of the Council of War that if the First Article be drawn up according to the foregoing Amendment; Colonel Adlercron may sign that, & the remaining Articles of the Convention.

NAM, 8707–48–1 p.92

105

Colonel John Adlercron to Lieutenant-Colonel Samuel Bagshawe

[Copy]   Cuddalore
25 November 1754

I received yours of the 14th Ins^t, & notwithstanding your Explanation of the Extent of the first Article of the Convention, I yet disapprove of it: I should be sorry the Publick Service would receive any Injury therefrom; but the Interest of the East India Company shall never make me lay aside the Honour of the King's Troops (the first thing recommended) which is attacked when my Power is intruded. But not being willing in a thing of that consequence to rely solely on my Judgement; I assembled a Council of War to know their Sentiments thereupon, which you have herewith enclosed.

I must own I do not think my Conduct since on this Coast could give the least reason for the Gentlemen of Madrass to imagine I would in any particular exert to their detriment the Power given me by His Majesty; on the contrary, a little more Confidence is what I flattered myself I had & deserved ...

NAM 8707–48–1 p.93

106

Colonel John Adlercron to Lieutenant-Colonel Samuel Bagshawe

[Copy]   Cuddalore
27 November 1754

I received yours of the 20th. Ins^t, & can say no more on the Subject of the Convention than what I have already done. By a Letter I received the same day from the Presidency tho' dated the 16th. Ins^t, it appears to me that my presence is absolutely necessary at Madrass; I am determined to leave this Saturday or Sunday for that purpose; & hope soon to have the pleasure of seeing you ...

NAM 8707–48–1 p.95

107

William Kellett, Regimental Surgeon, to Lieutenant-Colonel Samuel Bagshawe

Cuddalore
3 December 1754

I did not think I should ever desire your absence from the Regim.^t & yet I could not help being uneasy whilst your Departure from hence was doubtful[.] The happy & I may say surprising Influence y.^r Presence had at Madras confirms the Justness of my Sentiments; I fear y.^r too great Application contributed not a little to y.^r Disorder, which we [here] had the pleasure of hearing by the same post was removed; how disagreable a Suspense did this [free] us from! I may venture to say that at any time your Loss would be a general one, but at such a Critical Time as this, self Interest would make everyone feel it more sensibly, & indeed I have not met with one who did not seem to shrink at the Apprehension of y.^r Danger. I should have sincere pleasure in being able to give you a good Account of the Health of the Regiment but the Sickness was too violent to allow me that satisfaction. I have only the consolation of my own Mind, of being touched with their Distress, of using my utmost Endevours & Diligence & getting all the Insight & Assistance this place affords; I must also assure you that all the Mates have attended with the utmost exactness & Care. There are many reasons to be given for this Distemper raging amongst us with uncommon Violence; as the excess of Debauchery which reigned for some Time amongst us, the constant heavy Rains, the excessive Dampness of the Barracks & the intolerable Badness of the Provisions. These Causes combined with some others were sufficient to produce a Disorder of a bad kind[;] in the beginning of the bad Weather the Symptoms were less violent & gave way so readily, that I was in Hopes I had fallen on a certain Method, but I soon found that the Disorder kept pace with the Season in Violence & that scarcely a man came into the Hospital without a Fever attended with a surprising Dejection of Spirits, intolerable Pains in the Bowels & perpetual Tenesmus

& a violent Suppression of Urine; this last was a very trouble-some Symptom & what occasioned me most Uneasiness as it hindered me from using the proper Evacuations. I must also say that many contributed to their own Deaths by neglecting to come into the Hospital till their Strenght was quite exhausted; this was particularly the Case of Mead of your Company, poor Serjeant Bothwell died fairly of a Decay of Nature[,] he came into the Hospital without any other Complaint than Weakness & the next Morning after eating his Breakfast was found dead in his Bed. We at last began to feel the ill Effects of a crowded Hospital for tho all imaginable Care was taken to keep it clean & airy yet it was impossible amongst so many people afflicted with the same noisome Distemper to hinder the air from being tainted; as soon as I found this to be the Case, I removed all that were on the recovery to the Barracks, giving Cots with them & soon found the good effects of it, we now have only twenty two Men in the Hospital, all on the mending Hand, except one Wallace an old Stander, & the sick we sent out are recovering very fast with this fine weather, in a short Time I hope we shall be in a very healthy State & continue so. I performed an Operation on one Barlow a Grenadier who had a very large Collection of Matter on his Liver, & it succeeded; there was another with the same Disorder but he refused to submitt, till it was too late to attempt it. I should not attempt to trouble you with so long a Letter, at a time when you are engaged in Affairs of so much Weight, but that I know you interest yourself in the minutest Things which concern the Regiment. I sincerely wish that all y^r Toil & Fatigue may turn out to y^r Satisfaction in the End, however you are sure of the Approbation of y^r own Breast & the Applause of the World ...

JRL, B2/5/176

108

Ann, Dowager Lady Caldwell to Lieutenant-Colonel Samuel Bagshawe

Castle Caldwell
19 December 1754

I take the first opportunity to Enquire after my Dear Colonel Bagshaw; and at the same time Indulge my self with the pleasing hopes, that providence has heard the prayers and good Wishes for your Health and preservation of all that have the pleasure of being known to you, particularly of poor Kitty's & mine; She look'd Very thin and pale when she came to town, which I was not Surprized at, nor did she improve much while she stay'd; which was not longer than her Brother Jack[64] could get leave to go with her, and the Child[65] could be conveyed to town; he Improved greatly while he was with us ... he had been very ill before he came and look'd thin & puney, but soon recovered and is a most lovely Engaging Child; so great a favourite with your Uncle, that his Whole pleasure seems to be centr'd in him, and his fondness of him Daily Encreases, I hope their being in Darby Shire will rather advance than Hurt your Interest with your Uncle, as he upon all Occasions Expresses his aprobation of Kitty's behaviour and Conduct, She has the good fortune to please all the persons in the Neighbourhood, particularly Mr Clegg & Mr Evat Which I look upon as a Circumstance of the utmost Consequence as they both have a Very great Influence on your Uncle; and they will certainly make use of it for your Service ... Your little Sammy I hear is a Very fine Boy; as his Nurse at Bandon turned out a Very bad one; and no proper notice taken of your Children after you left the Country, my Cousin Uniack[66] was so good as to send her Chair Servants and a Nurse, for him. She has taken him under her protection to Youghal where no necessary Care is Wanting, which he shows by his Healthy looks and lively Spirits; he was in so Weakly and Dying a Way when they took him there they thought he would not recover; My Dear Coll. may be assured he shall be as properly Conducted in life as his years will permitt, but I trust in god you will soon return to receive your proper Charges, and that your friends will have the pleasure of delivering them Safe into your hands; how happy it would make me to have the least prospect of hearing from you and having it under your hand that the Watery Element and Distant Climate has been favourable to your Constitition and our Wishes ...

JRL, B2/3/276

109
Lieutenant-Colonel Samuel Bagshawe to Colonel John Adlercron

[Copy]   Cuddalore
                                              28 December 1754

Sir

My Return to Quarters having finished the Command which carried me to Fort S.t George, I take the liberty to represent to you that being the second in Command on this Coast, I do with all becoming Deference apprehend the Second Post of trust belongs to me, and that Tritchanopoly being a place of the greatest Importance next to where you are, and A Garrison, is my Post, and I think myself obliged in honor to the Kings Troops, and in Justice to my own Reputation to desire you will please to take this Matter under your Consideration, & give me orders to repair thither, to take the Command of that Garrison, I am with Respect & Fidelity

Sir
Your most obedient
and most humble Servant
Samuel Bagshawe

JRL, B2/5/184

110

Colonel John Adlercron to Lieutenant-Colonel Samuel Bagshawe

[Copy]   Cuddalore
                                                    5 January 1755

Since you desire that my answer to yours of the 28th December may be in writing; I think proper to acquaint you that I cannot approve your going to Tritchinopoly. I shall enter in my Book yours of the above date & this my Answer to it ...

P.S. I accidently heard last Night that a Field Officer was to attend the Parade every Morning. I should be glad to know by whose Orders.

NAM, 8707–48–1 p.103

111

Lieutenant-Colonel Samuel Bagshawe to Colonel John Adlercron

[Copy]   Cuddalore
                                                    5 January 1755

My Answer to the Postscript of your favour of this Days Date requiring to know by whose Orders I attended the Parade is this.
  The Parade being composed only of the Men of your Regt I thought it my Duty as Lieut Colonel to see to it they were dressed in a proper manner to mount Guard. I am sorry it has given you Offence but with due Submission I think this could not be unknown to you till last Night & then you heard of it by Accident, since I waited on you every Morning I could meet with you to make a Report & saw you and made you a Report five Mornings out of Seven, and on one of them representing to you that some of the Men mounted in black some in white Rollers[67] and desiring to know whether they should not appear

162

in the same manner, You gave Directions for their appearing in white Rollers.

I have received your Orders by the Adjutant not to attend the Parade and am with all becoming respect ...

JRL, B2/5/184a

112

Lieutenant-Colonel Samuel Bagshawe to Sir James Caldwell, Bart

[Draft]   Fort St David, Cuddalore
                                                            3 March 1755

The last letter I did myself the honor to write you was from Fort St George, this is from Fort St David; I had then as much to do as I now have little, I speak of publick business, for I am now greatly employed in writing to one or another of my Friends. The Convention between the English and French, and the Disposition it is imagined both are in to Peace give[s] a Change to our thoughts which seem more employed about our Return to Europe than the making of Conquests; however I have the Pleasure to tell you that while War was the Subject, I had an Opertunity to make such Enquirys and obtain such information of the State of Affairs in this Country, the Cause of the late Wars, the Share the English and French had in them, the Motives that enduced them to join the Indian Princes and what they have gained at last by it, that I am prepared for War or Peace, satisfied to stay, much more satisfied to return home. I have good reason to be certain the Arrival of the Kings Troops was of the greatest Service to the Affairs of the East India Company and productive of some of those pacifick Measures which have been pursued since our Arrival, And yet because we have not apeared in Action, they will not be forward to own any Obligation, and when we return home, as the Gazettes will not be filled with the slaughter of so many thousand on one Side and so many on the other, our good friends of England and Ireland will be apt to consider us a sett of people who have done neither good nor harm, Nothing to be blamed for and Nothing to be praised for, and there shall be very humane and good people of this Party, not reflecting that the Sons and Grandsons of those who must have been Slain in such an Engagement may hereafter do essential Service to their Country, and I fancy myself that I [would] rather have my Name left to Posterity as the Builder and Promoter of Hapiness in a little Village of Thirty Houses than as the Depopulator of as many Provinces. In this way I am consoling myself for the thousands I might have gained if the War had continued, and which if I survived might have been purchased with the Loss of an Arm and Eye or t'other Leg; As the Case is, if we are called home within a reasonable Space I hope to be able to eat heartily with you of a Piece of Mutton and Potatoes, or a good Jack, or some Wild fowl of your own killing at Castle Caldwell.

I beg my respects and best Wishes to Lady Caldwell[.][68] I hope on my Return to find the Family encreased with new Relations ...

JRL, B2/5/218

113

Lieutenant-Colonel Samuel Bagshawe to an Unknown Correspondent

[Draft]   [Fort St David, Cuddalore]
                                                      [1755]

As every Man must upon some Ocasions be the Trumpeter of his own Praise, I take the liberty to say that from the Day I was ordered to serve in the East Indies I bent my whole Study and the little knowledge I have to promote that Service; While upon my Passage I employed my time to form Dispositions suitable to the Nature of the Service on which the Troops were to be employed & the Enemy they had to deal with, as soon as I landed I lost no time to recover that lost at Sea & to fitt the Men for Service[,] Nor did I fail to acquaint the Company's Servants that we were ready to take the Field whenever they should require, & I had put the Garrison Duty on such a footing that it received no Alteration when Colonel Adlercron arrived, And when he came I no way Slacked my Attention or Diligence, Yet he was pleased to quarrell with me & take away the Comand of the Reg.[t] from me because I would not submit to terms which I think were unmilitary & noway necessary. He afterward refused to let me go upon a Service to which I was entitled by the Seniority of my Rank, and has on all Occasions taken pleasure to thwart Mortify and contradict me; When I was sent to Madrass he promised to hear the Charges, he now refuses and denys his promise and has convinced me he aims at depriving me of my Comission and would be glad of my Death.

The Company's Servants have frequently employed Junior Officers on lucrative Comands to which I am entitled but this I ascribe to their Partiality for their own Troops, their Resentments that the Kings are sent hither & that they can exercise an independant and in some cases a superior Power, as also a fear least by being employed the K.[s] Officers should get some knowledge of their Affairs & the transactions in this Country.

I do not pretend to be divested of private Interest; the Injury done to it is one of the Motives which induce me to complain, I should have been glad, I want to obtain a few Thousand pounds, my Family wants it, if I die they lose three thousand five hundred pounds, their Circumstances cannot afford such a loss, I should have been glad to obtain such a Sume, but I would have gained it with Reputation, I never would have lost sight of the Companys Interest or ever sacrificed it to my own private Affairs[.] I have other Motives that weigh with me more than my private Interest, I wanted to gain a Reputation to be of use to me when I should return to Europe, I have endeavored all my Life after Military knowledge but have been able to gain very little except a few gleanings from what I have read, I have no Experience, I was so fated in the last War not to be able to get to Flanders not even to Scotland & the Expedition to Britany only convinced me I had Resolution enough to look at an Enemy; here I should have had to do with an Enemy more ignorant then

myself worse disciplined & worse armed, and against whom
Europeans seldom fail of gaining success; Nine Parts in Ten of
Mankind do not consider what the People are against whom a
person obtains Success provided Success is obtained and
though Judges of military operations are not so easily imposed
on even these Judges will give a Man credit for what benefit he
gains by the Service when such Success in obtained, As a Body
of Troops who have never Seen Service but have been well
disciplined are fitter to be sent against an Enemy than a Crowd
of Men who are ignorant of the Use of Arms. These Reasons,
others I could give that tend to the same purpose, & My private
Interest in some part are the Motives which induce me to be
greatly dissatisfied with the Treatment I meet with in this
Country & desire to leave a people who chuse to prefer their
own private prejudices and Passions to all other Considerations.

It is with great Reluctance I write on these Matters, I am sure
I must do it awkwardly & with so little Inclination that though I
think it necessary to prepare Letters I do not do it with
an Intention to send them If I can obtain any reasonable
Acknowledgements or a reconciliation, I never am easy while at
Variance with any Man and though perhaps I may be wrong
sometimes in my resentm^{ts} I never fall out with any one before I
think I am ill used by him & have ever desired & Wish to do all
the good I can to every one with whom I am concerned ...

JRL, B2/5/240

114

Lieutenant-Colonel Samuel Bagshawe to Mrs Catherine Bagshawe

[Draft]   [Fort St David, Cuddalore]
                                              7 October 1755

My dear Kitty

I do not know if I have acquitted myself as I ought in my last
Letter but this I am sure of[,] I am not wanting in Affection

however I may be in Expression[.] I love you and I admire you for your affectionate Friendship and Generosity, Your Regard for me, your tenderness, your generously depriving yourself for my sake of all those Enjoyments that please at your time of Life, & wch your Birth promis'd to bestow on you and must ever endear you to me & procure you honor and Esteem from all Who know you. I would in this letter if I was able give you a fuller Acc^t of my pres^t State but I must tell you one Thing & desire you will mention it to our common friends that no exception may be taken at my Silence[,] I never sit down to write that I do not bring a painful Complaint on my Bowels so that I write as little as possible. The Climate has had that Effect on me I expected[,] a genl. Relaxation which wth out causing a Confining Sickness never suffers me to be quite well, I use a great deal of Exercise to wch I attribute under Providence that I am as well as I am, I constantly rise by Candle light, am on horseback by break of day & ride again in the Evening. I have tryed diff^t Methods of living, I have lived after the Manner we did at Quart^{rs} sometimes a little freer, I found this did not hurt me but yet did not make me easy & well. I have now altered it to an almost perfect abstinence from Wine[.] I see Comp^y[,] the Allowance I have for my Table making that necessary but I live by Rule from which I do not intend to depart if it continues to agree with me for any Person or consideration whatever & the more so as it is a Regimen you recomend & fancy is best for me ...

JRL, B2/3/29   * * *

115

The Petition of Lieutenant-Colonel Samuel Bagshawe

[Draft]   Fort St George, Madras
                                          23 November 1755

Petition of Lieu^t Colonel Samuel Bagshawe to George Pigot[69] Esq. President to the Select Committee for Affairs of Country Government &c

Gentlemen

I give you this trouble to represent to you a great Injustice I think I receive, and that an Injury is done to my honor and Reputation when Troops are sent out on Service under the Command of a Junior Officer: And by laying before you what I believe is a true State of my Situation in this Country I hope to obtain your Confidence and Assurance that the like shall not be offered me for the time to Come. I have too great Respect for you as a Body, and hope I stand too well in your Esteem as to receive such unkind Usage by Contrivance and Design.

I am the eldest officer on this Coast after the Commander in Chief and if the Customs of all the States in Europe are of any Weight, I have an undoubted Right to Comand any Party or Body of Troops (equal to my Rank) sent out for the Service of the East India Company, Where the Commander in Chief does not act himself, and until I am convicted of want of Courage, Capacity and Conduct, I cannot be set aside without the greatest partiality and Injustice. I will wait on you in Council to prove this more circumstantially if you think proper, and depend on your Justice to weigh this matter duely, and to receive such Reparation for my part in my future Treatment as is worthy you and will establish me[.]

I believe the Merchants of England are superior in Wisdom as well as Riches to those of any people in the World, Yet I will presume to say, their Credit and Esteem with other Nations depends on their Integrity and the Justness of their Actions not on their Riches or Understanding, and I hope the Gentlemen who represent the most considerable Body of Merchants in Great Britain, will not refuse even to a Single Person that Equity they would observe to a Community: I came hither at the hazard of my Life, and I came wth Inclination[,] it is not my fault I have not endeavoured to be useful, I always have been, and now am ready to go on any Service you shall think for the honor or Advantage of the East India Company. I desire to be favored with an imediate Answer and am with all becoming Regard and Respect

Gentlemen
Your most obedient
and faithfull humble
Servant
S.B.[70]

JRL, B2/5/261

116

William Kellett, Regimental Surgeon, to
Lieutenant-Colonel Samuel Bagshawe

Fort S! David, Cuddalore
20 December 1755

I am extremely obliged to you for the Acc! you favour me with of
y. Situation in point of Health, nor can I help feeling some pain
mixed with Admiration at y. long Letters wrote with so much
Ease on so affecting a Subject; I rejoice at y. being so well in
every other respect, I think it a very promising Sign for from the
regular flow of the Blood, may be expected a happy Alteration in
a Disorder so recent when assisted by proper Medicines, in
Diseases of this kind, proceeding from an internal Obstruction
from some irregular Secretion of the Juices, the Method of
Cure is very simple & regular, consisting in Evacuations of all
kinds & the strongest stimulative nervous Medicines, not only
internally but outwardly apply'd to the Nose to promote violent
sneezing, by that means to give a shock to the Nerves & assist
them in trowing off whatever oppresses them; the first process
you have gone through very smartly, there is nothing more I
could [have] done, except a Seton[71] in the Neck, which is a
capital Operation in all Disorders of the Eyes, either from
external or internal Causes; I have seen great Success attend it
in both Cases & indeed it is Wonderful what happy Changes will
follow a Discharge seemingly of so little Consequence; Issues
for the same purpose are often made in the Crown of the Head
& the Temporal Artery frequently opened; I find you are now
beginning the second process of y. Cure in a Course of nervous
Medicines, may their effects be prosperous! I can say nothing of

native Cinnabar[72] from my own Experience, having never seen it used, but this I can assure you of that it is a most powerful attenuating Medicine & with proper Magagem.[t]: very happy Effects may justly be expected from a Medicine capable of assisting Nature so powerfully in her Operations; I hope before this reaches you some good Omens of Success may appear from its Use. True native Cinnabar is very dear, but the small Quantity you can use makes it in that respect very trifling; there is a factitious Cinnabar made by Chymically uniting Sulphur & Mercury; this is very cheap & looked on as much safer, yet fully answering the Intentions of the other, in truth I believe the native is now seldom or never used in Medicine, it was observed on its first use to produce several uneasinesses in the Stomack, none of either kind came out to me ...

JRL, B2/5/276

117

Lieutenant-Colonel Samuel Bagshawe to Henry Fox, Secretary at War

[Copy]   Fort S.[t] David, Cuddalore
13 January 1756

By the last Dispatches I had the honor to represent to you some hardships I thought I suffered in point of Command. As this Afair is become still more interesting to me I hope you will be so good to excuse my giving you this fresh trouble.

There is at the time I write this Letter and has been some Months past a body of English Troops in the field from three to five hundred Europeans, a Train of Artillery and a considerable number of Country troops assisting the Nabob against the Polygars[73] who refuse to pay their Tribute; The Kings Troops are not thought of, nor the Rank of Officers at least considered; The Command is given to a Captain of the Companys Troops whom the Council here have made a Major[74] (of which it may be necessary to say something before I conclude this Letter). When

I was ordered to Fort S! George to Preside at a General Court Martial I took that Opertunity to write a Letter to the Genl. Council (or Select Committee as it is now called) of which I have the honor to send you a Copy with the Councils Answer. I have asked several of them, what fault they have to find with me, Whether they doubt my Courage, Conduct or Capacity, they say no, and some that they see no reason why I am not employed, and wish that I had been sent out at the time their Major[,] Lieu! Colonel Heron was employed, and some of them hint as if it was intended to employ me, but I have had too much Experience of Transactions here to be amused or not to know that Nothing is to be depended on that is not absolutely directed from home; I am in the Kings Service and that is an objection [that] will ever remain untill the Companys Servants are bound by Orders they cannot or dare not break, or that the Necessity of their Afairs may influence their Councils; but at this Distance I humbly presume Matters of Importance should not be left to the Caprice of Persons who after all that can be done, will have it too much in their Power to be Arbitrary; if Afairs abroad were always in the hands of Men of generous Principles improved by a liberal Education, such Cautions would be needless, but as Power both Civil and military may sometimes fall into the hands of Men of mean Capacities and little Minds, it is for the benefit and hapiness of People whose Lot it is to be dependant that the Good as well as the Bad be kept within just Bounds and hindred from doing publick Mischief or private Injuries under the Sanction of publick Authority. I here beg leave to introduce the hint I gave above.

The Companys Servants greatly resent that a person is sent over hither as Commander in Chief of the Company Troops which they think an Infringement of their Charter by which they consider themselves invested with a Power of giving Laws to all who shall come on the Coast, they also think they might Name what Degree of military Officers they please, but as they are not sure of this, I am perswaded if they succeed in the Atempt of naming a Major they will apoint others of a still higher Rank, at least to have one whose Comission shall be superior to the Commander of the Kings Troops.

However the present Commanding Officer has little more than the Name for they form Operations; send Troops on Service; apoint Comanding Officers; Change Garisons &c without consulting him, and most commonly without acquainting him till after their Orders are put in Execution.

In the Instructions to the Commander in Chief it is said— Whereas the East India Company have directed a certain Number of Persons employed in their Service to form themselves a General Council in order to consider of and resolve upon a proper Plan of Operation, You will assist the said Council therein, and when such a general Plan shall be settled on by the said Council &c—I believe it will hardly be proved that the Commander in Chief was ever desired to assist at any one Council, and now they have got or pretend they have got a curious Salvo to shut him out; by the Orders received last Year from the Directors this General Council is changed into a Select Comittee for Country Afairs and each Member is obliged to take an Oath of Secrecy, so that the Commander in Chief cannot be admitted without making them guilty of Perjury.

As I only write on publick Matters to gain your good Opinion, by shewing I endeavor after such knowledge as shall fitt me for Service, and as I have spoke freely of the Companys Servants that by representing things plainly you may better judge on what Principles Afairs are transacted, I think myself also bound in justice to acknowledge their Merit and to declare that the Gentlemen of whom I have spoke so freely are in their private Characters sensible good natured Men, hospitable and generous, and some of them in particular M[r] Orme and M[r] Palk[75] exceeding well acquainted with the Afairs of this Country and [the] Interest of the Company, but whether that in a Body they act by particular Instructions with respect to the K[s] Servants or that they fear Innovations, and are jealous if these shall obtain a Share of their Power it may continue in their hands, but so it most certainly is, they are not the same Persons in business and in private Life ...

* * *

JRL, B2/6/7

118

Lieutenant-Colonel Samuel Bagshawe to William Bagshawe of Ford

Fort S! David, Cuddalore
10 February 1756

Dear and honoured Uncle

I cannot thank you enough for the kindness which Kitty says you shew to her and the Child, as these are Instances of your favor in which I am so nearly concerned and on which I sett the highest Value; If it please God to permit me to return to my native Country, I think I shall not fail to give you every Proof in my power of Gratitude; indeed I ever had an Inclination to serve you, though I am afraid I was sometimes unhappy in the expression.

The State of health I have enjoyed in this Country has not been the most eligible, however thank God it is no Worse. By the bills I send Kitty, I hope you will believe I endeavour to be a good Husband, my Circumstances might have been better if I had met with the Justice I think due me. As Writing is an Exercise that hurts me very much, I hope you will allow me to keep any Observations I have made in this Country to help out an Evenings Conversation over a Pipe (if our Dame will give me leave to smoke) in your smoking Parlour, for I have been obliged since I came to India to take now and then a pipe of Tobacco for the benefit of my health.

Our Country Men of the East India Company and our Neighbours the French are acting the part of knaves and Fools and we who are innocent very likely may suffer for it ...

JRL, B2/3/172

119

Medical Certificate of the State of Lieutenant-Colonel Bagshawe's Health

Fort St George, Madras
18 October 1756

We do hereby certify that Lieu.^t Colonl. Bagshawe of Colonl. Adlercrons Regim.^t has had a very bad State of Health, since his Arrival in India, and by a violent Disorder in his Head, which he was seized with at Madrass in the latter End of the Year 1755, he lost entirely the Sight of one of his Eyes, and has the other very much impaired; in August 1756 He was again attack'd with an acute Inflammation of his Eye, attended with a most obstinate Head-Ach which threw him into a Nervous Fever, out of which he is at present by the Help of Country Air, slowly recovering, but the Pains in his Head and Eye still continue, and at times are extremely severe.

We therefore earnestly recommend to him, to return to Europe as soon as possible, it being our Opinion, that the Clymate will render him unfit for Service, be destructive to his Constitution, and even put his Life in the greatest Hazard, and that the least which can happen will be the loss of his other Eye.

William Kellett
[Andrew] Munro[76]

JRL, B2/6/116

120

Leonard Morse to Lieutenant-Colonel Samuel Bagshawe

War Office, London
19 July 1757

It is with great pleasure that I find since you left Town that your Pretensions to a Regiment are so much better than I had the honour of knowing before; I shall be, as I once observed to you,—extremely happy in having it in my power to write You such a Letter as Colonel Whitmore[77] had not long Since. If the Regimenting the Battalions takes place, as is now talked of, and seems more than probable it will, I shall make it my business to give You early Information, and if I thought I could be as secure of being your Agent, by means of Sir Robert Wilmot's application, which I flatter myself I could procure, or the Duke of Devonshire's thro' him, as I think you are of a Regiment soon, I would not in vain attempt to say how happy You would make me. I have a natural Interest in Lord Ilchester,[78] Lord Digby[79] and Mr Fox, but as they have so long made a point of pushing for Mr Calcraft, I cannot promise myself that in this case I may be able to get them to apply to You ...

JRL, B2/2/423

121

Lieutenant-Colonel Samuel Bagshawe to Sir Robert Wilmot

[Draft]   Chester
                                                           24 July 1757

I hope your usual Goodness will induce you to forgive the Freedom of this Letter. I called at Chatsworth as I said I would in my way through Derbyshire and I just mentioned to His Grace that I had seen you before I left Town but I had little opertunity and when it came to the Point less Resolution to say anything for myself. The Favors I have received from the Devonshire Family have come so purely from themselves without Aplication and there was so great a Delicacy in the Temper of His late Grace it hurt him to be sollicited, And as His Present Grace shews he possesses the other good Qualities of his Father there is all reason to believe he inherits this also, so that I fear to offend by Aplication[.] I am therefore resolved to leave myself to His

Grace's own Motion to do for me as he shall judge proper, but as I cannot be indifferent about Reputation and cannot help being concerned least any [advantage] should be taken of my coming from India to hurt it, I hope you will excuse this trouble—I think you have been very greatly my Friend, and it is very plain you could have no View nor Interest present or future in being so, I never had it in my Power to serve you nor do I see how I ever shall, You must therefore either have thought there was something of the Spirit of a Soldier in me or some honesty in my Disposition that deserved to be encouraged, I know no other Motive you could have to give me your friendship, of course when you find these Principles are not in me y.ʳ friendship must cease, what I therefore most earnestly desire is that if anything has been said or surmised to my disadvantage I may be brought to a speedy & an open Examination or Tryal or any Enquiry that may shew me faulty if I am at fault. I do not pretend to be free from Errors in Action and Judgement, but I am not conscious that I have been wanting in Integrity or Zeal for the Service, and the more publickly my Conduct is examined the more agreable it will be to me. If the greatest persons in the Nation are exposed to Censure how then should so inconsiderable a Mortal as I expect to escape it, but yet it is hard to suffer in Reputation or preferment meerly from Calumny. I beg you will [believe] what I am going to say, and when you find it not truth then never to believe more, that when I left India I suffered all the Misery represented in [my] Case, and do now firmly think if I had staid there I had by this time lost my Life or at least my Sight, yet in this Condition I protest to you I would have staid, if there had been an Apearance of doing any Service, but the Companys Servants seemed positively determined a Kings Officer of my Rank should not be employed and as every time they sett me aside they were conscious they were doing an Act of Violence it must be some check to their Deliberation & the publick business in some Measure obstructed so that Sickness out of the Question the greatest Service I could really do them was to come away ... As Matters now Stand, if my Rank in the Army deserves to be considered and if His Grace of Devonshire would be pleased to recomend me to H.M.ˢ Favor for a Reg.^t I will endeavour to acquit myself to give Satisfaction and I hope I am indifferently well qualified for the Care, Discipline & Service of a Reg.^t and hope [I] may also yet do some Service for the publick, however though [I may] not succeed in promotion I beg I may not be [denied] an Opertunity to Justify my Reputation and preserve the good Opinion of my Friends ...

JRL, B2/3/834

122

Sir James Caldwell, Bart. to Lieutenant-Colonel Samuel Bagshawe

[London]
9 August 1757

... It gives me great Surprise & Concern that you should Apprehend that you lay under any Reflection for leaving India, every Body that I spake to is sensible nothing could have saved your Life but your returning home & it would not have been Consistent with the Character of a good Christian or Subject to have stayed to Perish by a Climate when there was a Prospect of Escaping it & by that Means having it further in your Power to serve your King your Country & your Family & you may be assured my Dr Colonel by everything I have heard or can Imagin It will not be the least check to your Preferment[.] I have heard the Duke of Devonshire frequently spake in the Kindest Manner of you & I believe he will be always Strongly in your Interest[,] how ever infatuated the Rulers of our Country may be at Present they Cannot be so unjust & so Blind to [their] Interest as not to Consider the very few of those that have with true Bravery Suffered, percivered & still greatly suffered in the service ...

* * *

JRL, B2/3/391

123

Lieutenant-Colonel Samuel Bagshawe to Leonard Morse

[Draft]   [Buxton]
                                                 16 August 1757

By the Date of your Letter it came to Buxton a little after I left it
to go to meet Mrs Bagshaw Coming from Ireland, I found it at
Chester—I am very much obliged to you for your friendly
Opinion of me and Wishes on my behalf, which I have reason to
aprehend are more favourable than my Fortune as I have not the
least Intimation that any Promotion is intended for me & since
so much time has passed & no Declaration, I suppose the
proposed Augmentation is blown over—

As to my Agency I do assure you I should with pleasure see it
in your hands, but I need not acquaint you how Seldom the
Colonels have it in their power to name their Agents, I will deal
so frankly as to tell you that if a Reg^t had been given me & the
Matter left to myself, I should have named a particular person[80]
for whom I have professed such a Regard but my Expectations
of a Reg^t have been & are so faint, I can hardly pronounce the
Name to myself—I have a perfect Respect for the Persons you
Name your Friends & next to the Regim^t nothing could give
me so much joy & Satisfaction as His Grace of Devonshire or
Sir Robert Wilmot to recomend an Agent to me & I be allowed
to accept the person they should name. You will oblige me
much to favor me with a Letter if anything extraordinary
happen ...

JRL, B2/2/425

124

Lieutenant-Colonel Samuel Bagshawe to John Payne, Chairman of the Court of Directors of the Honble. East India Company

[Draft]   Ford
9 December 1757

I acquainted you with my departure from London ten days before I left it, I was obliged to go at the time apointed, You took no Notice of me or my Letter then or since. You will please to pardon me if I mention some things [that] have hapned to me in the East India Companys Service, I claim no merit from you for going to India, HM was pleased to order the Reg.^t to which I am Lieu.^t Colonel thither[,] I went thither in obedience to his M Commands—but from the time the Reg.^t was directed to prepare for the Voyage & till my Return I studied to the utmost of my Power the Companys Service, & I think I can point out ocasions where I might have served the Company, during my stay in the Country I experienced repeated Injustice, No regard in the least paid to the Rank I held in the Army, the Custom I believe of most or all of the Nations in Europe when Troops are ordered on Service and for no other reason I could ever conceive but because I was an Officer in the Kings Service. I also suffered greatly by the Climate & lost one eye & was advised to return immediatly to Europe as the only means to save the other & my Life. I offered to run this hazard & only desired common Justice to be done me. My Sickness exposed me to great Expence, I was also obliged to pay my Passage home, a thing [unknown] in the Service and to give a hundred pounds for it and my Expences before I arived in London amounted to two hundred and Sixty Pounds almost as much in Six Months as my whole Pay amounts to in Value, I have since been at great Expence for the Recovery of my health, what must have become [of] me if I had not been supported out of my private Fortune; I told my Case as far as my Arival in London to you and to the Secret Committee, I waited on you and I wrote to you[,] y.^r Books will show you the Apointments made to your own Officers on such Ocasions[.] I have been treated with Injustice by your Servants, I am Slighted by you, What shall I say in my Country & to my Friends when I speak of the East India Company? What would you say in my Circumstances, I know I am a person of small Consideration when weighed against the Directors of the East India Company, but the greater and more considerable you are the less it becomes your Dignity to treat with Contempt a person who has suffered as I have done & who has Strove to serve the Company faithfully ...

JRL, B2/2/814

125

Lieutenant-Colonel Samuel Bagshawe to William, Viscount Barrington, Secretary at War

[Draft]   [Ford]
9 December 1757

Y.ʳ L.ᵈ Ship receives this trouble as my Duty to acquaint y.ʳL.ᵈ Ship I have recovered a good Degree of health, & that I am fitt to go on Service; I should be glad to be excused Serving in a very hot Climate[,] I have suffered already so much in one & it agrees so ill with me, but I am all Obedience to HMs Commands & I hope it will be no Objection to my Serving somewhere that the Corps to which I belong is not yet arived from India.

JRL, B2/2/48

126

John Calcraft, Regimental Agent, to Lieutenant-Colonel Samuel Bagshawe

London
12 April 1758

According to my Promise I am now to inform you that it is Said with Certainty; The 2ᵈ Battallions will be Regimented & Soon;

Wherefore, So high as You are on the Establishment, You shou'd I think Remind your freinds of Your Pretensions which are very Strong, and will I hope be Regarded. If in any Shape I can be usefull here, I beg You will command me; But I must beg you not to mention to any One that this Intelligence comes from Me—

JRL, B2/2/442

127
Lieutenant-Colonel Samuel Bagshawe to John Calcraft, Regimental Agent

[Draft]   Ford
18 April 1758

I cannot express how much I am obliged to you for your favour of the 12th. Ins^t & the Information you there give me which is of the greatest Consequence to me, Yet I am so particularly circumstanced at this Time that whether I succeed or am passed over I cannot make any fresh Application[,] my Friends know my Inclination[,] they have assured me of their Friendship when Ocasion offered[,] what can I do[,] I fear to offend by a further Sollicitation & I have beside the greatest confidence in their honor, perhaps you may hear me mentioned and then a Word from you may do me great Service and [as] you will have early intelligence of what passes if you find I am likely to be one in the List I hope you will interest yourself for Maj^r Ford[,] it will greatly lessen the Satisfaction I should receive from Promotion if he does not succeed me ...

JRL, B2/2/442a

128

John Calcraft, Regimental Agent, to Lieutenant-Colonel Samuel Bagshawe

London
22 April 1758

I had yesterday the honour of your letter of the 18th.—I own, I wish you had been here to have presented a Memorial to His Majesty or that you had reminded your freinds of your Application; Though I don't at all know You will be the worse for not doing so—The Report is, that the Regiments are in a great measure to be given by seniority if so, You Stand very fair; But I don't believe the Matter Settled yet—You may be sure that in case of your Success Major Forde shall not be neglected & in that Event if you have not Other Engagements, I shall be very proud to serve you as Agent, & ever ready to make the most Gratefull Return if you are kind enough to accept my Services ... Whenever I have heard your name mention'd on this Occasion, I have not omitted to express my knowledge of your Inclination & Ability to Serve ...

JRL, B2/2/446

129

Lieutenant-Colonel Samuel Bagshawe to John Calcraft, Regimental Agent

[Draft]
Ford
25 April 1758

I have this day received your favor of the 22ᵈ and by what I else learn suppose the Colonels are by this time fixed & that you now know whether I am of the Number or not. With Respect to the Request you make for the Agency, Your Merit, Capacity & Connection would make it an honour to me to have such a person to manage the Affairs of the Regᵗ but I need not mention to you that these Apointments are now reduced to a Method & indeed it is very far from being unreasonable if when a person by the Credit of his Patron & Friend obtains Promotion to accept a person whom his Friend should recommend. The D. of D. is my Patron, Sir Rob.[t] Wilmot has long been a disinterested Friend—It will be my request when I Obtain a Reg.[t] that the Agent may be agreable to them. I will deal so honestly with you to tell you I did intend to propose a Young Gentleman to their Favor but I believe it will not suit his Occasion to undertake an Agency, If you will please to be of the Pains to see Sir Rob.[t] Wilmott & prevail with him to mention it to the D. of D. His Graces & Sir Roberts Aprobation will absolutely determine mine. To speak of Things one wishes may happen as if they had hapned, I beg the favour of you that if I am named for a Reg.[t] & you are the Agent that M.[r] Roberts may receive it into his Division of y.[r] Office and when you have an Oppertunity to recommend my Friend Ford That you will remember the Succession[,] Cap.[t] Hepburn for Whom we both have a friend-ship is the oldest Captain[,] is a very good Officer and will be very acceptable to the Corps ...

JRL, B2/2/448

130

Leonard Morse to Lieutenant-Colonel Samuel Bagshawe

War Office, London
28 April 1758

Enclosed is a List of Colonels as Settled yesterday, very many are in your situation; but as you have the advantage many have not, of no one being put over your head I hope you will be prevailed on to think tolerably of the disappointment which your last letter seems to intimate you expected. The Duke of Richmond[81] is I think the only one younger than you who gets a Regiment; and you know there is no answering for the influence of the Nobility. Do not believe my dear Colonel that in saying this I can suppose you will presently be able to think indifferently on this matter, tho' I could much wish you to do so ... I saw Sir Robert Wilmot this morning who wishes much with me to hear that you feel not greatly disappointed; and seems to think you will, as no one is put over your head ...

JRL, B2/2/449

131

Lieutenant-Colonel Samuel Bagshawe to Leonard Morse

[Draft]   Ford
2 May 1758

I was this Morning in my Nursery to Reform the Springing of my Young Trees Where I found Branches that were Thieves [whose] substance was derived from [the] Robbery [of] their Brother Branches. I cut them off without Mercy or hesitation, some y^t had very poor heads & others that were of a cankered sower Disposition & what [others] were unseemly in my Plantation, [I] either cut off or have [had] them removed to try what Effect a Change of Soil may make upon them, Some fine shoots that were of a good Stock & have a promising appearance although unduly shot up I have spared in hopes when properly cultivated they may become good Trees, while at this Work I reced y^r Letter of the 28th[,] in the wrath of my Disapointment I could not help saying to myself the K—has been doing in his G—ds. what I have been doing in my Nursery—Patience is a Sovereign Remedy but very bitter to the Palate, many of my Brethren are in a worse situation than I am, if the Court frowns upon me the Country Smiles, I hope I shall soon be cured of any Ambition and of that [inclination] to lose a Substance in pursuit of a Shadow: If I had succeeded & you had come to see me you might perhaps have sometimes met with a Glass of claratt, now if you come you must be contented at all times with humble Port, but find your Welcome shall not be less hearty.

I beg my Sincere Respects to Sir R.W. & thanks for his Friendship[,] I am perswaded I had his good wishes—And I can forgive but I never shall forget the Speech, promise & performance of a certain great Scribe ...

JRL, B2/2/449a

132

Lieutenant-Colonel Samuel Bagshawe to William, Viscount Barrington, Secretary at War

[Draft]   Ford
                                                                                          5 May 1758

When y.ʳ L.ᵈSp. did me the honor to sit down by me & Assure me I might rely on your Protection and that you never forgot persons, I dare not think it the Speech of a Levée, because y.ʳ L.ᵈSp. was not obliged to speak thus to me so that I must believe my being passed over when fifteen Regᵗˢ were disposed of was owing to some particular Reason, I flatter myself my Pretensions are as good as many that are promoted whether considered in the view of Interest, Merit or Seniority; I was strongly recomended to y.ʳ L.ᵈSp. by the Duke of D. and I had as I believe y.ʳ L.ᵈSps. promise, I have done my Duty as punctually, I have been as ready to Serve & I have run as great hazards & I have suffered as much as any Lieuᵗ Col. in the Service & excepting that knowledge wᶜʰ is gained by the advantage of being employed in particular Services hope I am not inferior in Capacity to those younger Officers who have been preferred before me & with Respect to Seniority if Promotion was to go in that Channel, I think there are only Eight L.ᵗ Colˢ now serving Who are Seniors & there has been Eleven Junior Officers including the Artillery promoted to the Rank of Colonel. I know I am not so active as many others yet when I met with my Loss & which hapned to me from my own readiness to promote the Service I was as active a

Man as most in the Army; The Favor I now ask of Y.ʳ L.ᵈ Sp. is to tell me with the frankness becoming a Man of Quality & your high Station what is the bar to my promotion because I suffer greatly in my present Situation from Anxiety of Mind & Neglect of other Pursuits which might be of Advantage to me. I hope y.ʳ L.ᵈ Sp. will not think me unworthy an answer[,] I have ever served the K. with fidelity & Affection to the best of my power ...

JRL, B2/2/50

133

William, Viscount Barrington, Secretary at War, to Lieutenant-Colonel Samuel Bagshawe

London
11 May 1758

I have received your letter of the 5.ᵗʰ instant & in return I can only assure you that I did bring you under consideration when the Regiments were disposed of. I am a little surprized that you should be so much disturbed at your want of success upon this occasion, as I do not see that any one here has been put over your head, except the Duke of Richmond & the King's Aids de Camp, whom his Majesty has always chose without a strict regard to Rank ...

JRL, B2/2/51

134

Lieutenant-Colonel Samuel Bagshawe to William, Viscount Barrington, Secretary at War

[Draft]
Ford
20 July 1758

It is a new thing to me to be so long idle & from my Post[,] I should hope that in so great a Variety of business now on Foot some sort of Employment might be found for an Officer who is desirous to serve, and who used to be esteemed as well qualified, as others of his Rank. It will befal me as to a Boy kept from School by the Poverty of his Parents, when he returns he sees the lower Classes in the higher Forms and has the further Mortification to find that they are really better Schollars[.] I am making a great Progress in Ignorance: There are many Officers abroad who have learned something from me who now may, or very soon will be able to instruct me, I lament more the Loss of knowledge than the Loss of Preferment, In a little time I shall be ashamed to serve: As I cannot help presuming Your Lordship could relieve me from so disagreable a situation, I beg your Lordship will be pleased to deem me worthy your Protection ...

JRL, B2/2/52

135

William, Viscount Barrington, Secretary at War, to Lieutenant-Colonel Samuel Bagshawe

London
31 July 1758

I have this moment reced. your Letter & I have forwarded it already to Lord Ligonier,[82] whom I have on several former occasions reminded of you ...

JRL, B2/2/53

136

Leonard Morse to Lieutenant-Colonel Samuel Bagshawe

War Office, London
15 August 1758

I wish nothing more sincerely than that it was in my power to tell you without hesitation that your presence in Town is necessary.

Lord B. is a very complaisant man; his Letter to you was of his own writing, consequently could not want his usual politeness— the 66th Regiment is yet undisposed of, and that is the only thing they can do for you; I cannot apprehend that you are forgot, tho' it may not be impossible that there may be wanting a proper remembrance of you; I cannot learn the reason, if there be any, for keeping that Regiment so long open.

I shall be very sorry to say any thing my good Sir which may prevent your coming to Town, as the pleasure of seeing you would be a Self interested motive, (which is generally a prevailing one) for wishing you to come. But I consider the Journey is long; to you it must be tedious, and without any doubt is very expensive—

Your application must be to Marshall Ligonier; that indeed Lord B.'s short letter gave you to understand. The D. of Devonshire is in your neighbourhood; his application by letter to Lord Ligonier might do the business, and without your presence to Sollicit it; Your Rank and Services cannot be a Secret to any one of distinction in the Army; and your pretensions at this time, particularly for this Vacancy, as good as any ones; those before you having been past by have little pretension and I fancy the case must be remarkable if a Junior gets it, unless it be one of the King's Aid de Camps, who you know are lately made Seniors—

Sir Robert Wilmot is out of Town, or I should have given you his opinion; I at the same time apprehend he would not much recommend to You another Journey to Town on uncertainties—

I do not remember to have heard whether the Duke of Devonshire is far from you; It may be his Grace may know how to advise in this matter; and I dare say his letter will have due weight, either in procuring your promotion on this occasion, or a reason for its being longer kept open—

I need not repeat to you my dear Sir how most sincerely I wish your welfare and satisfaction, and could I see you a Colonel I flatter myself I should then see my Friend with abundance less anxiety than must at this time hang on his brow ...

JRL, B2/2/459

137

Captain David Hepburne to Lieutenant-Colonel Samuel Bagshawe

London
19 August 1758

Dear Coll.

I am sure you will forgive my seeming neglect in not writting to you of late when I tell you I have been deeply Ingaged with the India Comp^y above a month past, & all to get my poor little Trumpery out of their Clutches, I have not language to describe their trifling and disobliging behaviour, I was obliged to trot backwards & forwards, from office to office & from day to day, & had not the Shaddow of a favor to ask of them, only to be allowed to bring a few Necessarys Ashore, at last, as if they had made me a present, I have got my own property into my possession. They have seized and kept a single Dozen tea Cups which I brought home for my private use, that are not worth 18 shill. & which I scorn to ask them for—

***

JRL, B2/2/264

138

Lieutenant-Colonel Samuel Bagshawe to William Bagshawe of the Inner Temple

London
29 August 1758

... I have made a sudden Journey to London, I had a mind to let it be seen that I am fitt & ready to go on Service if they chuse to employ me. On my Arrival I find a Reg^t which had been some time vacant given to a younger Lieu^t Colonel[83] to whose pretences for such a preference I am quite a Stranger, this has determined me now I am in Town to know what I have to expect and if I cannot get Promotion to quit the Service. If they should be ashamed to sett me aside, there is a probability it may fall to my Lott to go abroad, And as I would be prepared for such an Event, I beg you will tell me how far I may trouble you in my Family Afairs; The Charge I would lay upon you in my Absence is the Education of my Children and to inspect the Accounts of the Agents to whom I must commit my Afairs, and that if you will accept such a Charge you will instruct me how I must give you a proper Power; as to the Children, the finding out a good School will be your chiefest trouble (indeed an important trouble) in other respects they will be sufficiently taken care of by their Mother, but in matters of business She is to be imposed on by any one that has much Cunning and little honesty, for meaning no Evill herself She has no thoughts of suspecting any in others and so easily becomes their Prey ...

JRL, B2/3/232

139

Lieutenant-Colonel Samuel Bagshawe to William, fourth Duke of Devonshire

[Draft]   London
                                          5 September 1758

Your Graces usual Goodness will I hope excuse my giving you this trouble to acquaint you with the Situation of my Affairs since I came to London—On my Arrival I heard that the Vacant Reg.^t was given away to a Younger Lt Colonel. I have waited on Lord Barrington & Marshal Lord Legonier, Lord Barrington told me Lord Ligonier had wrote him that he had recomended me to the K., but that His Maity. had determined to give the Reg.^t to Lafausille[83], Lord Ligonier told me he had recomended me to the K. but then His Maity. said how could I serve wanting a Leg & and an Eye? & on further Discourse, told me I was considered as not fitt for Service—This Declaration leaves me very little to expect while Ld Ligonier Commands[,] And obliges me to seek to Your Grace for what I shall do[.] I cannot continue in the Service under such Circumstances. Your Grace may be able to reverse this Sentence against me, And with y^r Graces protection, somthing will be done for me. I would not give y^r Grace the trouble to write to me but beg you will please to signifie your mind to Sir Robt Wilmott. I have been advised in Confidence by a Genl. Officer (whom I may name to y^r Grace[,] Genl. Napier) to give in a Petition to the K., I wish y^r Grace would please to say whether you aprove of this Step or whether I should ask leave to sell, I shall be entirely governed by what y^r Grace shall recomend ...

JRL, B15/1/28

140
The Petition of Lieutenant-Colonel Samuel Bagshawe

[Copy]   [London]
                                          [October 1758]

To the King's most Excellent Majesty
                    The Petition of Lieu^t Colonel Samuel
                    Bagshawe of the Thirty Ninth Reg^t of
                    Foot commanded by Col^o Adlercron
Most humbly Sheweth

That your Majesty's Petitioner has Served Twenty Seven Years of which Eleven years in Gibraltar, Brittany, and the East Indies.

That he lost a Leg in the Expedition to Brittany under the command of Lieut. Genl. St Clair, and one of his Eyes in the East Indies, where he was in danger of losing the other likewise.

That when the Regiment he has the honour to Serve in was ordered to the East Indies he was in an extreme bad State of Health and his private Affairs in great disorder, but his Love and Zeal for your Majesty's Service would not allow him to think of Staying behind; having however lost one Eye, and in the utmost danger of losing the other he was obliged to get Leave to come to England where he has happily Recovered.

That as soon as he found himself well, and fit for duty, he acquainted Your Majesty's Secretary at War, and the Adjutant Genl. therewith, desiring to be put upon Service as the Regiment he belongs to was ordered home, and could not for some time be fit for duty. Upon the Troops going to Cape Breton he applied to Field Marshal Lord Ligonier as well as to the Secretary at War desiring to be employed there, as he did also when he heard of the design against Crown Point.

That he begs leave to appeal for his character to Field Marshal Lord Ligonier, Lieut: Genl S.t Clair, Lieu.t Genl. Lord Rothes[84], The Duke of Devonshire, Lord Barrington, and Major General Napier; And being now in perfect good health

> Your Majesty's Petitioner most humbly
> presumes to lay his Case before Your
> Majesty and to beg that in consideration of
> his Service and his Sufferings Your
> Majesty would be graciously pleased to
> honour him with the Rank
> of Colonel, or any other Mark of
> Your Majesty's favour and approbation

And Your Majesty's Petitioner as in Duty bound will continue to Pray &c

JRL, B15/2/25

141

Colonel John Adlercron to Lieutenant-Colonel Samuel Bagshawe

London
30 November 1758

... I arrived here with M.rs Adlercron and my Daughter this day Week and tho' every day since attempting to see the Great

Folks, could not till yesterday know the Destination of the Regiment: Lord Barrington who received me very graciously informed me we were to be on the Irish Establishmen.ᵗ and that I might send to the War Office for a Beating Order to Recruit in Great Britain: As Men are very scarce on this side of the Water, I purpose applying to the Duke of Bedford[85] for leave to Recruit in the North of Ireland for a number of Men. Major Forde having accepted of the Command of the Company's Troops at Bengal, contrary to His Majesty's Instructions and the Orders I left him to follow us by the first Ship, and his not having sent home the Regiment's Accounts will distress us much as M.ʳ Calcraft says he can't settle with the Regiment till he hears from him; this Neglect of Major Forde's surprises me much as I have always thought him very exact. The Regiment now being fixed on the Irish Establishment, I have appointed Cap.ᵗ Desbrisay my Agent, and Major Hepburne purposes the next Week setting out to join the Regiment. As for you, Sir, you have my consent to remain with your family and [I] hope you'l be better provided for, before there is a necessity for your going to Ireland.

I have not had the least hint from any of the Great Folks of my Conduct being censured whilst in India, tho' I am certain the Company's Servants wrote many falseties concerning my behaviour to them; if His Majesty will look into my Journal, which I have given to General Napier to peruse they will see the Treatment I have received from my first coming to the Time of my leaving the Country.

I have seen Lord Holdernesse, who gave me a very kind reception; this morning I was at Lord Ligonier's Levee, who is now a Great Man. M.ʳˢ Adlercron desires her Compliments to you; We both join in desiring you will make them acceptable to M.ʳˢ Bagshawe ...

JRL, B2/2/39

142

Lieutenant-Colonel Samuel Bagshawe to Colonel John Adlercron

[Draft]   [Ford]
                                                 4 December 1758

Dᣟ Sᣟ

I most thankfully acknowledge your obliging favor of the 30ᵗʰ & the Indulgence you grant me which however I will not expect to be continued to me when business shall require my Attendance, I have never willingly omitted any essential part of my Duty and while I eat the Kˢ Bread I will not refuse the Kˢ Service: I do not much Wonder that you meet with no open Attacks from a certain Quarter and although Calumny like a Fog may cover the Earth [yet] when Truth like the Sun appears it is immediatly dissipated[,] the only thing to be apprehended is some places may be so shaded that the Rays of truth cannot be admitted, there the Mist must continue till such Obstructions are removed ... We jointly desire that [Mrs Adlercron] you & Miss Adlerⁿ will [let] Ford be your Road on your Return to Ireland & make some Stay will us: We live in a healthy Country & pleasant enough in the Summer Season & I have found great benefit from Buxton a Bath in our Neighbourhood: As I still think that if you had not allowed me to return to Europe at the time I left India I must have lost my other Eye if not my Life you will believe me sincere when I assure you I am

               Dᣟ Sᣟ Yᣟ obliged & most humᵇ
               Servᣟ
               S.B.

JRL, B2/2/39a

143

Major David Hepburne to Lieutenant-Colonel Samuel Bagshawe

London
7 December 1758

Not only the Severe Weather we have had of late, which has almost demolished me, but also an Unexpected event (which will surprize a gentleman of your feeling disposition) has quite unhinged all my views and Imployed the time my health would allow of, to carry my point, and prevented my writing to the only sincere friend I believe, that I have in the World. To be plain, they are going to unmajor me again, for tho' I was appointed to that office by Col. Adlercron's Commission, which was thought Sufficient by most people here, Yet Maj^r Forde having applyed to his Friends in power, they dispute C. Adlercrons Sufficiency, and Insist on Fordes keeping his Commiss^n in the Reg^t notwithstanding his having accepted £5000 in Lieu of it, as well as his great appointments in India, and as the Reg^t is now on the Irish Establishment, it is feared that Mr Fox will prevail on the L^d L^t to Continue Forde the Major. Could Adlercron be perswaded to lay the Case before his Majesty it would soon be ended in our Favor—But not to trouble you longer with grievances, the last act as a Field Officer, I believe I shall ever be guilty of, is now to write to the Command^g Officer at quarters by Col. Adlercrons Directions, to send over Serj^t M^{c}kenzie as you desire—some people are of opinion, that if this business of the Majority is Contested, tho' perhaps Forde may not keep it a third dog may come in for the bones, if so, I am perswaded you will think I ought to get away from a Situation in which I must serve with a degree of contempt: that I never will; & if I am not let down easily, I thank God I can bring my desires & wants within a narrow Compas[,] peace & obscurity I can very well bear—I would mention something about the Reg^t to you Dear Sir if I knew anything of the Matter, we are established in Ireland, & that by the Industry of Mr Adlercron it is said, but no orders or directions how we are to be disposed of, or recruited, have as yet been given, the L^d L^t is in the Country, & we know not where to apply. It is impossible to express the Confusion that the Accounts of the Reg^t are in, Maj^r Forde has sent no Manner of Accounts & Mr Calcraft says he has drawn for more money than he should, in short we must take the last Gentlemans Word for every thing, nor does it appear as yet, that we have the Smalest Certain Fund to begin the recruiting on. I fear greatly my dear Col. that you will have your share of plague with regard to our Reg^{tll} Affairs, your knowledge & Authority must be used in Settling those of Importance, the Common details of druggery I should willingly undertake if I am thought worthy of being a Field O. but must beg to be excused where neither Authority, Credit, or profit will fall to my lot ... I shall only Add, that to the disturbances of my Mind, which I get the better of hourly, I am far from being in good health[,] an Impenetrable Fogg has hung over this place several days[,] All the Old, & Crazy have Suffered greatly by it, Col. Adlercron is not well, no one knows what will become of the poor 39th if you do not exert yourself in its Favor ...

JRL, B2/2/267

144

Lieutenant-Colonel Samuel Bagshawe to Mrs Catherine Bagshawe

London
16 December 1758

My dear Kitty

I am puzled what Interpretation to put upon the Treatment I meet with, I have been three times at Devonshire house without gaining admittance, and twice at Sir R W^s and though I left word yesterday Morning by Sir R^s Servant to desire he would let me know when I could see him, I have not heard a Syllable from him: I think not to give myself much more trouble about one or the other but to ask leave to Sell, I shall with difficulty bring myself to believe this all Accident, however I will still keep in remembrance our Friends Advice, while my hand is in the Lyons Mouth: Why am I used in this manner? I cannot charge myself with any such behavior to any one dependant on me, I long for a Deliverance: I wish the Matter which drew me to Town was finished[,] I would not stay a Moment longer in Town, & heartily repent I suffered myself to be seduced to it: and that I may be the better punished I do not intend to partake of any of the Amusements it affords.

You will imagine from the Contents of this Letter that I am much out of humour, I am somewhat vexed, but only a temporary Vexation & that will leave no essential Impression: more contempt than Rage, such as a fine lady may feel when an inferior Beauty attempts to make her uneasy—while my Kittys mine what signifies all the little Flirts of Fortune, no Matter though it blusters abroad, if all is peace within, fair Weather is pleasanter after a Shower; & Sickness gives a Relish to health: Thinking on you my Kitty has quite calmed my Spirits & I am quite at ease & with as much Sincerity & warmth of Afection as you can desire, My Dearest Kittys Saml. Bagshawe[.]

JRL, B2/3/32

3
1759–1763

'Every Regiment in Common Occurrences has an Equal Right to favour and Protection ...'

The Pitt-Newcastle war ministry had embarked on the year 1759 in confident mood. The capture of the French-Canadian fortress of Louisbourg the previous July had signalled a decisive end to the disappointing opening phases of the Seven Years' War. Now, a two-pronged assault on the heart of Canada was about to be launched, a major expeditionary force was poised to strike at French possessions in the Caribbean and the situation in Germany, while not brilliant, was far from discouraging. Then, in February, intelligence reached London of French plans to retrieve their sinking fortunes by an invasion of the British Isles. Two main attacks were planned—one against Essex and the other on the west coast of Scotland, supported by a diversionary raid on Ireland, to be commanded by Commodore François Thurot. In the event, only Thurot's operation took place; one of Bagshawe's recruiting officers, Lieutenant Hercules Ellis, was caught up in it [152].

British troop-numbers had grown dramatically during the war, but most of these men were committed abroad. It was estimated that only about 10,000 were available in England to resist a French landing, with scarcely 5,000 more in the whole kingdom of Ireland. As autumn approached, the likely time of the French attempt, recruiting was given top priority. The City of London organized a successful subscription scheme for raising men, and the Duke of Devonshire proposed that noblemen raise regiments as they had done in 1745; (Matthews Sewell, it will be recalled, had served in one raised by the Duke of Bolton). The old king, George II, resisted this idea, as did his Commander-in-Chief, Lord Ligonier; neither man wanted to loosen his grip on military patronage, or allow officers with money to steal a march on deserving but poorer men, but by the beginning of

November the idea of raising men for rank had taken root in Ireland as well as England.[1] As the Lord Lieutenant, the Duke of Bedford, reported;

> I know no other Resource but that of raising New Corps, which can only be effected by giving the Nobility and Gentry of this Kingdom, the Encouragements which have been given in Great Britain, to engage them by Rank & other Emoluments to prevail on their Tenants and Dependants to enter into the Army, and thereby bring into it, a better Class and Rank of People, than would otherwise enlist themselves into it, but on such an Emergency as the present one, & under the Command of their own Landlords and Neighbours.[2]

One of the first of the Irish 'Nobility and Gentry' to respond to this call to arms was Samuel Bagshawe's brother-in-law, Sir James Caldwell, already deeply engaged in his futile quest for an Irish peerage. Caldwell offered to raise '... an Independent Troop of Light Horse in the nature of Hussars'[3] and hastened to London at the end of November to plead his cause before Lord Ligonier and the Great Commoner in person.[4] About 7 December, his proposal was cordially accepted.[5] The previous week, in the course of transmitting two more proposals to Pitt, Bedford remarked;

> I have likewise had an intimation given me, from the eldest Lieutenant Colonel of Foot in the Service, that he is desirous of raising a Regiment having the Rank of Colonel, but the particulars of his offer are not yet come to my Hands. As soon as I receive them (if they appear to me to be reasonable) I will immediately transmit them to you.[6]

The lieutenant-colonel referred to was Samuel Bagshawe, and his proposal to raise the unit which was to become the 93rd Regiment of Foot [145], was sent to London on 18 December.[7] It was promptly accepted, and the new corps was placed on the Irish Establishment with effect from 5 January 1760. It comprised a colonel, lieutenant-colonel, major, six captains, a captain lieutenant, eight ensigns, a chaplain, surgeon and mate, 27 sergeants, 27 corporals, 18 drummers and 630 private men in nine companies. The annual cost to the Irish exchequer of the new unit was £13,371: 3s: 4d.[8] Bagshawe's commission as colonel was dated 17 January 1760.[9]

Bagshawe's brother-in-law, Henry Caldwell, who was shortly to accept a captain's commission in the 93rd, was greatly surprised to hear of '... your Design in Raising a Reg^t after such usage & that by a Scheme so Disadvantagious to you in Point of Interest [.] I must own,' he went on, 'I think it is difficult not to resent ill Usage but then at the same time Cannot but think it Great in making a proper Distinction & not punishing ones Country for faults her Ministers only are Guilty off (I mean only those of War)'[10]—an obvious reference to the Secretary at War, Viscount Barrington's casual treatment of Bagshawe in 1758 [132–33].Samuel too was evidently disturbed at the lengths he had to go to in obtaining the colonelcy he considered already his by right of merit and service [147].

According to a statement authorized by Kitty Bagshawe in 1763, it cost her late husband £3,000 to raise the 93rd [205]. If the regiment had been disbanded within three years, he would have had £660: 18s of this sum refunded on account of swords and accoutrements he had provided.[11] He would also have expected to make somewhere in the region of £500 profit per annum from clothing the regiment, but in fact it took well over a year for any money to appear on this account.[12] Bagshawe had also expected his initial investment to be partly compensated for by subscriptions from his junior officers, the original plan being for them to raise men in return for their commissions, but the Duke of Bedford used the 93rd as a source of patronage and he had precious little say in the men appointed.

Among the vice-regal clients dumped on Bagshawe was the troublesome and impecunious Lieutenant Francis Flood, nephew of Warden Flood, Attorney General of Ireland [157–58]. It proved next to impossible to wring money out of Flood at any time; likewise a number of the other subalterns, some of whom proved to be notably wayward and incompetent [155–56].

The beating order for the 93rd Foot was issued on 5 February 1760.[13] As was usual, a cadre was formed by drafting in from other regiments on the Irish Establishment a quota of drummers and private men with at least a year's experience, '... expert in their Excercise, [who] can Read and Write well, are Sober and well Behaved, Strong and Active, And in every Respect Qualified to be Serj^{ts} or Corporals in the Reg^t ...'[14] It was intended to enrol only 'Able Bodied Protestants' and to that end, the infant corps was formed at Charlemont and

Armagh. By mid-April, 531 rank-and-file had enlisted. Most of them came from Dublin, Carrickfergus, Armagh, Belturbet, Galway and Antrim. The majority were classed as 'labourers', but there was a significant number of weavers, shoemakers and tailors, as well as the occasional butcher or bricklayer and one man, Private Thomas Meares, aged 33, who was described as a 'Scribler'.[15] At the beginning of May, the regiment was only 39 men short of its establishment.[16] It was mustered for the first time at the end of that month,[17] and reviewed in its summer camp at Kedra, near Cahir, on 24 July. Bagshawe, who had been under canvas with his men for nearly a month, left for Derbyshire immediately after. The 93rd remained in camp until 11 August and then marched for Cork, which was to be the scene of its martyrdom as an effective unit.[18]

In his important study of the Bagshawe Papers, James Hayes took a benign view of the 93rd,[19] and indeed it was probably no worse than the generality of regiments raised for rank at this time. This is not saying a great deal, however, for in order to make sure of their commissions by completing their units on time, officers enlisted the kind of outcasts and derelicts they might previously have rejected.[20] So, although Edward Windus, Bagshawe's lieutenant-colonel, issued strict recruiting instructions and kept an unfailingly sharp look-out for papists [156], the record suggests that he was less scrupulous when it came to quality-control. As early as June 1760, a 63 year old soldier named John Bowland was discharged on account of consumption. Another, Matthew Wheatly, aged 60, was '... Infirm and Unable to learn his Exercise'. A number of younger men were reported as suffering from blindness, lameness in the legs and hands, pains in the legs on marching and 'Obstinate and Scorbutick ulcers'.[21] A similar purge in May 1762 uncovered such unlikely warriors as Private Keith Carr, '... Very infirm & much troubled with Worms', William Grace, who suffered from epileptic fits and a rupture, Spicer Harris, an old man quite 'worn out in the Service' and John Knowlan, aged 50, afflicted by 'Piles of many years standing.'[22]

By this time, regimental morale was at a very low ebb. With the exception of Thurot's raid on Carrickfergus in February 1760, the threat of a French landing had been lifted by Admiral Hawke's great victory at Quiberon Bay on 30 November 1759. The troops mustered for home defence were henceforth re-deployed in Germany, in the

Caribbean, on the coast of France and in Portugal, though not necessarily in their parent corps. Far from every regiment having an equal right to favour and protection as Colonel Bagshawe argued [173], the policy was to draft the best men from the young corps into seasoned battalions. From the point of view of government this was eminently sensible, for it was a waste of precious manpower to leave it at the mercy of inexperienced subalterns and novice n.c.o.s, but having persuaded themselves that their investments would bring them glory and profit, the military undertakers were disgusted to find themselves reduced to the level of perpetual recruiters.

The 93rd suffered the first of three swingeing drafts as early as November 1760, when Lieutenant-Colonel James Molesworth, Cork's lieutenant-governor, picked out 109 of its best men [167].[23] In February 1761, Molesworth took another 109 [171]. In the opinion of Lieutenant-Colonel Windus, this double blow, coupled with the effects of natural wastage, '... tore the Reg^t to pieces' [172]. In March 1762, a rumour circulated that the regiment was to be drafted in its entirety. Bagshawe issued a bitter remonstrance [189]. In the event, 297 men were taken, leaving a mixture of old men and the rawest of the new recruits [196]. In April, the regiment could only muster 188 rank-and-file, 45 of whom were sick.[24] Everything, as Windus was forced to admit, was '... vastly behind hand.'[25]

Like most other colonels, Samuel Bagshawe spent much of his time away from the regiment, leaving it in the safe hands of his two field officers, Windus and Major Robert Preston. Both men sent detailed reports to their absent commander, whose hand is encountered far less often in this section of the correspondence. W. H. G. Bagshawe concluded that the colonel kept many of his papers at his residence in Mary Street, Dublin, at this period, and that they were in some way dispersed after his death.[26]

Outwardly, Bagshawe's prospects continued to improve throughout this time. The Duke of Devonshire responded to his request for a seat in the Irish Parliament [147], by bringing him in for the 'potwalloper' borough of Tallagh (Tallow), Co. Waterford, in the general election of 1761. Tallagh, which returned two MPs, was part of the vast Irish inheritance which had belonged to the Duke's late wife, Charlotte Boyle, daughter of Richard, 3rd Earl of Burlington.[27] Lieutenant-Colonel Windus thought that the voters there '... must go as the Duke of Devonshire pleases'[28] but in fact the borough was in '... a very doubtful and floating condition.'[29] At first, Bagshawe and his running mate, Sir Robert Deane, were opposed by a coalition of local gentlemen, but the Duke's men on the spot, Sir Henry Cavendish and the vicar of Tallagh, Thomas Dawson, succeeded in buying off the ringleaders.[30] The contest helped establish Tallagh's reputation as an expensive constituency,[31] and despite soothing noises from his patron [170], the election may have cost Bagshawe over £500.[32]

Despite restorative visits to Buxton, the colonel's health had been precarious ever since his return from India. Shortly after the Irish Parliament was prorogued in April 1762, he took an obstinate cold, and spent some time at Blackrock Bay, Dublin, in an attempt to shake it off. As his strength continued to wane, he resolved to take a cure at Bath, but even before his arrival there, his condition had worsened considerably. His liver was inflamed, his legs were swollen with dropsy, and he could take almost no nourishment. Medical opinions were obtained from London; from Michael Crane, King's Apothecary [204], and the 'father of army medicine' Sir John Pringle.[33] Lodgings were booked for him in the capital and he set out from Bath in a 'bed machine' on 13 August, attended by an apothecary (Mr West) and a nurse.[34] The first night was spent at Devizes and the second at Newbury. On 15 August, he arrived at the Crown Inn, Reading. A local doctor, Mr Russell, was called to his bedside and Crane was summoned from London. Next day, 16 August, Bagshawe indicated that he wished to make his will. Witnesses were hastily summoned. He was now so weak that he could not complete the will in his own hand, and at about five pm he died, leaving Kitty, who had accompanied him throughout his last journey, in a distracted state.[35]

Bagshawe left the bulk of his estate, real and personal, to his eldest surviving son, Samuel. Kitty was bequeathed the sum of £200 per annum and allowed to live at Ford until such time as she remarried or Samual Bagshawe junior reached the age of 25. The colonel's remaining children, John,[36] Richard,[37], William,[38] and Ann,[39] received annuities, as did his sister Frances. In 1763 Kitty, with the assistance of her brother Sir James Caldwell, petitioned in vain for additional support for her family [205]. Sad to say, in later life, disagreements with Samuel junior and the weakened condition of the Ford estate left her dependent for a time on financial assistance from her cousin, Captain William Trench, (subsequently the Earl of Clancarty), a former officer in the 93rd.[40] None of Samuel Bagshawe's sons followed him into the army.

145

The Proposal of Lieutenant-Colonel Samuel Bagshawe

[Copy] [Dublin]
[December, 1759]

To His Grace John Duke of Bedford Lord Lieutenant General and General Governour of Ireland.

The Proposal of Lieutenant-Colonel Samuel Bagshawe

That he is desirous to raise a Regiment of Infantry at his own expence. Of able bodied Protestants. To consist of nine Companies. Each Company of 3 Serjeants, 3 Corporals, 2 Drummers and 70 Private Men.

That he is willing to furnish Swords and Accoutrements for said Reg.ᵗ at his own Expence, provided the Regiment subsists three years. But if reduced before that time the Swords and Accoutrements to be at the expence of the Publick.

That he has had the honour to serve the Crown of Great Britain thirty years, near eleven of which as Lieutenant Colonel, which he purchased, and went abroad with that rank to the East Indies.

It is requested that in consideration of this proposal and length of service Your Grace will be graciously pleased to recommend him to His Majesty to have the Rank of Colonel—
Signed
Samuel Bagshawe

PRO. SP63/416/225

146

Captain William Montgomery, Regimental Agent, to Lieutenant-Colonel Samuel Bagshawe

Dublin
25 December 1759

Since you left this [place] there are orders come over for two Regᵗˢ more to be placed on this establishment to be commanded by Col. Blaney[41] & Sir Ralph Gore.[42] From what I have heard I have reason to believe your proposal will be accepted, In which case you will have great difficulty in raising your men as these Regt^s will have the start of you if they use proper diligence. If your proposal is accepted wou'd you choose to have an express sent to you so soon as the information arrives, or is there anything whatsoever that you can think of wherein I can be of service to you. I am very greatly oblidg'd to you for your reccomendation to Sir James Caldwell who has apointed me his Agent. He is placed on a very favourable establishment for his pocket as he is in every Way on the same footing with all the Dragoons on this establishment in regard to contingent & Warr. men & profitts arising from the cloathing.

As you will probably have the reccomendation of several Officers & that I am certain you wou'd choose those that wou'd do most credit to your Corps, I take the liberty to inform you, that Lieu^t Whiting of Genl. Handasides Regt^t[43] & who is at present a gentleman at large in the Lord Lieut^s family, has aplied for a Company in one of the Regt^s to be rais'd. He is reccomended by Lord Rothes to the Lord Lieu^t. If you can get him you will get one of the best men in this country & every way quallified for the Service & one who will do honour to your Regt^t . . .

JRL, B2/1/2

147
Lieutenant-Colonel Samuel Bagshawe to William, fourth Duke of Devonshire

[Draft]   [January 1760]

. . . Sevl. Off^{rs} & others having given in Proposals to His Grace the D. of B. to raise Regt^{ts} on the present Situation of Affairs in this Kingdom[,] I have also offered to raise & accoutre a Reg^t at my own Expence—It is a little Severe after my Sufferings & Service not to obtain Promotion on other Terms but I am determined to have Patience, perhaps at length it will be seen I do not deserve the treatm.^t I have met with.

Your Grace if you please has it much in y.^r Power to assist me [in] this Attempt & to procure me Amends for past Disapointments [by giving me] Your Graces Interest & recomending me to be chose a Memb.^r of Parliament for one of the Boroughs under Y.^r Graces Influences or for some other in which the Speaker[44] could procure me to be chosen[.] I am willing to be at the Expence & the Speaker will find me a steady & a resolute Friend[.] I hope to be favoured with an Answer from Y.^r Grace [unless your] Grace is determined to be no ways my Friend ...

JRL, B15/1/29

148

Major David Hepburne to Colonel Samuel Bagshawe

Galway
18 January 1760

I do with the utmost faithfullness and Sincerity Congratulate you on the Success of your desires & Merit & do most heartily wish & pray for the Continuence of all good to you & yours. I am perfectly sensible of your kind & generous Intentions to have served me, had it been in your power,[45] & Shall ever gratefully remember the Obligations I already am under to you, My dear Sir. I have not been much the favorite of Fortune, as you justly observe, habit therefore, as well as reason will Inable me to bear every disappointment that may befall me. Providence May perhaps Intend it for my benefit, if I make the proper use of it. Be so good Dear Sir to advise me, if I should not ask leave to come to Dublin to solicite for Leave to quit the Service if I am set aside[,] you know Sir I have long wished for rest & ease, my health declines Apace, & I am now greatly Afflicted with the gravell. I will also honestly own to you that I do not think myself very fit to be a Major, that Office requires a person of more readyness & activity than I am at present, I should have made a

much better L.ᵗ Col. if it had pleased the Stars. I will be entirely
governed by you Sir, Condescend to give me your Advice, for
tho' I am very tired of the Service, I shall ever make it a matter of
Conscience to do my duty to my best, if my good friends think I
should continue to do any. God help the poor sealed 39ᵗʰ[.] Now
you have left it, I know not what will become of us ...

JRL, B2/1/6

149
Lieutenant-Colonel Edward Windus to Colonel Samuel Bagshawe

Waterford
9 February 1760

Sir,

I received the favor of your kind letter, & propose to set out very
soon in order to kiss your hands, & receive any Commands you
may be pleas'd to honor me with.

The Commanding Officer at this Quarter has allowed me to
Name two of the Queen's,[46] agreeable to the Government's
Order, to be Serjeant & Corporal in your Regiment. They are
young, active, strong, write well, & exercise well, & if you should
be at a loss for a Serjeant Major, I am in hopes the Serjeant may
be soon fit for that Post; They set out tomorrow.

I beg leave to assure you I shall think myself happy in being
under your Command, & am with the greatest respect &
Esteem,

> Sir,
> Your most Obedient
> And Most
> Humble Servant
> Edwᵈ Windus

JRL, B2/1/17

150

Recruiting Instructions for the 93rd Regiment of Foot

[Copy]   [February–March 1760]

Recruiting Instructions for the Off.^rs of his Majesty's Ninety third Reg.^t of Foot Commanded by Col.^o Saml. Bagshawe

No. 1   To Shew your beating Order to the Comanding Off. of the Troops if there be any in the Place, & to the Chief Magistrate.

No. 2   You are to Inlist none but such as are certifyed by a Minister of the Church of Ireland or by a Protestant dissenting Minister, to be protestants, and Born of Protestant parents, & to take particular Care the Certificates are not Counterfeit.

No. 3   All Recruits are to be able Bodied, Sound in their Limbs, free from Ruptures, Scald heads Ulcerous Sores or any Remarkable deformity, None to be Inlisted who cannot wear his hair, who is in knee'd, Splay footed, or Subject to fits, A Surgeon to examine the Recruits, & his Certificate of their Soundness in every Respect to be Sent to the Reg.^t with the Certificates of their being Protestants, their Attestations, & Return of Necessaries. Three Pounds will be allowed for Every Recruit approved of & subsist.^ce from the day they join the Reg.^t only.

No. 4   None to be taken who have been in the Service Except he be under 35 years of age, the Discharges of such men to be sent with them to the Reg.^t otherwise they will be supposed to have been Drumed out, & of Course will be Rejected.

No. 5   No Strolers, Vagabonds, Tinkers, Chimney Sweepers, Colliers, or Saylors to be Inlisted, but such men only as were born in the Neighbourhood of the place they are Inlisted in, & of whom you can get and give a good Account.

No. 6   Every Recruit to be attested in the Presence of an

210

an Officer, who is to Sign, as a Witness to his Attestation.

No. 7 None to be Inlisted between twenty & thirty five years of age under five feet six inches, & from Sixteen to twenty years of Age under five feet five inches in their Stocking feet, & care to be taken that the Standard be just, & none under Sixteen or upwards of thirty five to be Inlisted for the Regiment.

No. 8 All Recruits are to be furnished with Necessaries out of their Bounty money, that they may join the Reg.ᵗ as free from debt as possible, & Strict Charge to be given to them, & to those who conduct them to Quarters, to take particular care of their Necessaries on the March, if any should be in debt, on Acc.ᵗ of being well provided with Shirts, Shoes & Stockings, fit to appear as Soldiers, the Recruiting Off.ʳ to send an Acc.ᵗ of his debt, Sign'd by himself, to the paymaster, by the Serj.ᵗ or Corpl. that conducts the Recruits to the Regim.ᵗ

No. 9 No more than thirty pounds at a time to be drawn for, besides the Sub.ᶜᵉ of the Parties, an Acc.ᵗ to be Sent to the Reg.ᵗ & another to the Agent, of the application of the money drawn, Every Month, or Oftener if Occation Requires.

No. 10 The Subsist.ᶜᵉ of the Recruiting parties to be Stopped Monthly by the Agent from the Comp.ʸˢ they belong to, the Recruiting Off.ʳ is to draw it from the Agent, & to Subsist them Accordingly; & to avoid any Confusion in the Acc.ᵗˢ, the Agent is not to pay any Subsist.ᶜᵉ to the Parties or Recruits that may pass through Dublin; but the Off.ʳ must send it with the Serj.ᵗ or Corpl. who conducts the Recruits to Quarters, & if any Serj.ᵗ or Corpl. so Employ'd Embezzles any Money he is Entrusted with or disobey any order of the Recruiting Off.ʳ such Off.ʳ is to Acquaint the Commanding Off.ʳ of the Reg.ᵗ with the Nature of the Offence by Letter that the delinquent may be kept with the Reg.ᵗ & Tryed by a Court Martial, in which Case another will be sent in his Room.

No. 11 To avoid, as Much as possible Inlisting such as have Deserted from other Corps, it is Recommended to the Recruiting Off^{rs} that they Require all Recruits to make Oath before the Magistrate, (at the time of Attesting), that they never were Inlisted before, nor Ever Rec^d any Money on Any Such Acc^t, Except such (of course) who can produce a Discharge.

No. 12 Great care to be taken that the above Instructions are Strictly Attended to, & if any Recruits are Rejected, the Off^r who Inlisted them will have no Allow^{ce} for them, but will be charged with a fortnights Subsist^{ce} to carry them home.

No. 13 If a Recruiting Off^r thinks it Necessary to Change his Recruiting Quarters he is to give timely Notice to the Adjutant of the place he is going to, & when he will be there.

No man Attested, to be Discharged, but by a field Officer.

Edwd Windus
Lt Col of the 93^d Reg^t

JRL, B2/1/20

151

Major David Hepburne to Colonel Samuel Bagshawe

Galway
15 February 1760

You would doubtless have had great reason to be offended, had the refusal of some people here, to Comply with your desires (relating to the Men you wanted from the 39th) proceeded from any thing personal, or in the least like a slight to Col. Bagshaw. I sincerely believe that it was intirely owing to the wretched condition the Reg^t is in at present, & that diffidence which you know Dear Sir young officers will naturally have, who act for

other people & Command Companys, not their own. I can
faithfully assure you Sir, that your name & memory is in a high
esteem, I may say veneration, in the 39th, as in any Society, who
ever had, or will have the happyness of knowing you ... I know
not whether I shall obtain leave to come to Dublin ... I have
again wrote to the Genl. about it, But Dear Sir be so kind as to
tell me, why you would dissuade me from quitting the service,
for which I really am so unfit. I declare to you my Dear Col. with
that sincerity I would appeal to my maker with, as well as what is
due to a gentleman, whose worth and friendship I have had so
many proofs of, that my principal motive, is a consciousness of
my incapacity to do the duty as it ought, & next, that habitual
desire men at my time of life have to ease and quiet. But I shall
ever be guided by your advice, being very certain of your good
Intentions to me, & all Mankind ...

[PS] I am far from being well, besides my gravell complaints,
I have a violent Inflammation in my right foot ...

JRL, B2/1/23

152
Lieutenant Hercules Ellis to Colonel Samuel Bagshawe

Ballynure
27 February 1760

Sir

I Cant Doubt of your Hearing of the French landing nigh
Car.fergus & their taking the Town & Castle, Ive sent you a
Copy of the Capitulation, Mon^{sr} Thourot wth 3 Ships the largest
about 30 Guns landed about a thousand regular forces, (tho
they mention 1500) at Killroot about two Miles below the Town
on Thursday the 21st Ins^t about Eleven a Clock undiscovered to
be French 'till the most of them was landed as they Kept up
English Colours, upon their being formed they Immediately

marched up to the Town w[th.] two peices of Canon w[ch.] they forced some of the Country people to draw upon Carrs in the front of their Army & began the Attack ag[st.] the Castle about three in the Afternoon after beating back some of our small Guards from the Gates w[ch.] they Exchanged several shot with, we held out about an Hour w[ch.] was a long time Considering the Ammunition we Had, for the most that any man had was Six rounds & a great part of that was made up after the Action began.[47] I was About a Mile in the Country when I heard the News, and Immediately went in and joined, tho no Way prepared but w[th.] my Sword 'till one of our Soldiers fell & I took up his Arms & Ammunition, & upon my Calling to them if they would Hold out they all said they had no Ammunition & at that time they were reduced to one round, Upon w[ch.] Coll. Jennings[48] w[th.] the rest of us ordered a Parly to be beat upon w[ch.] the Cap[t.] of the Hussars who was in the front[49] Called out no Parlee no Parlee, but their Commanders thought proper to Accept of it, & Signed to the Terms you see, tho the Verball Agreem[t.] was that the Castle and Amunition shoud not be given up and Coll. Jennings who behaved like an Able Genl. & had several discharge of shot particularly pointed at him, told them he w[d.] have Died in the ruins of it had he thought they w[d.] not [have] kept up to their first Agreem[t.] but was obliged to Acquiesce, & promised for Himself & the rest to perform the Agreem[t.] & hoped that they w[d.] do the same, but when they saw the Poor force we had who actually all behaved Gallantly, they were out of all patience, & was for tearing the Capitulation when Coll. Jennings talked to them about plundering the Town and Destroying the Powder in the Castle, w[ch.] they have Almost Intirely Done, And the reason they gave for it was that they were not provided w[th.] provisions & their Genl. said he did not Know but he w[d.] take the Mayor to France, they Embarked on Monday night the 25th and made us Attend the whole night to Cover their Embarkation, they are still at Anchor in the Lough nigh the Town, and has the Mayor Mess[rs.] Spaight & Gill as Hostages for 2000£ ransom for the Town. M. Thourot I understand Differed w[th.] the French Genl.[50] about landing, he was for landing nigh Belfast & Attacking both places at once to Cut off any

Communication between the two places, & had they Done it they woud have Undoubtedly taken both places being no way prepared wth arms or regular forces & neither places in any Posture of Defence.

By the Best Information I can learn they had upwards of Seventy Killed wth five or Six Officers wth their Genl. left behind wounded & we only four or five killed & about as many wounded wth an Officer or two Slitly wounded, I was Disired by Coll. Jennings to go to the Country about 5 or 6 Miles to get Quarters for the Officers & Men as there was other regulars Coming to town & the Town in Prodigious Distress for all Kinds of Necessarys, It would give me great Pleasure had I your Approbation in this Affair as you may see I Coud not write Sooner thinking it my Duty to Do what I Coud in the Service of my King & Country & w^d be glad to know your Commands how I shoud or ought to Act for the future, Ive lost some Valuable things not having time to remove them but that I do not Value Doing my Duty.[51]

I had an Acc^{tt} of the Corpor. & Drum you Intended me being Come to Belfast since I came here, I have got Six Men, 'tested According to my Instructions before this Afair Hapened & a Promise from Some More, I shall not Add but am with great Esteem

> Sir your most Obed^t
> & most obliged h^{ble} Servt
> Her^s Ellis

JRL, B2/1/28

153

Lieutenant Francis Flood to Colonel Samuel Bagshawe

> Kilkenny
> 2 March 1760

According to your Orders, I send you inclosed a return of the Men I have inlisted. The two Men you sent to assist me in

Recruiting have hurt me very much, as [they] have suffered Men to escape on their March to Quarters. Michll. Carty was in the charge of Thomas Carroll, the first Assistant you sent and suffered him to Escape from Ballinakill, Pat Higgins escaped from the second man you sent to assist me, and I can asure you I gave each of the Deserters two Guineas as [they] were realy fine Fellows. I have sent safe to your Regim.^t fourteen Men, and am in great hopes you'll not let me be a looser by the two men that escaped from my Party.

I have sent all the Attestations and Certifycates in the most exact conformity to your Instructions to the Commanding Officer at Newry which henders me from filling up my Returns, as I do not remember the dates of the Attestations and by whom attested and Certifyed –

After the Assizes I wo^d be Oblidged to you to admitt [me] to go to Watterford, as some of my Family has estates in that County where I immagine I sho^d have success. . . .

JRL, B2/1/30

154

Lieutenant Francis Flood to Colonel Samuel Bagshawe

Kilkenny
23 March 1760

Sir

This Moment I received the favour of your letter by the Serjeant and am much surprized you have not received my Returns which I have taken care to send you, since I came here I have inlisted fifteen Men, and I can assure you I inclosed you their Returns—but very likely [they] have Miscarry[ed]. . . I have been never informed of my been Oblidged to raise Ten Men at My own expence and have by this post wrote to my Uncle the Attorney General who recommended me to the Duke of

Bedford for the Lieutenancy and whom I am Asured will Furnish me with a sum Necessary to Raise Ten Men if it answers his Agreement, I now inclose you my Account, and a Return of four Recruits[.]

Believe me Sir that there's nobody wo.^d take more care to provide good and proper men for the Service of your Regiment and to do everything Agreeable to your Instructions than I, and that I shall with all pleasure lay hold of every Oppertunity to give you proofes of the Esteem with which

> I am Sir
> Your most Obed.^t
> humble Servant
> Fra.^s Flood

JRL, B2/1/42

155
Lieutenant-Colonel Edward Windus to Colonel Samuel Bagshawe

Charlemont
24 March 1760

... Before this reaches you, you will have rec.^d the returns of all I have approv'd of, but I must Observe, That the officers don't follow their Recruiting Instructions exactly, wch not only retarded my sending the Returns as I intended to you, but Obliges me to write to them to be more exact. They have sent some of five feet two inches, & several from that to 5f–4, but think we should not take them less than 5f–3 in my own private opinion, but as their Instructions direct them to take none under 5f–4, under 20 years of Age, They should keep up to it & they should do the same respecting the Age, except you allow them a Discretionary leave to go beyond 36 y.^{rs} of age. Mr Crawford[52] has not observed the above Articles of his Instructions, not sent any Returns of them or of their necessaries with them, & Mr Ellis has omitted sending the Certificates of his, for want of which I have not yet Returned them, but hope to get all Rectify'd by the 1ˢᵗ of next Month[.]

I am sorry we are to have any Charge of the French Prisoners, as we are not Disciplin'd & don't know what to say to being Encamped before rais'd, & Disciplin'd, a little at least . . .

***

If we are to do Duty on French Prisoners (which I hope you will evade) I must send the Old Arms, I suppose, with them, & some Cartridges, but we can't get Cartridge paper to make them unless you can procure an Order for some of what is in Store here, & what is One Flint pr. Man? which is all they have allowed us yet.

We are very Unfitt to do duty, & all our Serjᵗˢ & Corplˢ being Recruiting, I hope, will be a Sufficient Reason against it, how can we be Answerable for our Men 'till Disciplined?

The New Arms that came down (150) are exceeding good ones indeed. I suppose we shall soon have more.

I wish the Cloathier⁵³ was to go Naked 'till your Regiment was Cloathed. . .

JRL, B2/1/43

156

Lieutenant-Colonel Edward Windus to Colonel Samuel Bagshawe

Charlemont
26 March 1760

Inclos'd I send you two returns of Recruits, One from Lᵗ Caulfeild,⁵⁴ the other from Enˢ Cook,⁵⁵ & must Observe to you wherein they have acted in Open Opposition to the First, & most Material Article of your Recruiting Instructions, by Inlisting Papists, knowing them (I may say) to be such; & who even (were that any sort of excuse for it) never read their recantation. I have marked them P̲a̲ in the returns, & they all very ingenuously Acknowledge to me (having examined them closely,

& separately) that they were Papists, & went to Mass at different Romish Chappells, viz.ᵗ at Holy Cross, at Thurles, At Monstereven, at Kildaning, & other places, 7 told me the names of their Priests, & acknowledged they never were at Church in their lives ... This is so flagrant a piece of Disobedience in the above named Officers, & so Contrary to the L.ᵈ L.ᵗˢ Intentions, as well as Lord Rothes's & yours, That I have not only rejected them, but have sent them with the Corporal (who conducted them here) to you, That you may learn from them (as I did) all the particulars, & to take what Notice you think proper of the behaviour of the two Officers.

I am really of Opinion when Officers go home on the Recruiting Service, they are not quite so Diligent as when at a strange place, & never tire of living with their Friends, Consequently don't take all the pains they should do to forward the Business they are sent on, & I believe in that I am not singular in my Opinions, I don't mean that all Officers do so, but very young Gent.ⁿ are apt to be a little Giddy, & to mind their Country Diversions more than Recruiting, whereas in other places where they live at their own Expence, they must mind their Business more, or run in Debt, wᶜʰ indeed is with Difficulty avoided.

Out of Ten inlisted by En.ˢ Cook, One <u>Dunn</u> Deserted on his way here, & all the rest (Goldin & Forrester Excepted) are Papists, One of which, at least, (Laurence Mᶜᴰonald) must be known by En.ˢ Cook to be so, as he was a Sarvant of M.ʳ Cook's Father, & lived in the House with him. If the Certificates are not Forged, but Actually sign'd by M.ʳ Lane, Curate of Drom, I know not what he deserves, but it can be no sort of Excuse to En.ˢ Cook, whose Instructions are expressly against taking Papists or Roman Catholics, & who ought to be very certain of their being Protestants, & born of Protestant Parents, it was easy to find out that those he inlisted were Papists, they knew each other to be so ... they all acknowledge it, & En.ˢ Cook must have known some, or all of them to be Papists.

The Returns Came just as you see it, torn & not Sign'd, whether designedly so, or not, I don't know.

As no doubt you will write to these two Officers, I beg you will

Order them to Sign their Returns, to send proper Ones, Attestations and Certificates, & to Mark on the back of the Attestations & Certificates the Mens Names.

I have Rejected Pat McCormack, being very Old & not Strong. He acknowledged to me that he was born in the year of the Battle of Almanza,[56] & calls himself 53 years of age, & I must beg leave to Observe, That very few Returns of Recruits come where the Age set down on them, agree[s] with what the Men declare themselves to be, nor the Height either which you will see in James Thompson, Bart. Collins, & Jno Cranny.

Lt Caulfield has Acted in an Extraordinary Manner, not only by inlisting Papists but by sending Certificates for Dwyer, Collins & Cranny, sign'd by Felix O'Neile, who is no Clergy-man, but One who keeps a Bleach Yard at Monstereven ...

JRL, B2/1/46

157

Lieutenant Francis Flood to Colonel Samuel Bagshawe

Kilkenny
29 March 1760

I received the favour of your letter and do remember that I wrote to Mr Ponsonby when I was at Galway, as I did not chuse to apply to my Uncle the Att^y Genl. because he got me my Ensigns Commission, but two days after I wrote to the Speaker, I received a letter from my Uncle to let me know that my Lord Duke had given me a Lieutenancy (by his application) in your Regiment, but I wrote to him about what you mentioned, and inclosed I send you his Answer ...

JRL, B2/1/49

158

The Right Hon. Warden Flood, Attorney General of Ireland, to Lieutenant Francis Flood

[Dublin]
[March 1760]

I shewed Mr Secretary Rigby[57] your letter this morning who says Col^o Bagshaw is mistaken in what he writes to you; that it is true that it will be looked upon as a matter of Merit in you & y^r friends to help the Regim^t to as many good men as you can, & upon as easy terms as they can be got, but the expence is in no sort to be charged to or born by you, & this you may let ye Col. know, or if you please may send him this letter, certain it is my Ld Lieutenant mentioned nothing of any such condition to me when he promised me this Commiss^n for you, nor since …

JRL, B2/1/48

159

Lieutenant Charles Crawford to Colonel Samuel Bagshawe

Newry
31 March 1760

According to your Orders, I have sent Inclos'd a Return of all the Recruits, I got since I came here, But one Man, as I have not yet got his Certificate nor has he been Attested,

I Rec^d a letter from the Agent informing me that I was to raise 20 men at my own expence, I will do everything in my power to oblige & please Coll^n Bagshawe as far as my fortune will permit, but my sittuation is such at present as will not allow me, to lay out so much money, at this present time, I will give you sufficient security for any sum you are pleased to charge me with, for the Raiseing of that number of Men; As for my Recruits being so low a standard I am very sorry it is not in my power to help, I have offer'd as great Advance money as any Party here & have taken all the pains I cou'd, considering the badness of my Party & that so small, as a serjeant, & the worst Drum in the service, I do assure you I was never Knowingly Guilty of any neglect of your Orders, but as I had not the Recruiting Instructions cou'd not be punctuall to them ...

JRL, B2/1/50

160

Captain Thomas Gaylard to Colonel Samuel Bagshawe

Kedra Camp
5 August 1760

Sir

I shall take it as a particular favour if you will give your Consent that Lieu.^{t} Hazard[58] shall Recruit for me. Belturbut, Inniskillen & Cavan are Contiguous to him, he is willing to do me this piece of Service, & I hope you will not be against his endeavours to befriend me, particularly as you must be sensible, that at this time when the Company I have the Care of is just on the point of being perfected with every Necessary, and what danger there is of its falling off from being Compleat (in every necessary) they now have, and the many other Inconveniencies which must attend my leaving it. Col.^{o} Windus has no objection to this Change but would the rather act by your opinion. I beg therefore you will be kind enough to give me your Answer by Return of the Post, as My Company does not march to Cork till Tuesday and your Letter will reach [me] this Monday Morning, Your Compliance with this my Earnest Request will greatly Oblige
　　　　　　Sir Your Most Obed.^{t} Humble
　　　　　　Servt
　　　　　　　　Thos Gaylard

JRL, B2/1/146

161

Lieutenant-Colonel Edward Windus to Colonel Samuel Bagshawe

Kedra Camp
6 August 1760

We are to march the 11th, 12th & 13th to take our Camp Equipage with us & deliver it at Corke. I have therefore sent the Q^r Master there to fix that matter so that the Storekeep^r may be ready to receive them as each Divi^n marches in, & to settle about our Barrack & to see for a House proper for a Hospl. as well as to Engage the Number of Carts wanted by the Reg^t to come for our Baggage as they are not to be got in the Neighbour[hood]...
Between our Selves, I shall be very glad to have C. G... d recruiting, He is ever grumbling & refractory, & it is with great difficulty I can get him to do anything. I have had an other Contest with him, to get him to pay the Taylor for making his Company's Gaters, & was obliged to send several messages to him about it, before I spoke to him ... Capt Caldwell[59] wants to go to England to Recruit, but without an Order we can't Recruit there, it has been some time put a stop to, & the Regiments on this Establishment were Order'd to Recruit in Ireland.

In the Distribution of Quarters at Corke, I have taken my own Company into the Barracks with me, which is the practice I have been used to, & what General Fitzwilliam[60] always thought I had a right to do, so after some Grumbling among the Captains, they drew [lots] and the Companies that are to be Quarter'd on the Town are Capt Urquhart's,[61] C. Schuylers,[62] & C. Trench's.[63]

If I was not to take my Company into the Barracks with me, I have no right to a Quarter for my self, as my right is derived from being Capt of my Comp^y

If I took a Quarter for myself in the Barracks, my Comp^y being out, I must turn out some Captain whose Comp^y would lie in the Barracks, wch is as arbitrary, as taking my Comp^y with me.

The Off^{rs} & men should be Quartered as Contiguous as possible, & if my Comp^y was in the Town, & I in the Barracks, (wch I think absolutely Necessary) I must be reduced to ask a favour of some Capt (perhaps C. G-d) for a spare room, for my servant to be near me, which in case of Sickness, & many other Cases is so necessary, & the reverse so Inconvenient, & I should be sorry to be reduced to the necessity of asking a fav^r especially as I think I have a right to have my Company with me, & I have other occasion for my Serjeant to give him Directions about the payment, as well as Managem^t of my Company, & I think he should be near me, in case I should want him, at any time of the Day or in the Evening. These reasons weigh with me, & I think it is more proper that the Cap^{ts} should be Governed by me, than I by them.

C. Gaylard came to me just now, & wants me to let Lt Hassard go recruiting in his room, wch I told him I could not take it upon me to do, for you had fix'd it before you went that the Eldest of each Rank should go, & every One take their turn, & I could not alter it …

JRL, B2/1/147

162

Lieutenant-Colonel Edward Windus to Colonel Samuel Bagshawe

Kedra Camp
7 August 1760

By not hearing from you since you left Clonmell, I suppose this, & Other Letters I have wrote to you will not reach you in Dublin. I hope however to hear from you in answer to some things which I mentioned in my Last. C. Gaylard wrote to you to desire Lt Hassard might recruit for him & expects an answer on Monday, but I hope you have not Comply'd with his request, nor left it to me, for I shall be glad to have him away from the Regiment, He promotes Drinking & sitting up too much for young Off^{rs} to keep him Company, wch they will do, besides many reasons wch I need not mention to you.

I find you are to have Brigade Major Preston for your Major, wch was Offer'd to him, fine times when Major's Posts go a begging.

We are order'd by Government to send a Return of our Arms Serviceable, Unserviceable, & wanting so I shall return the Number made Unserviceable by Cocks &c breaking, but None wanting, depending upon Mr Truelock[64] wch is a poor Dependence you will say, & I hope this is done in Order to have them made Serviceable at the Governm^{ts} expence.

I shall send off the Recruiting Parties on Monday & Capt Gayl^d, Lt Ellis, & En^s Croker,[65] wch last says he, has some Men ready waiting for him ...

[P.S.] We have had such immoderate falls of rain these few days past, that has fill'd up all the Pores of the Earth, & the Companies about the Center of the Regiment were this Day obliged to Lave the Water out of their Tents with wooden bowls, & in order to carry it off, we have been obliged to cut a trench from the Center Street close to the Gravel walk, to the left of your Tent ... and so to carry it off that way towards the rear, & several other Trenches ...

JRL, B2/1/148

163

Lieutenant-Colonel Edward Windus to Colonel Samuel Bagshawe

Cork
1 September 1760

Inclos'd I send you the State of your Regim^t & in another Cov^r I send you a Copy of the Recruiting Instructions, such as Occurr'd to me, if you chuse to make any Alteration, you have only to let me know, & they shall be Observ'd, some Reg^{ts} allow the Recruiting Off^r £2, & pay, from the date of their Attestation, others £3 & pay only from the time of their Approbation wch latter I take to be the best method, & it corresponds with the last Order of Governm^t

We have a great many Old men, who I fear never will be able to exercise, & who I would by no means Chuse should join the Battalion at the time of Review. I would therefore continue to recruit to purge the Reg.t of them, but I fear our Fund will not Answer as we want upwards of 60 men now besides what may desert.

We go on very well in our Drilling, twice a Day, & the very Awkward are out 3 times a Day, I have secured a Market house for Drilling in, all the Winter, & I have taken an Hospital sufficient for 70 men, & a good Loft to exercise a good number, so I have by this means, a very proper place for all Malingerers, or for any who Misbehave, where they are Confin'd & exercised 3 times a Day, kept on half Diet, washed & kept Clean, & made Sick of the Hospital, not Sick in the Hospital; Those who are really sick are treated properly, & exercise is good for all who do not keep their beds.

I am out every Morning at the Drill, at Six o'Clock, we mount guard at Eleven, where I see the Companies & examine into the particular dress & appearance of every Man. We begin to dress better than we did, & as I see every Man's Hair be comb'd, oil'd, & properly tyed, & his Hat well put on, They must Contract a Habit of Observing my Directions in that, as well as other matters, & the Officers, observing what I would be at, must give their assistance, as they see their men before I inspect them. In short I am in hopes we shall cut as good a figure as our Rags will admit of, for we shall be in Rags long before the Review, except wee could have our new Cloathing on before we are Review'd which I would take care to save after the Review, [by] covering the Lapells & Cuffs with the Old, & in that Case, we shall Cut a very good figure, & I will answer for the Discipline; & if this can be done, I think your Regiment will be talk'd of, which, I hope, will do both you & me some Service.

I am teaching four pretty large Squads, & the Grenadiers, the method of Firing, Advancing, & Retreating, One in the rear of the Other, with the Officers superintending, & the Serjeants & Corporals paying attention to their own Squads, so that, by this means, every Squad is sure to do alike, to step together, & all must do it with the same signal of the Drum, & keep the same time. I only begun today, & by pursuing it, as I know of none so good, they will at any time be fit to join, Every Squad, tho separated at a little distance, must do alike, & learn the same thing, & get equally forward, being (before) taught the use of their arms & fitted for this method, wch. is a sort of graduation before joining ...

JRL, B2/1/149

164
Lieutenant-Colonel Edward Windus to Colonel Samuel Bagshawe

Cork
3 October 1760

Inclos'd I send you the present State of your Regiment, by which you will see we have lost some men since our Arrival at this place. I have sent Ensign Lowe[66] & a Party with him, as he promises to get me some Men, I have sent Cuff & Finagen to Dublin, to take up Deserters, & pick up men for us, I find it would Cost for a tollerable long Advertisem^t. 10s: 10d, the first time, & 2s: 2d every time after & I hardly think it worth while, as few are got by advertising, but in that I shall do as you please, but there are such a Number, that I fear it will bring a Discredit upon us, let me know your sentiments on this, & I shall act accordingly, having yet done nothing in it. I expect Major Preston here on Monday ... I have apply'd for Capt. Caldwell who intends going to England, he wanted to recruit there, but that we can't do, or indeed afford to do.

I shall carry on the Drill in such a Manner during the Winter, as I am in hopes, will make your Regiment make as good a Figure, at least, as our Neighbours. I hope you will let me pitch upon a Cock for the next Hatts, for what they had at first, was such as would (by no Means) Stand, & I would have no Man in your Regiment whose Cock won't Stand to a bit of Hat, let it be ever so Old. I have ... alter'd it to the 3d [crease] & the Ladies say our Cocks are much Mended for it, so do the Men, & we all find it so.

Our Cloathing is in very bad Order, & you must expect to see us in rags, except Mr Nixon sends us a large quantity of Cloath & lining to mend it with, & Mr Ford[67] sends us lace. I have been obliged to order a second pair of linnen Drawers p^r Man to make them look decent & clean, for their cloath Breeches are worn out, & they will be starved with cold this Winter in the linnen ones. I have ordered Tops of Leather to be put on the gaters when they go out to exercise & save the knees of Breeches & Stockings, We begin to get their Hair in tollerable order, wch I see every morning, that it be well comb'd tyed & oil'd to make it look smooth & well, & before next Review, it will all be long enough to plat & turn up under their Hats ...

JRL, B2/1/155

165

Captain William Montgomery, Regimental Agent, to Colonel Samuel Bagshawe

Dublin
21 October 1760

... Cap^n Schuyler & Lt Cawfield are the only officers who have satisfied the demands you left me upon them. And Cap^n Joas is to send me a Draft on Scotland for his debt. The others promise fairly to pay soon. By this you will see the necessity of sending me directions concerning the pay^t of the cloathier's Acc^t which comes to £1227: 10: 2.½ & for the pay^t of which he has been often with me, & has press'd me greatly, on Acc^t that the cloathing was delivered so long ago. It will be right to pay him a good part of the money soon. If he was to receive £1000 on Acc^t & the remainder when you come over and have had time to satisfie your self as to the justness of his demand. What money I have of yours may be applied in part & the rest either remitted to me or if more agreable to you I can get it here on your cloathing warrant which is the usual way. There will be half a year's cloathing paid in February or March next so that you will not have much interest to pay & no expence in the negotiation. But of this you are the only judge & whatever directions you give me I shall follow. You will know that the cloathing warrant is in the cloathiers name & must be assigned to you by him before it becomes your property. In the doing of this the cloathier always takes care to be satisfied in his demand either in money or by an obligation to pay him.

Let me know whether you are to pay for the forrage caps, or if they are to be charg'd to the men, the price is 1^{shg} 8^d and is an Article in the cloathiers Acc^t

Lieu^t Daley[68] wrote me in answer to the demand I made upon him. That he wou'd enquire of the Primate[69] whether at the time of his recommendation there was any mention made of his raising men on his getting his preferment. I have save'd him that trouble & the Primate told me that it was particularly mentioned he shou'd raise men as a consideration for his preferment, had you known this you might have burthen'd that gentleman with a larger number than I believe you have done.

I had forgot to acquaint you that Lieu^t Merydith[70] has paid the £28 he was indebted to you ...

JRL, B2/1/156

166

Colonel Samuel Bagshawe to Captain William Montgomery, Regimental Agent

[Draft]   London
                                          11 November 1760

I have reced y^r obliging favour of the 21st Oct^r & thank you for the kind Office you have done me with the Primate, wch corresponds with Lt Dalys & his Bro^{rs} behaviour when they first came to see me, I then told them Lt Daly was to raise Thirty Men for his Lieutenancy & at that time they did not seem to make any Objection, their doing it [afterwards] made me apprehensive they might have applied to the Primate & that his G:. disapproved of their raising Men & I had rather lose the Whole than desire Terms which might be disagreeable to him or disoblige persons who might be very useful to him.

As to M:. Nixon be so good to do as you say [and] raise as much Money upon y:. best terms you can upon the Cloathing Warrn:. as is necessary to make him easy. I did expect to have had Money p:.d me from persons by whom I am disappointed, however with y:. half a Year's Cloathing I think I shall by that time have money p:.d me to enable me to discharge all demands upon me, & please to apply my Pay & whatsoever Money comes due to me to this purpose, and pray be so good to ask L:.t Hazard for his Money w:.ch became payable in Oct:.r, he may perhaps for the sake of Delay inform you he wants to quit & that I have wrote for him to give in his Resignation but in the mean time I expect him to pay in his Money & he shall have it again w:.n leave is obtained for him to sell out, & that I expect he shall pay the Interest I am obliged to pay for the Money you raise for Nixon for his Sume from the day it becomes payable.

I did not promise to pay for the forage Caps, if it is usual for the Colonels to provide them, I will, else the Soldiers must pay for them ...

JRL, B2/1/156a

167
Lieutenant-Colonel Edward Windus to Colonel Samuel Bagshawe

Cork
23 November 1760

I deferr'd sending you the Return 'till I could give you an Account of the number of men given to the Royal[71] & Handasyds Reg:.ts[72] which indeed has effectually demolished us. L:.t Governor Molesworth[73] was order'd here to superintend the

230

Embarkation, & to pick out such men of your Regiment as he thought fit for immediate service, & he was order'd to take the whole of what was wanted from this Regiment & in case we had not a sufficient number, he was then to have recourse to Genl. Adlercrons Voluntiers. Upon which he has given 94, & taken the names of some others, but he thought the remainder of the Regiment so unfit, That he made application to Makay[74] & got 37 of Genl. Adlercrons, & we are to supply the place of all who may desert between this, & the day of Embarkation, as they are Order'd to Embark Compleat, so that it is impossible to say what Number we may lose in the whole, & those the pick'd men of the Regiment as you may judge by their having recourse to Adlercrons, when they had taken all they liked, in short we are reduced before our time, & now they may Establish us as a Regiment of Invalids as soon as they please ... We shall want a great many men, I have therefore sent out more parties to recruit...

***

Our Captains suffer greatly by giving these Draughts, the Debts of those of Captain Schuyler's Company amount to about £15 & we all suffer, & to mend the matter, we are obliged to send them Compleat in Necessaries, even those who are greatly in Debt, which is so much loss to each Captain. I have stickled for them as much as I possibly could.

Since I wrote the above, The Two Regiments are Embark'd ...& I am very busy about getting them to Give me Receipts, for the Number of Men we have given, & the species of Cloathing they have taken which when their Confusion is over, & I can get them to settle with me about, I shall let you know, but as their Cloathing came to them but lately, & they did not deliver it to the Draughts before this day, I have not yet been able to get them to sign the necessary receipts, nor will they do it 'till they return the Cloathing, but I hope to get all done tomorrow morning... it has been a most Confus'd piece of business indeed ...

JRL, B2/1/161

168

Lieutenant-Colonel Edward Windus to Colonel Samuel Bagshawe

Cork
5 December 1760

Inclos'd I send you the present State of your Regiment, by which you will find we want on the face of the Return 205, from wch take off 27, i.e. the 3 Contingent Men p^r Comp^y which makes the N^o we actually want 178. If we are to be paid for our Draughts, we must recruit as fast as we can, which indeed we are doing, if we are not to be paid for them which I believe will be the Case, it will be the better for us, as we shall be allow'd to keep the Draughts in our returns as Effectives for some time, at least four Months to pay for them, & the growing Fund, I hope, will answer very well for us.

The Order of Government was, That the Draughts should not take away any of your Cloathing with them, but Col^o Molesworth told me he had wrote his reasons to the Government for allowing the two Reg^{ts} to take them, & I have wrote to Montgomery to see you have Justice done you in resiect of the Cloathing, & as it was very bad I presume you will not be displeased at their taking them.

I am glad to find, That the Duke of Devonshire sets you up for Tallow, & by what I can learn, we shall have several Sitting Members in the Reg^t. Standing Ones there is no doubt of ...

JRL, B2/1/163

169

Lieutenant Francis Flood to Colonel Samuel Bagshawe

Floodhall
24 January 1761

I hope you will excuse the liberty I take in troubleing you with this letter, as it wo^d give me the utmost concern to do any thing that sho.^d be disagreeable, I must beg lave to let you know that Mr Montgomery has aplyed to me for the Ballance of my Recruiting Account due you at a time my Famly is in distress, being concerned in a Contested Election, and on receiveing Mr Montgomery's letter, I aply'd to my Father for the Ballance, he told me, that as he had stud candidate for the Corporation of Callen, it was not in his power to discharge the debt at the time desired but that he wo.^d certainly discharge it in three Months, I therefore make my aplication to you hopeing you will be so kind to give me that time to discharge the Ballance of my Account—A favour which you may depend shall ever greatfully be Acknowledged with the Utmost gratitude & Respect ...

JRL, B2/1/182

170

Sir Robert Wilmot to Colonel Samuel Bagshawe

[London]
28 February 1761

I have the Duke of Devonshire's Commands to acquaint you that, as he has reason to believe the Parliament of Ireland will soon be called, It will be proper for you speedily to repair to that Kingdom, but if the meeting at Derby should be fixed for Any Day within a Week or Ten Days at the farthest from this day, His Grace will be glad to see you there; if the meeting be later, His Grace desires you will write to some Friend to signify How you would have declared your self in case you had appeared at that Meeting ...

When you get to Ireland, You will apply to Sir Henry Cavendish,[75] Who has taken all proper Steps to secure you at Tallagh, to which place you are to repair as soon as possible after your arrival in that Kingdom—The Duke of Devonshire is afraid your Election will be attended with some Expence to you, however His Grace will talk with you upon that point afterwards; but the Mony will certainly be well laid out if your Success be thereby secured, which I heartily wish, and of which I have no doubt, if you appear soon amongst them, for Strangers have certain Prejudices to combat & surmount ...

JRL, B2/3/844

171

Lieutenant-Colonel Edward Windus to Colonel Samuel Bagshawe

Cork
2 March 1761

I could wish you had an Opportunity of Letting Lord Rothes know your Reg.^{t} was not so remarkably weak as Others, particularly Colonel Rufane's 2 Battalions, late Lord Forbes's;[76] They wanted about 300 when they came here, which N.^{o} was augmented to 381, the Number of Draughts they received at the time of Embarkation. We suffered as much upon this Occasion, as we did, upon the last, 109 more of your Regiment being pick'd out, so that we can't be looked upon now as a Regiment, before the Draught to the 1st, 16th, 76th & 90th Regiments, we wanted only 76 men of being Compleat, including Deserters since we left Camp, besides many who deserted without joining the Reg.^{t} & men are now very hard to be got. Captn Joass writes me from Dublin, That the Recruiting Parties there take Boys of Five feet two, & men grown up of 5 feet five Upwards of 26 years of Age & have but very indifferent Success ...

***

I shall send the Agent an Account of what N.^{o} Each Reg.^{t} received of your Draughts, as they took our Cloathing, wch I hope you will be Considered for, notwithstanding they were very bad, as they would have made Waistcoats for the next year ...

***

I shall now set about repairing the Cloathing, having got Materials from Nixon for that purpose, that the men we keep, may have something to set them off, as they have not youth to do it . . .

If you can find room, & it be not too much trouble, I should be much Obliged to you to bring me 3 y^{ds}: & ¼ of the best Scarlet Cloth, for I cannot get any good here, & 6 y^{ds}: & ½ of Shalloon, Major Preston tells me, by making use of his Name, Job Ray in Tavistock lane will give you the same as he sends to the Cameronian Regiment,[77] w^{ch}: is the best he ever saw, & the Cheapest. I hope he will pack it up so as not to rub or wear by Carriage . . .

JRL, B2/1/190

172

Lieutenant-Colonel Edward Windus to Colonel Samuel Bagshawe

Cork
17 March 1761

I sent the last Return of your Regim^t: to the Agent to deliver it to you upon your Arrival in Dublin, & I wrote to you giving you an Account of the Draughts <u>taken</u> from you, to the Amount of 109, of which 95 were given to the 76th: Reg^t:[78] & 14 to Morgans.[79]

Colonel Makay writes to Major Preston, to let him know, That he understands Col^o: Molesworth has exceeded his Orders, in taking any from Adlercrons, or yours, but Volunt^{rs}:. He only got 76 Voluntiers from Adlercrons, & just that Number turn'd out, (the Day the Regim^t: was Order'd under Arms) as Voluntiers, but the Next day, Colonel Molesworth, with the Commanding Off^{rs}: of the 76th: & 90th: Reg^{ts}: picked out 33 more, & it seems in Case did not get Volunt^{rs}: enough to Compleat the two Regim^{ts}:, Colonel Molesworth was to have recourse to the Regiment Quarter'd nearest to Corke. I only think proper to apprise you of this, that when you arrive in Dublin, you may there inform Your Self perhaps, What Col^o: Molesworth was Order'd to do upon that Occasion,

& whether he exceeded them, to the prejudice of your Reg^t or not.

They have tore the Reg^t to pieces, we have now only 346 men, & I could wish 60 of them were Discharged being Unfit for any thing. Some of them have been in the Hospl. ever since we came to Corke, & are actually Incurable. In short I must heartily wish you & I were in a Young, Old Corps, which is in every respect, better than an Old, Young Corps.

If it were not for fear you might think me a Quack, I would take the Liberty to beg you to bring me ... some Pectoral Balsam of Honey, for Cough etc, & some Pectoral Lozenges of Tolu,[80] also some Elixer ... for Rheumatism being often troubled with both Disorders, & I am much troubled with Headaches. I am afraid you will think me very troublesome, therefore, I shall stop here ...

JRL, B2/1/193

173

The Memorial of Colonel Samuel Bagshawe

[Draft]   [April 1761]

To Their Excellencies The Lords Justices Genl. and Genl. Governors of Ireland

The Memorial of Colonel Samuel Bagshawe Humbly Sheweth
     That Agreeable to an order of the 20th Octr 1760, One hundred & nine pick't Men were Draughted from the 93^d Regiment of Foot (which your Memorialist has the Honour to Command) to Compleat the 1st Batt^n of the Royal & the 16th Reg^t of Foot, then goeing on forreign Service, that by the Countermand of that Service & the Return of those Regiments to Ireland that Emergency has Ceased—
     That Another draught was made of the like Number of Men to Compleat the 76th & 90th Regiments of Foot, which has Served almost to Ruin the said 93rd Reg^t

Your Memorialist therefore Pray your Excellencies will be pleased to Recommend the State of the 93^d Reg^t to his Excellency the Lord Lieu^t that the Men draughted to the 1st Battⁿ of the Royal & 16th Reg^{ts} of Foot, and an Equivalent Number for those who since have been otherwise Disposed of by those Regiments may be returned back to the 93^d Regim^t, The Service for which they were drafted being Countermanded.

Your Memorialist also Pray that the Cloathing Detained by those Regim^{ts} with the Drafts may be Returned, or a Sufficient Recompence made for such Cloathing, And that the Debts of the Draughts may be paid, Or that your Excellencys will be pleased to Consider in what manner the Captains of the 93^d Reg^t may be Indemnified as it is a loss they cannot well sustain, & for wch no Provision is yet made, Which is Humbly submitted to your Ex^{cies}

Samuel Bagshawe

Reasons Offered why the Draughts taken from the 93^d Regiment to Compleat the 1st & 16th Regiments should be Returned back to the 93^d—

Every Regiment in Common Occurrences has an Equal Right to favour & Protection

It became the 93^d Regiment Chearfully to Submitt to an Exigency of Government—

The 1st & 16th Regiments being Returned to Ireland, The Service Countermanded, that Exigency has Ceased, and they are again under like Circumstances as the 93^d as Appears by their being lately Draughted ... and the 93^d has good Reasons to Claim their Draughts back again, Otherways Regiments under like Circumstances will be Differently Treated, The Service also will Suffer, for if a Certain Number of Officers are sent [from] the 93^d Reg^t to Recruit and a like Number from the 1st & 16th three times the number of Recruits may be raised.

The Officers of the 93^d Reg^t are as well Disposed to be Employed on Service as those of any other Corps can be, and it is hoped, they are as well Qualified, but if they are only to be

Employed to raise Recruits their Military Talent must lie Buried. They are Deprived of the Means of Improvement and of Distinguishing themselves and Exposed to a most Vexatious kind of Life and to Continual Losses from Desertion &c, as is Daily Experienced by those who have a Number of Recruits to Raise & Discipline—

JRL, B2/1/203

174

Lieutenant Francis Flood to Colonel Samuel Bagshawe

Kilkenny
22 April 1761

I have rec^d a letter this day from Lieu^t Coll. Windus wherein he mentions that you are much disobliged at my not paying in the Ballance of my Recruiting Account due you. This makes me immagin that you did not receive the letter I troubled you with some time ago to make an Apolagy and to beg you wo^d give me time untill After the Elections[.]

I am truly sencible of your kindness in forbearing untill this time and I must beg lave to tell you Sir, that the money wo^d [have] been paid long before this, but my Family has been and are at this time, Ingaged in a disputed Corporation, which has been very expencive to them, However I know that this is no excuse for you, and that your Money ought to have been paid, I am Ashamed to be so troublesome, but on my Aplication to my Father, he told me this day, that my two Brothers been Ordered to Germany, he was Oblidged to give them what money he co^d well spare, which has distressed him a little, but that he will pay my debt and all other demands that may be made against me by the End of May, or the beginning of June Certainly, I hope you'll be so kind to forbear untill that time, and I shall ever esteem it as the greatest favour ...

JRL, B2/1/206

175

Major Robert Preston to Colonel Samuel Bagshawe

Cork
26 April 1761

Sir,

Colonel Windus made me very uneasie when he returned from you at Tallough by telling me that you was Displeased with me, on account that I had never write to you since I came into your Regiment, And no Doubt had that been the case you would have very good Reason, But Sir so soon as I knew for a Certainty that I was Major of your Regiment, I wrote to you from Limerick, mentioning that Tho' I was not made by your nomenation,[81] yet that I hoped on account of an old acquaintance, that I was as agreeable as any other that would have been put in upon you, and that in a few days I was going to Cork to join your Regiment, This Letter I directed to you in Derbyshire, I own that I never have write to you since I joined the Regiment, But that is far from any wanting Respect to you, For tho' there was great reason to write and to Complain to you of what was doing to your Regiment, yet as Colonel Windus was on the Spot, I thought it would have been Interfering in his Province, for me to Report such things to you. But I wrote to severall others mentioning what had been done, and what good Cause you had to complain of the way your Regiment was used. Be assured Sir that since I came to Cork, I have Imployed myself Intirely about the Regiment[.] Collonel Windus might have Informed you that I Seldom Scarce ever go to take the Devertion of the Town, And that while I am in the Barracks, I am Constantly Imployed in Doing what Little I can about the Regiment, I beg you will belive me to be

Sir
your most Humble and
most Obedient Servant
Rob. Preston

JRL, B2/1/208

176

Major Robert Preston to Colonel Samuel Bagshawe

Cork
15 May 1761

I am favoured with yours of the 5th. May,[82] and am very much Obliged to you for the Kind Sentiments you have of me, Which I shall alwise Endeavour Shall Continue, I was very Certain When Collonel Windus spoke to me that the Smalest Explanation would put everything to Rights[.] It would have been very odd, That a Freindship, which has Subsisted these many years, Should Cease upon my being Major to your Regiment, To the Contrary, I am very Hopefull it will encreass.

We are very Bussey in preparing the Few men that they have left of your Regiment, To be fit for being Reviewed, And I hope the Reviewing Generall will say that we have not been Idle, You will not have above Two Hundred men in the Ranks[,] The rest must be reviewed in the Royall, Handysides and Rufanes Regiments ...

JRL, B2/1/218

177

Major Robert Preston to Colonel Samuel Bagshawe

Cork
23 May 1761

Yesterday I called together all the Officers of your Regiment, and Read to them that part of your Letter in Relation to the Purchasing the Company[,][83] Flood the eldest Lieu^t sayd he was willing to Purchass the Captain Lieutenancy if he did not get the Company which he thought he had a good Right to, Croker the second Lieu^t was not here, Att this the Lieu^{ts}. were all wishing it

might Come to them, So in that there is no Difficulty, Two
Ensigns Smith[84] and Spaight[85] were both willing to Purchass
the Lieutenancy, I told them that I did not know whether they or
two others that are not as yet joined were the Eldest (for we have
Delayed adjusting the Rank till they arrive) But I desired them
to look out for a Purchessor for their Ensigncy which I believed
would be Difficult, for the World is greatly Changed since you
and I knew it for one is affronted now a days if offered any thing
less than a Company[.] I told them likewise that none but who
had a Proper Character would be admitted to Purchass, The
Officers asked what would be [the] difference of the Prices from
one Rank to another[,] I answered that you in your letter had
desired to know what the opinion of your Officers was upon that
Subject and that I had Delayed writing you my opinion till the
Lieut.ᵗ Collonel Returned [,] But that to Satisfie them they
should know my Opinion, which was, That the only foundation I
had to go upon, was that a Lieutenancy in a young Regiment was
Better than an Ensigncy in an old one for that Severall Ensigns
in the old went Lieuᵗˢ into the Young, That I valued an Ensigncy
in an old Regᵗᵗ at £450, The Difference from Lieutenant to
Captain Lieutenant at £200[,] from Captain Lieutenant to
Captain at £350, That I valued the Ensigncy at £300 and from
Ensign to Lieuᵗᵗ at £150, I told them that as yet I [knew] neither
the Lieuᵗᵗ Collonels nor your Opinion of the Matter[,] But that I
would soon and that they might be Providing Sums about that
Value. Flood had Receved a letter from you the post before, but
he thinks that he will get the Company whether you will or not,
and has write a Memoriall to the Government upon it, It was not
in my Power to Convince him that the Captain Lieuᵗᵗ had a
better right than he.

***

JRL, B2/1/221,222

178

Captain William Montgomery, Regimental Agent, to Colonel Samuel Bagshawe

Dublin
25 July 1761

... Some days ago when at the Muster Office I saw your Memorial relative to the Drafts. On some very serious conversation with Mr Mangin[86] I found that if your Memorial was laid before a Board of General Officers that for certain every shilling of the vacant pay of the Drafts would be made a saving to the Publick, excepting the Levy mony usually allowed for raising men. That it was very uncertain whether the Drafts would be return'd & for certain the vacant pay be checqued. As your Reg.^t wants at present the whole number of Men Drafted & that the pay of said Drafts comes to a considerable sum, which will be a sufficient fund to make the Reg.^t not only compleat but replace all the bad men; The risque therefor the memorial runs of having the effect I have [made] mention of, has made Mr Mangin recommend the Memorial to be withdrawn till I receive your further orders. The Memorial is returnd to [the] Secretarys office (with the permission of Lord Rothes) & may be had from thence on having your answer ...

JRL, B2/1/232

179

Captain Alexander Joass to Colonel Samuel Bagshawe

Dublin
25 August 1761

When you was in this Country I ask'd your leave to dispose or exchange my Company, if I should happen to find a Convenient Opportunity of a purchase or Exchange for my Advantage, which you was very kind to consent to. I think it my duty to Inform you that I am now on a Scheme of buying the Fort Majors place of Stirling Castle in Scotland, & have applyed to Colonel Windus to sell my Company for £1000 British, on Condition of my succeeding to the other, which is to be hop'd you won't think an unreasonable price. Capt.ⁿ Lieu.ᵗ Woolocombe[87] has refus'd buying, Floods father has given Security for his Sons debts, the young man says his father will give the Cash, this I very much doubt, I imagine Lieu.ᵗ Lombard[88] will be the purchaser, I beg your Concurrence in this as I think it an Excellent Opportunity of settling myself at the Eve of a War ...

JRL, B2/1/235

180

Lieutenant-Colonel Edward Windus to Colonel Samuel Bagshawe

Limerick
1 September 1761

You will see by the Inclos'd Return that we both lose & get men. Lord Rothes was pleased to ask every Corp in Ireland for 2 Grenadiers, to make up his Losses in the Gren.ʳ Comp.ʸ of his Reg.ᵗ of Guards,[89] as none refused, You may imagine I did not, so I have given him two as Appears on the back of the Return, for which he gives us five Guineas each, & a Guinea to each Man.

Cap.ᵗ Joas has apply'd for leave to sell, in Order to make a purchase of a Town Major's post, in Scotland; & L.ᵗ Flood's Father, I apprehend, will lay down the Difference between his Commission, w.ᶜʰ will be 400 Guineas, & £1000 Brittish, w.ᶜʰ Joas expects for his Comp.ʸ if it meets with y.ʳ Approbation, & his Majesty's Consent, I don't know if any of the Ensigns will give 200 guineas difference, in w.ᶜʰ Case, we must find an Ensign to give as much; if none of the Ensigns will, Joas tells me of a very good young Man, an Ensign in the Royal Irish,[90] who will give the 400 Guin.^{s} & sell his own Commission. Capt Joas hopes you will approve of all this & give leave for the Scheme to go forward, & being in great haste, is in hopes you will signify y.^{r} Approbation as soon as possible, that it may be Carried into Execution.

I expect your Cloathing down any day, as Mr Nixon, before I left Dublin, promised it should be here yesterday ...

JRL, B2/1/236

181

Lieutenant Francis Flood to Colonel Samuel Bagshawe

Limerick
4 September 1761

As Captain Joas purposes disposeing of his Comp.^{y} in your Regiment and as I am inform'd that the Capt Lieu.^{t} and Mr Ellis who is eldest Lieutenant has refused to purchase, it has been offered to me as been the next in seniority by Coll. Windus, upon wch I wrote to my Father and he has agreed to lodge the money. I therefore thought it my duty to inform you of it, hopeing you have no objection to my purchising, I am truly sencible of a late indiscretion I have been guilty of by running indebted to the Regiment, but hope you will impute it to my youth, as you may depend I shall never be guilty of a thing of that nature while I have the honour of serveing under you, or while I continue in his Majesty's Service. I discharged the Ballance due to you and your Reg.^{t} three weeks ago, and have got a receit from Mr Montgomery and I now waite for your Aprobation to purchis Captain Joas's Company ...

JRL, B2/1/238

182

Lieutenant Francis Flood to Colonel Samuel Bagshawe

Limerick
15 October 1761

I received you kind favour of the 28th of September,[91] and am greatly Obliged to you for makeing choice of me to purchase Cap:^t Joass's Company, as all my Senior Officers have declined —I shall rely intirely upon you in forwarding the Commission as there is no delay at my side, my money being lodged six weeks ago, and as my Lieutenancy is disposed of to Ensign Watts,[92] if you approve of him, his money is ready ...

JRL, B2/1/247

183

Lieutenant-Colonel Edward Windus to Colonel Samuel Bagshawe

Limerick
18 October 1761

I am extreamly sorry I am under the Necessity of acquainting you, that L:^t Meredyth is a most Unhappy young Man, being frequently engaged in Quarrells, & thereby bringing a Discredit on the Corps. He has had five since the 1st of Sept:^r & the Officers here would no longer associate with him, or suffer him to continue any longer in the Mess.

As matters are therefore come to such a Crisis with him, I should be wanting in my Duty were I to suffer him to continue any longer with the Regiment. I have therefore given him leave to go where he pleases, & he tells me he will try to persuade his Friends to procure him a Change into some Regiment abroad, or going on Service, which being a more active Life may possibly suit him better, & be of use to him.

I have kept him under my own Observation since the Regiment march'd from Corke, in hopes of bringing about a reformation in him, that I might have it in my power of acquainting his Friends with it, & thereby, be of some kind of Service to him, as I know he lays under their Displeasure, but I must own my advice has had no kind of weight with him, any more than that of Major Preston, Cap.ᵗ Caldwell, & others.

I cannot send him to any other Quarter, as he there would have no Superior, & of course Command a Comp.ʸ, which I should be sorry to entrust him with the care of. I must therefore return him on the recruiting Service, 'till I can get out a Licence for him, & I hope his Friends will get him transferr'd to some other Corps, but I fear they would leave him just where he is, & do nothing for him, if they knew the reason why he is sent from the Regiment.

I have taken all imaginable pains to make him sensible of the tottering Situation he was in (after the Affair at Corke)[93] with his Bro.ʳ Officers: & upon every Occasion since that time (of which he has given me many) have given him most Serious Advice to Conduct himself as other Officers do, & refrain from Drinking, as he knows it never fails to lead him to do some wrong headed, Outragious thing; When sober, he cannot keep away from a Billiard Table, or when Drunk, out of a Bawdy house, where he is very apt to Draw his Sword upon Friends or foes; tho' he seldom meets any of the former there, or any where else. In short, he has made himself despised by the people of Corke, & this place; as much as he has Disagreeable to his Brother Officers.

I hope you approve of the Step I have taken in respect of him, as I would Chuse, on Account of his Friends, (some of whom I have great esteem for) to proceed with Mildness.

***

JRL, B2/1/248

184

Lieutenant-Colonel Edward Windus to Colonel Samuel Bagshawe

Limerick
27 October 1761

Upon the receipt of your Letter,[94] I called the Officers together, & read to them that part of it relating to Lieu. Meredyth, a Letter I rec.^d from him, & anuther he wrote to Capt.ⁿ Caldwell, & I must say that I think they have long since Shewn great Moderation & forbearance on account of his Youth, but they are now Convinc'd of the Impossibility of his behaving well, that He has shown how much he despises the repeated Advice given him by several of his Bro. Officers upon many Occasions, that One thing was no sooner overlook'd, than he run into Another, That He is of a morose, Obstinate Disposition, & very Quarrelsome, that he has brought a Reflection on the Corps, which they are Convinc'd would greatly increase, were he suffer'd to remain amongst them, & as a proof of his making very light of his present situation, He was no sooner told, that as the Officers had spoke to me, to desire he might no longer Continue in their Mess, for they would not keep him Company, He was therefore at Liberty to go where he pleas'd, for he should not stay here to do Duty with a Set of Gentlemen he was on so bad a footing with, & reminding him of their overlooking his bad conduct at Corke upon Account of his Youth, & his Letter promising future good behaviour, I say Notwithstanding all I said to him, & his [seeming] repentance of what he had done, which I have reason to think was not real, He went as Unconcern'd as ever to his daily haunt the Billiard Table, from thence in the Evening to a Dancing School, where he made a Disturbance, & by Dancing banish'd all thoughts of his Situation, & after that, to Crown all, [sat] down to Drink with one Fitzgerald a Barber with whom he Drank three Bottles of Clarett, he afterwards when going away made so light of it, that he swore his Friends should do something for him, or he would make them glad to get rid of him. These & such like has fixed the Officers in refusing to keep him Company, or looking upon him as an Officer in the Regiment, & beg they may not be plagued with him again, & they further think him very mean spirited in asking to join the Corps again.

I dare say Sir, you will approve of the Behaviour of your Officers upon the Occasion ...

JRL, B2/1/252

185

Major Robert Preston to Colonel Samuel Bagshawe

Limerick
24 November 1761

I esteem the Letter I Riceved from you,[95] And am Greatly obliged to you for your Friendship, and it shall alwise be my Constant Endeavour to make a Gratefull Return. As for my Vews or Schemes, They are so Vague that I can Scarce be said to have any, I have no Conection with any great man, Any Interest that I can pretend to have, Is with Some and they very few of my Superior Officers, and that only from a long Service, and attention to my duty, And they Very Probably have nearer Conections of their own[.] You may be sure that I would Reather be in an old Regiment than in a young one, For I should neither like half pay nor being out of the Army In which you know that I have Spent all my life; And that was the Reason I came with Reluctancy into your Regiment & forsaw that Erskine,[96] who was by much the oldest Major in the Service would soon be made a Lieu.[tt] Collonell, And altho' every one told me that my going into your Regiment would not preclude me in the 26th, I thought otherwise and the Consequence Showed that I did not Judge wrong; A very little after Sir Robert Arnotts[97] being made Major of the 26th, Morris of the 2[d98] Dyed upon which I wrote to the Duke of Bedford, and should have been very glad to have got it, Altho' that I knew that Generall Montagu was against it, But I likewise was Certain, That if I had got it, that I was by no

248

means Disagreeable to Generall Montague otherwise I would not have asked for it, Besides everything at that time in your Regiment Conduced to make me very much Discontented; Leaving a Regiment that I can say without any great Vanity I had a Considerable hand in the Breeding up, A Major being made in it to which I thought I had a better Tittle, Your Regiment to which I was Major Turned out into the Barrack Yeard, and all the Best men picked out of it, I many times wished to God that I had never seen nor heard of it, But now Sir those Impressions are wore off, And as I have the Good will and Friendship of you and Collonell Windus, I thinck myself very happy, much more so than going into a Regiment where it may happen at least for Sometime that I should have the Ill will and dislike of my Collonel, Lieu^{tt} Collonel and all the Officers, And which some time or other Probably I must have to go through for your Regiment cannot be supposed to Stand a long time. And now Sir that I have write you the Reall State of my mind, I shall acquaint you with the only Vew or Scheme that I have formed, which is that if I have your Consent, To go to Dublin in the Beginning of Jany for a fortnight or Three weeks—In order to Show those that I have the Honour of being Known to, that I am not Dead; Besides I want to have some Conversation with you in Relation to your Regiment, In Many Particulars of which I shall be greatly at a Loss till I know your Sentiments ...

JRL, B2/1/268

186

Lieutenant Francis Flood to Colonel Samuel Bagshawe

Limerick
5 February 1762

I hope you will pardon me for being so often troublesome to you but being lately inform'd that the purchase I lately made with Capt^t Joass in regard to his Comp^y has not gone forward although my money has been lodged four Months ago, I must beg lave to take the liberty of Asureing you that it has been a very unexpressable disappointment to me, for had I not been under an ingagement with Capt Joass, I co^d have got with great ease a Company in one of the New Reg^{ts} as may apeer by a letter I lately received from the Lord Chief Justice. As my Chief Study has been to act in all particulars agreeable to you, and as I have been ever ready since I have had the honour of Serveing under you, to do every thing for the good and service of your Reg^t haveing always a strict attention to my duty, wch the several Commanding Officers can tell you, I therefore hope you will be so good as to recommend me to the Speaker & to my relations who are in the House of Commons (as you shall find I have deserved) as you may guess my disapointment has been very hard on me and wch must ever lay me under the greatest obligation to you, And which shall be ever remmembered with the highest Sence of Respect and Gratitude ...

JRL, B2/1/304

187

Major Robert Preston to Colonel Samuel Bagshawe

Limerick
23 February 1762

When I wrote last to you I was so Perplexed with the orders I had Receved to send all the Companys of your Regiment out of Town except one, That I did not know what to do with one hundred and Twenty Recruits that I had here in this town, and so I ordered them all to their Respective Comp^{ys}[,] But Collonel Windus's Letter that I receved last Post has Revived me by letting me know that you are permitted to have in this Town in Numbers to the amount of Three Companys[,] one in the Barracks and two in the town, This gives an opportunity of carrying on the exercise of your Reg^{tt} upon the Scheme almost that I had formed which was for me to go to Clare Castle with the recruits of the four Companys at Gort and Clare, And Collonel Windus with the Adjutant with the Recruits of the other five Companys here, My going away Breaks this a little but not much.

My Scheme is one which if you approve of may easily be put in Execution, Clare Castle which I know well, having been Quartred a year in it, is by much the best Place in Ireland for Breeding Recruits in, It is two miles from a Town, and there is a Wall Round the Barracks to hinder men from going out at night, It will hold all your Recruits extreamly well, Therefor I would take the two Comp^ys that are there just now up to the Town and Send the Adjutant with all the Recruits down to Clare Castle, Collonel Windus will have the Serjeant Major and Serj^tt North the Clerk with him in this Town, And when he goes to see what the Adjutant is doing with the Recruits he will have but 18 measured miles to ride ... or if he wants the Adjutant, to send in the afternoon for him, he will be with him by the time he rises.

***

I have receved Great Complaints from the Comp^y at Dingle against the Serjeant and his Wife[.] I have ordered Poor Ellis when he can get time to go there and Inquire into them, If the half of them be true I would have wrote to you for [an] order to Reduce that Serjeant to the Ranks—for I would not have given him the Honor of a Court Martial ...

JRL, B2/1/313

188

Lieutenant Francis Flood to Colonel Samuel Bagshawe

Ross Castle
28 February 1762

I am realy Ashamed to be so often troublesome to you but as you have been hitherto particularly kind to me, imboldens me to ask a favour, I have been lately Married to a young Lady in the

County of Clare, with the Consent of my Father and friends, and have got a pretty good fortune. I was but five days in the County Clare and my time was so short that I cou.^d not settle halve the business that was necessary on such an occasion. I have not been absent from the Regiment these twelve Months, and if you wo.^d be so kind to give me lave of Absence only for a fortnight I shall ever greatfully acknowlage your goodness, as the Major will not admitt me without your aprobation ... I must intreat your answer by next post ...

JRL, B2/1/314

189

Colonel Samuel Bagshawe to the Right Hon. William Garrard

[Draft]   Dublin
                                                                  4 March 1762

This last year 218 Men were culled and taken from the 93.^d Reg.^t under my Command in a very unprecedented manner. This year the whole Reg.^t is to be incorporated with another Reg.^t going on foreign Service, There is something so particular in this Treatment as must bring a dishonourable Reflection upon the Reg.^t from those who do not know the Corps but from those that Do and [know] that I am the Eldest Colonel of Foot on this Establishment & of course the first to be ordered on Service, the Disgrace will fall on me; I have ever served the Crown of GB faithfully & well & am not conscious that I deserve any Mark of Contempt or Displeasure[,] Indeed if the abilities of a soldier lies in his Heels I confess I am wanting but His Majesty's Service has not yet Suffered either by my hands or by my Head, I therefore beseech you will please move H. Ex.^y [the] Ld L.^t that I am willing and desirous to be employed, [that] I & my Officers may go on Service with the Reg.^t or that this Draught may not be made

in a manner which must cover me with a shame and Disgrace
~~which I think I have no way deserved~~ ...[99]

JRL, B2/1/316

190

Major Robert Preston to Colonel Samuel Bagshawe

Limerick
[7] March 1762

By last nights post I receved an order to go Directly to Cork,
which you know I have been Expecting for this some time.

All my Schemes and all my Pains about your Regiment is
gone to the Devill[,] But God be Thanked I can begin again—
after a few oaths that I gave last night I find myself quite easy,
When I was an Adjutant I had twice the Modling of the 26[th.]
Reg[tt.], and why not now as Major have twice the Modling of the
93[d.], I am both Ready & Willing, it is my Superiors Business to
Command[,] It is mine to obey—Windus comes now in for his
Share of the Trouble, He went great game with me upon his
arrivall telling me that like an old Soldier he came in when all
the Trouble was over, I am sorry that he has now the Joke
against him, and should have been very well pleased to have
shared it with him in assisting him ...

JRL, B2/1/319

191

Lieutenant-Colonel Edward Windus to Colonel
Samuel Bagshawe

Limerick
7 March 1762

You have Struck me Dumb, & I have not one Word to
say, except that I am no longer to be Surpris'd at anything.

I shall not be able to make a pun for a Month to Come, hey ho!

The Order being issued, I am persuaded you won't be able to prevail upon the Gov.^t to send us as a Corps, in that case they must reverse the present Order, & give another, for we as well as the 2 Reg^{ts}. Order'd to Portugal, would want a great Many Draughts no doubt, None of y.^r Officers however, but must approve of your Remonstrance.

I beg you will procure me a Copy of the Order for the Manner we are to give our Men, whether with Cloathing or not, We have such a Number of Recruits, furnished w.th Necessaries, that our Captains will suffer greatly, I hope we are not to Compleat our Men w.th Necessaries, for having more than Compleated & now inlisting to make good our Desertions, we cannot be supposed to have any Stock purse, nor would I Acknowledge that we had any, & it becomes now so absolutely necessary to Make up the Accounts with the Utmost Expedition, & divide what may be in the Agents hands, I wou'd give him Orders to say he has none but is advancing Money to Carry on the Recruiting business.

***

I wish you may soon be able to inform me, what is to become of us after we have parted with our Men, & where we are to be quartered, That we may fix upon the head Quarter, where the Major, the Adjutant, & I will be to form & Discipline the Recruits as they come up, for I do suppose we shall be order'd to recruit as the 5 young Corps are.[100]

I suppose we shall be favor'd with Lt Governor Molesworth's Comp^y again at Corke, where he will be much more Disagreeable if possible than heretofore ...

JRL, B2/1/320

192

Lieutenant-Colonel Edward Windus to Colonel Samuel Bagshawe

Cork
19 March 1762

You need not doubt my inclination to give the Bad as well as the Good men, but what will that avail when some body (perhaps the L.ᵗ Gov.ʳ) will come down & pick out such only, as he & the Commanding Officers of Armstrong's[101] & Blayney's,[102] shall think fit for the Service they are going on, especially when they know three other Reg.ᵗˢ have 200 Voluntiers each ready for them to make up their Numbers, & I shall be told he has instructions from the Gov.ᵗ so to do, what in such Case, will all I can Urge avail?

We shall be at a very great Loss & the Greatest Confusion if you do not Order every Officer here, for without them we cannot settle the Accounts of the Comp.ˢ ...As soon as Montgomery Sends us an Account of the Noneffectives, we will put it in such Order, as will permit us to make a Distribution without Censure, w.ᶜʰ I think can very well be done now, having fill'd up Draughts, Deaths, Deserters & Discharged, within 19, w.ᶜʰ is more than Compleating the Reg.ᵗ[.] I beg you will hurry Montgomery with the Account, & don't let the Charges for Recruits, & for Subsistence of Recruiting Parties be blended together, if it be possible to avoid it.

I hope you or Montgomery will be able to send me a Copy of the Instructions given to the Person who superintends the Embarkation that I may know his power ...

I am told many men are very bare of Necessaries, & as we have a great many Recruits, many are in Debt, & we shall have many make away with their Necessaries, before they are Draughted, and it will be out of our power to Compleat them as the Captains will sustain a sufficient loss already. Yet if Molesw.ᵗʰ comes down, he will order them (as he did before) to be Compleated to the Regimental order, & tell me to take it out of the Stock purse, but I shall let him know we have no such thing, having more than Compleated to the Establishment, & the Captains can't do it out of their pay. I foresee we shall have some Squabbling, but I will have good Authority for it, if I comply with any Order to Compleat Necessaries ...

In my last, I mention'd L.ᵗ Flood's Applications to me, for leave of Absence from his Comp.ʸ of Light Infantry, that was then at Ross Castle, He was indeed at that time, from under my Command, however, in [the] Absence of Cap.ᵗ Schuyler (who came here to follow his private pursuits) he took leave and was seen at Ennis, by Blayney's Reg.ᵗ & I believe he will not march in with the Comp.ʸ of Light Infantry w.ᶜʰ is to be here tomorrow, if so, I shall when he comes, put him under an Arrest ...

Inclos'd I send you a Return of the State of the Reg.ᵗ as it was the 1s.ᵗ June, & as it was when we march'd from Limerick, w.ᶜʰ shews that we wanted only 1 man of being Compleat to 630 rank & file, & that we have by that means fill'd up all our Deserters which is more than Compleating ...

JRL, B2/1/323

193

Lieutenant-Colonel Edward Windus to Colonel Samuel Bagshawe

Cork
21–23 March 1762

You would be agreeably Surpris'd to find by my last, that I have made it out only One Man wanting to Compleat to 630 rank & file before we were Order'd to March to Corke; in Order to do it, I have included all I knew were inlisted, tho' not yet join'd, w.ᶜʰ will answer to the Return sent up to Gov.ᵗ of 46 inlisted since last fortnights Return, but in one part of my Letter, I believe it is Call'd 19 wanting, w.ᶜʰ is a Mistake. We have many Deserters & a few before the 14.ᵗʰ but I have made it appear as if none had, that we may show as Compleat as possible in case you show it to

Lord Rothes; & all our Deserters, I shall Contrive to have gone off since we were Order'd to march here.

Mar 23rd

The Above should have gone last post, but having no more to say then, I waited 'till this, to Acquaint you, That Colonel Armstrong this day told me he thought it best to take our Men as soon as we can give them, & desired to receive them, if Convenient on Thursday, wch being very Agreable to us, it is to be so Order'd. He wanted only to take such as are fit for Immediate Service, but I reminded him of the Tenor of the Order, wch runs, To deliver all our Men, so he is to take them all at present, & he writes by this post to Ld Rothes to let him know he Apprehends, there are some too young, & perhaps some too old for immediate service, & to beg to know what is to be done with them, so I apprehend will shall be Obliged to receive some back again.

He has demanded Arms, Accoutrements & Cloathing, & as they should indeed have been Cloathed long ago, it is the opinion of Severall Field Officers here, That we must Cloath them, nor Can it be refused, wch I am very sorry for, if you can get off this Article, we must have Authority to receive our Cloathing from them.

I shall in the Mean time take a Receipt for such a number of Men, Arm'd, accout^d and Cloath'd, specifying What Arms, Accout^{mts} & Cloathing they take, which I believe will answer all you desire.

I am glad this business will be done, at least I hope so, before Molesworth's arrival, & hope he won't afterwards take upon him to order us to provide them with Necessaries, wch is not at present talked of.

I want to know what is to become of us, wch I dare say you will find out soon, & let us know ...

JRL, B2/1/324

194
Lieutenant-Colonel Edward Windus to Colonel Samuel Bagshawe

Cork
28 March 1762

As you don't say when Molesworth is to be here, I am in hopes the Draught will be over before he comes, & as Colonel Armstrong expects an Answer from Lord Rothes by to morrow Night's post, I believe he will give Orders next day for our giving the Draughts on Wednesd^y ... He has told me to show him what men I please, meaning to do it in the most agreable manner ... so that I can't see how we can possibly Disagree, especially as you now think, Sickness, too much Age, or too much youth, are reasonable Objections to his taking men; if you had intimated this before, & not bid me stick to the Letter of the Order, in giving all our men, I assure you the Draught would have been over last tuesday, & now I can tell Colonel Armstrong he need not wait for Lord Rothes's Answer, 'tho I suppose he won't proceed now 'till he gets it.

***

Lt Flood came here last night, & I have Order'd him in Arrest, he wanted much to get off, but I told him he must make his Application to you, for I had acquainted you with it, & I would not do any thing in it, 'till I hear from you, for I did not know but you might report him to Ld Rothes, if this does not have a good effect upon his future Conduct, I don't know any thing that will. I have Order'd him to make up the Accounts of Capt Joass's Comp^y & pay the ballance.

***

JRL, B2/1/327

195

Lieutenant Francis Flood to Colonel Samuel Bagshawe

Cork
28 March 1762

Sir

I took the liberty some time ago to write to you from Killarny to beg you wo.^d admitt me to go to Ennis for a few days, & before I co.^d receive an Answer from you I rec.^d a letter from Ennis to let me know that my Wife was very ill, wch you may naturally suppose allarm'd me vastly, & wch oblidged me to lave Killarny, before I had the pleasure of hearing from you, in the mean while the Comp.^y rec.^d orders to march unknown to me, and when I heard it, I immediately set of for Quarters and arrived here in Six days after the Comp.^y had march'd into Town. Upon my Arrival here Lt Coll. Windus order'd me in Arrest for not Marching into Town with the Comp.^y I, understanding I had acted wrong, made Coll. Windus an apology wch he wo.^d not except of, as he said he had reported me to you and waited your Answer. I therefore take the liberty to intreat you'll be so good as to except of my apology, as it is the first Crime of that nature I have commited since I have had the honour of being in your Reg.^t and which shall be the last favour of that Nature I shall trouble you for again. Your kindness shall be ever acknowladged by him who is with the greatest respect

Sir,
Your Obliged and
Obed.^t humb.^{le} Servt
Fra.^s Flood

JRL, B2/1/328

196

Lieutenant-Colonel Edward Windus to Colonel Samuel Bagshawe

Cork
4 April 1762

I find Col. Armstrong had rec.^d an order, wch Contradicted the first, & left him at Liberty to make the Draught as he thought best for the Service he is going on, He therefore pick'd out of our Reg.^t only 297, & took all the Voluntiers from Adlercrons, Sr Ralph Gore's, & all but 12 of Strodes, so it Can't possibly be look'd upon, that all the rest of ours, are too Old & too young for immediate Service, for we have a great many still fit for it, but I do suppose they will lose many by Desertion, just before Embarkation ...[and] we are the Reg.^t to furnish the number to make them Compleat, I suppose, indeed we have many rather too young & weak at present, but I dont think we have 20 too Old.

I am persuaded Col. Armstrong did not write that we had many too Old but that he apprehended there might be some so, & some too young, & to beg he might be at Liberty to Chuse such as were the fittest for Immediate Service. He was looking for me, to show me what he did write, but not seeing me that night, he told me to that Effect next day. Another thing pray take Notice of, several who were neither too Old, or too Young, were not thought fit, on Account of being Pox'd, & others having sore Legs, which are often hidden disorders for they don't Acquaint the Surgeon with these things for fear of Confinement in an Hospl.. We are very busy at present Making up the Mens Accounts that leave us, & settling the Taylors Accounts, & several Accounts of the Companies, but I shall as soon as possible send you a Return such as you want.

If we are Dispers'd: it will (as it has done) occasion great Confusion in the Accounts, for want of Officers fit to Command Companies, & we shall have but very few that know (exclusive of keeping Accounts) how to Command in a Quarter remote from the head Quarters ... I could wish we could get into the

Barracks here, after the Regiments embark & Continue here the next Year, I think this can't be refus'd. If we must return to Limerick, I hope we shall be indulg'd with Barracks, for except a very few Old men, we are in the situation of Poles,[103] having mostly Recruits Undisciplin'd, & this has thrown us vastly behind hand. As to Old men, Seabrights[104] w[ch] is look'd upon to be as good a Reg[t] as any in Ireland, has more than we, before Handasyd's went to Dublin Gabbet[105] avow'd to me, they had 100 Old men in the Reg[t], look at the Cameronians & you will find many more than we have, & few Reg[ts] so few ... I really think this is a very Critical time for You to Struggle for us & to make a point of our being together in Barracks, & Considering the treatment of your Regiment, I think they Can't avoid Complying with so reasonable (& I may say so fashionable) a request, all the young Regiments being so indulg'd & they have as many old Officers as we shall have, & full as good Non Com[d] Officers. I have made a great Change in the latter, many being Unfitt for it, I have brought them to a Court Martial, w[ch] has Authoris'd me to reduce them, & I have made others, so that we now have scarcely a Corporal fit to make a Serjeant left.

**

JRL, B2/1/333,334

197

Lieutenant-Colonel Edward Windus to Colonel Samuel Bagshawe

Cork
18 April 1762

... As we can't set about Recruiting for a Considerable time, & are Order'd to do it, to replace the Drafts, The Growing stock purse will be full Sufficient to Answer the business of Recruiting, & all other Charges that ought to come out of it, & that Fund will be better than if Armstrongs and Blayneys were to pay us for the Drafts, as to the Arms and Accoutrements lost by

Desertion, I presume the Government will make you an Allowance for the One & give an Order to replace the Other. If any thing is to fall upon the Captains, I hope it will only be on those, whose Negligence deserves it, which I am sure must be your Intention.

When all the Charges are made on the Non effective Fund it will be greatly Reduced, & the Ballance to be Divided will be a mere trifle, or I am much mistaken. As to the Article of Cloathing, it was absolutely Necessary to Cloath every body to show them at the time of Draughting, not knowing who, or what they would be Oblig'd to take, or who you would Discharge. But we shall take the New Cloaths from such I suppose, when Discharged. I think it was a severe thing indeed to Order Y.^r New Cloaths to be given with the Draughts, but you must be Allow'd for them, there can be no Doubt. I wish we were in Barracks. I am at a Constant Expence of hiring a Lodging, for no Billet will do for the Commanding Officer of a Regim.^t

***

JRL, B2/1/338

198

The Memorial of Lieutenant Francis Flood

[Copy]   [Cork]
                                                      21 May 1762

To His Excie. the Earl of Halifax Lord Lieutenant General & General Governor of Ireland[106]

The Memorial of Lieutenant Francis Flood of His Majesty's Ninety Thirde Regiment of Foot Commanded by Colonel Samuel Bagshawe.

Sheweth that your Memorialist presumes humbly to lay before your Excellency that about Eight Months Since a Vacancy of a Company being Expected in the said Regiment by Captain

Alexander Joass' Declaration of his Intention to Sell out, the
Purchase was Offer'd to the two Lieutenants Immediately
preceeding your Memorialist in Seniority, who both thought
proper to decline it, that Colonel Bagshawe did then Offer it to
your Memorialist in his turn who Agree'd, And depositing the
Money in the hands of M.ʳ Montgomery the Agent, waited four
Months with great Impatience daily expecting Cap.ᵗ Joass would
obtain Liberty to Sell. That your Memorialist had Scarce
withdrawn his Money from M.ʳ Montgomery, when Colonel
Bagshawe inform'd him by Letter that the Company was ready
for him and required him to Lodge the Money, with which
request your Memorialist was taking the most expeditious
means to comply being only retarded by the difficulty of selling
his Lieutenancy for which however he has made an Agreement
and is now ready to pay in the Money. But that Colonel Bagshawe
after the many Inconveniences to which your Memorialist has
been Exposed in the Transaction of this Matter particularly that
of Neglecting to make Use of the Interest of his Friends with
your Excellency for a Company in the new Levies, has at length
signified to your Memorialist his pleasure that Lieutenant Ellis
one of those Gentlemen who Eight Months ago had absolutely
rejected the Purchase shall now have the Company. Your
memorialist takes the Liberty of representing to your Excie. that
his Behaviour in the Regiment has always been Unexception-
able, and for this appeals to the Judgment of his Brother
Officers that his Conduct can Stand the Test of Even the
Severity of those Rules which the Wisdom of the Legislator has
thought proper to Establish as the Sole Measure of Obedience
of an Officer and a Gentleman, and flyes to your Excies.
Protection Humbly hopeing that your Excie. will not Suffer such
an Infringement of that Regulation which has so long Govern'd
in the Sale and Purchase of Commissions to be made in
Prejudice of your Memorialist who without the Interposition
of your Excies. Authority is Strongly Apprehensive of being
severely Injured in this Affair ...

JRL, B2/1/356

199

Major Robert Preston to Colonel Samuel Bagshawe

Cork
30 May 1762

Since my last to you I have Receved two of Yours In Relation to
Mr Flood, That young man gives me more Plague than all the
rest of your Officers, He came to me upon Saturday was eight
days [ago] and told me his Wife was to be at Charleville upon
Tuesday and begged that I would give him leave to go out and
meet her, And I like an Idiot believed what he told me, Tho' I
might have known him better[,] But being a Complesant man to
Ladys I told him that as the young Lady was not accoustomed to
Travelling he might go forward to Limerick and Bring her all
the Road, and that he was to be here at furthest on Thursday,
But this day is Sunday and he is not arrived[,] he will be here
this night for I saw a Gentleman who spoke to him upon the Road,
So soon as he arrives I shall demand a Sight of his Memoriall
and send you a Copy of it[.] I in my last told you that I heard of
his having sent one to the Lords Justices, The Contents of it I
could not Learn, for the Man that told me of it would not so
much as look at the Memorial, I hope Mr Flood will not be so
wrong headed as to refuse me a Sight of it, which very Probably
he may, but you shall hear of it by Tuesdays Post ...

JRL, B2/1/359

200

Major Robert Preston to Colonel Samuel Bagshawe

Cork
1 June 1762

As I wrote you in my Last that Lieu^tt Flood would be in Town
upon Sunday night[,] he and his Wife too did arrive but I
did not see him till yesterday, When I let him know how

unbecoming a Soldier his behaviour was, And was obliged to Convince him to Read him the Articles of War, I told him that he must Show me a Copey of the Memoriall he sent Which he Sayd he would endeavour to do, but that he was not sure if he had a Copey of it, It was past seven this night befor he Brought me a Copey of what I Inclose to you[.] If there be nothing more than that which he gave to me it is absolute nonsense. There is a complaint against you hinted for the Retarding the Sale of Joass's Comp.[y], and likewise not a fair Representation of the Fact of the Alteration of Circumstances of poor Ellis, There is likewise a Call for a Character from your Officers, If he means the Head Officers of your Regiment, He is Damnably Mistaken, at least for me and I can say the same for your Lieu.[tt] Collonel— Whereas was Ellis to Call for a Character I should very readily say what I know to be true that he is a Dilligent Carefull Officer in the Station that he is in, Tho I do not thinck him fitt to Command Armys, You cannot Imagine what Pleasure it gives me that You have taken a Care of that Man ...

JRL, B2/1/363

201

Major Robert Preston to Colonel Samuel Bagshawe

Cork
13 June 1762

D.[r] Collonel Do you Imagine that if I had heard of any Officer in the Regiment using any expressions unbecoming, that I would have Passed it over, you would have heard it from me by letting you know that such an officer in your Regiment was in arrast, I am Constantly with the Officers of the Regiment[,] I hope they Like me, I am sure they do not Choose to offend me, And they know the sure way to do that is to give their Tongues too much Liberty—from which you may be sure that whatever Libertys they gave themselves it was not before me, But Sir it was out of their Power to say any thing before me, for no Sooner your Letter came to Flood, by which your Desings was known, That very same Day I let every one in the Coffee house know the whole of the Matter, Youngkers I do not deal with, Severall others Who I told all the matter to asked me if Ellis was a near Relation of yours, When I assured them that you had never heard off or seen the Man till he was in your own Reg.^{tt} They told me it was very extraordinary, and from them you have all the Praise that such a good action Requires, Flood when he got your Letter came to me and show'd it me, he sayed that you had not used him well, I did Indeavour to Convince him that to the Contrary you wrote a very kind letter to him, and told him that I hope he did not put himself in a Rank as an Officer with Ellis, But I believe he thincks Differently[,] he knows that he can Dance better than Ellis and can run in Debt better, He sayed to me that he Imagined that Collonel Windus had Write to you to his Disadavantage, I told him that I was affraid that Windus had not, But I assured him that if I had at that time Commanded the Regiment I would as my Duty Required me have acquainted you that he had twice left his Command without Leave, which I thought one of the greatest faults an Officer could be guilty of, When I sent for him to give me a Copey of his Memoriall, I let him know that all the Chief Justices[107] on earth had no Influence upon a Court Martiall, That he might have Interest to prevent the Sentence being put in Execution but that the world would see he had acted Contrary to the Articles of War, he sayed he did not know it, I told him I was the proper person for him to Consult with, and not the Young Boys that knew nothing, But I find that those young People thinck we old ones fools ...

JRL, B2/1/368

Major Robert Preston to Colonel Samuel Bagshawe

Cork
20 June 1762

I am very Sorry your Indisposition still Continues, I was in hopes that it would have been over Long ago, I beg that you will give yourself no Trouble in Writing to me except when you have Directions to send me.

You will see by the last Return that I had given Lieu.^{tt} Flood Leave to go to Kilkenny, he returned that night I last wrote you, and the next day he came and Delivered the Origional Memoriall that he had sent to the Lord Chief Justice to Transmit to the Lord Lieutenant, The Lord Chief Justice knew better than to send it, When he delivered it to me, I told him that I hoped for the future, that when he had an Inclination to write Memorialls, that he would Advise with People who knew the Service reather than with those that knew nothing of the matter, The getting that Memoriall gives me great Pleasure, As Severall of the Youngsters in the Reg^{tts} here did not thinck that Flood was in the Wrong—but his delivering it to me by his Uncles advise will I hope Convince them, as it has done Flood that he acted by Bad advice ...

When you are quite well I beg you will write me what you pay for your Soldiers Hatts, My Reason for Desiring this is, That the Hatts that came with the Cloathing are extreamly bad, and I believe I can put you on a way to be fully as Cheap served with much Better Hatts, The other day going into a Hatter in this Town to buy a Hatt for myself I had some Conversation with him upon the Badness of our Soldiers Hatts, He pulled out a Cargo of Hatts which he sayd he sold at Two and Two pence, Which he assured me would Stand the Cock and not Scabb as our Soldiers Hats do, and he likewise said that the Collonels paid to Page the Hatter at Dublin two and eight Pence for their Soldiers Hatts, I bought one of those Hatts which I have put on a Corporal's Head, So that I will know whether his Hatts be as good as he says they are ...

JRL, B2/1/371

203

Major Robert Preston to Colonel Samuel Bagshawe

Cork
20 July 1762

I am Extreamly Sorry that your Indisposition Increases And that you are obliged to go to Bath, I hope that the Waters there will soon Recover you that we may have you back again, I alwise wish that the Head of a Regiment should be near to it, It is much easier to follow directions than to give them, But besides that the Regard I have for you, makes me have a great feeling in any thing that affects you.

***

As to our Review we have a great number of Sick men, many that have sore legs which were we in Barracks I could soon get Cured, So that I do not think I will be able to show much above thirty file, Those can do any thing Generall Boscawen[108] has a mind to have them do, They can Exercise very well, They can march extreamly well both by the Slow and the Quick Step, Indeed our Quick step differs from other Regiments for we do not lift our feet and put them down in the same place but step full out, And as to firing I do not doubt but we will do that very well, I am at Present busy accoustoming them to it, the men dress very Tollerably and have plenty of necessarys, As to numbers that is not your fault, so I expect to make a very fine review. As to accoutrements we have more than we have men—I wish we could get Recruits as fast as we could get Accoutrements.

***

JRL, B2/1/388

204

Michael Crane, King's Apothecary, to Sir James Caldwell, Bart.

London
5 August 1762

...I receivd a letter from Mrs Bagshaw from Gloucester on the way to Bath, giving a very bad account of the Colonel; I find it a disease of the Liver, and I fear a Total breaking up of the constitution, I have desired he would try Bath water in small quantities, and under the inspection of Dr Maisey & if he thinks it will be of use to consult any body here, & will send the case, I will advise with whomsoever they shall approve, tho I think those waters most likely to mend his stomach, & without that is bro^t into better case, neither medecine can relieve nor food nourish...

JRL, B2/3/401

205

The Memorial of Mrs Catherine Bagshawe

[Draft]   [Bromley, 1763]

To the King's most excellent Majesty

The humble Memorial of [Catherine] Bagshaw Widow[.] Your Memorialist begs leave to represent that her late Husband [Samuel] Bagshaw Esqr was thirty years an officer in your majesty's Army

That he had the Command of a Company at the Invasion of the Coast of Bretaigny in France, and at port l'Orient being the very last in the Retreat he had the misfortune to lose his Leg which was Shot off by a Cannon Ball above the Knee, no other person in that expedition receiving a wound except himself, his misfortune owing to his being the very last in the Retreat.

That being still unwilling to quit the Service he purchased

the Commission of Lieutenant Colonel in the Thirty ninth Regiment; and when that Regiment was ordered to the East Indies, he chose rather to go with it than to accept of any Government or other Advantages at home, many offers of which were made him but he chose rather to do the duty of his Post in the farther Service of your Majesty and his Country.

That he continued in the East Indies above three years, and by the Fatigues he underwent and the unwholesomeness of the Climate he had the farther misfortune of totally losing the sight of one of his Eyes and greatly impairing the other; his Health was also greatly impaired and his Constitution broken. At this time he was the oldest Lieutenant Colonel in Ireland, from his Rank Services and Sufferings he had the greatest Reason to expect to be preferred to an old Regiment, and he might have even sold his Lieutenant Colonelcy for £5,000 yet he was so zealous in the Publick Cause that when an Invasion of Ireland was apprehended in the year 1759 he raised and accoutred a Regiment intirely at his own Expence having applyed for and obtained his late Majesty's permission so to do notwithstanding his bad state of Health made it highly improbable that he should live long enough to derive the advantages from his Command which might have made it eligible in a private view.

The Fatigue that he suffered in raising and disciplining the new Regiment totally exhausted the Small Remains of his Health which the Hardships he had endured, the wounds he had received, & the unwholesome Climate he served in had left him, and after languishing in a hopeless decay he at length died worn out in the Service of a premature Old Age on the 23^{d} of September 1762 in his Journey from Bath to London.

Your Memorialist most humbly Represents that the Sum for which his Lieutenant Colonelcy would have sold for being 5,000 added to the £3,000 which he expended in raising and accoutreing his Regiment make a neat Loss upon his Death to his Family of no less than £8,000 which is more Severely felt as he fell himself a Sacrifice to his zeal for the Service and left your Memorialist with five Orphans in a great degree unprovided for, an Estate in Derbyshire upon which they all depend being very greatly incumbered, by the Colonel's necessary Expences & by a vexatious Lawsuit which was commenced against him by one Newton who took advantage of his being abroad in the East Indies to distress his family and perplex his Affairs.

Your Memorialist therefore most humbly hopes that your Majesty will be most graciously pleased to take the Case of herself and Orphans into your royal Consideration.[109]

JRL, B3/16/130

Notes

Full publication details are given at the first mention of a particular book or article. In subsequent references an abbreviated citation is given where appropriate. Unless otherwise expressed, the place of publication is London.

Abbreviations

BJRL	*Bulletin of the John Rylands University Library of Manchester*
DNB	*Dictionary of National Biography*
DRO	Dorset Record Office
JRL	John Rylands University Library of Manchester
JSAHR	*Journal of the Society for Army Historical Research*
NAM	National Army Museum, London
NLI	National Library of Ireland, Dublin
PRO. SP	Public Record Office, State Papers
PRO. WO	Public Record Office, War Office Papers
PRONI	Public Record Office of Northern Ireland

Notes to the Introduction

1 R. Sedgwick, ed., John, Lord Hervey, *Some Materials towards Memoirs of the Reign of King George II* (1931), II, p. 525.
2 For the history of anti-army feeling in Britain see L. G. Schwoerer, *No Standing Armies! The Anti-army Ideology in Seventeenth Century England* (Baltimore and London, 1974) *passim* and A. J. Guy, *Oeconomy and Discipline: Officership and Administration in the British Army 1714–63* (Manchester, 1985), pp. 3–9.
3 I. Roy, 'The Profession of Arms' in W. Prest ed. *The Professions in Early Modern England* (1987), pp. 181–219, *passim*; J. Childs, *The British Army of William III, 1689–1702* (Manchester, 1987), pp. 69–73.
4 C. T. Atkinson, *The Dorsetshire Regiment* (Oxford, 1947), I, *passim*.

5 F. G. James, *Ireland in the Empire 1688–1770* (Cambridge (Mass.), 1973), pp. 177–78.

6 Guy, *Oeconomy and Discipline*, pp. 9–10, 35.

7 J. W. Hayes, 'The Military Papers of Colonel Samuel Bagshawe 1713–62', *Bulletin of the John Rylands University Library of Manchester*, XXXIX (1956–57), p. 372.

8 Recruiting policy in Ireland is examined by K. P. Ferguson, 'The Army in Ireland from the Restoration to the Act of Union', unpublished PhD Thesis, Trinity College Dublin (1980), pp. 68–75 and R. B. McDowell, *Ireland in the Age of Imperialism and Revolution 1760–1801* (Oxford, 1979), pp. 59–62.

9 Hayes, 'Bagshawe Papers', pp. 365–66; McDowell, op. cit., p. 62.

10 Atkinson, op. cit., pp. 39–40. As it was, only 100 rank and file embarked for Ireland; the remainder had either died or transferred into the independent companies serving in Jamaica.

11 J. A. Houlding, *Fit for Service: The Training of the British Army 1715–1795* (Oxford, 1981), pp. 4–98.

12 For exceptions to this rule, see Guy, *Oeconomy and Discipline*, note 39, p. 134.

13 J. W. Hayes, 'Lieutenant-Colonel and Major Commandants of the Seven Years' War', *Journal of the Society for Army Historical Research*, XXXVI (1958), pp. 3–13; A. J. Guy, 'Drafts for Portugal, 1762: Recruiting for Rank at the End of the Seven Years' War', *Annual Report of the National Army Museum* (1977–78), pp. 29–34.

14 PRO. SP63/416/253 John, Duke of Bedford, Lord Lieutenant of Ireland, to William Pitt, 18 December 1759.

15 JRL, B2/3/841 Lieutenant-Colonel Samuel Bagshawe to Sir Robert Wilmot, 17 October 1758.

16 J. W. Hayes, 'The Social and Professional Background of the Officers of the British Army, 1714–1763', unpublished MA thesis, University of London (1956), pp. 120–25.

17 JRL, B2/1/35 Major Robert Preston to Colonel Samuel Bagshawe, 16 May 1762.

18 Samuel Bever, *The Cadet, A Military Treatise* (Dublin, 1756), p. 163.

19 Houlding, op. cit., p. 110.

20 Loc. cit.

21 Ibid, pp. 114–15.

22 P. E. Kopperman, 'Religion and Religious Policy in the British Army c1700–1796', *The Journal of Religious History* (forthcoming).

23 S. R. Frey, *The British Soldier in America: A Social History of Military Life in the Revolutionary Period* (Austin (Texas), 1981), pp. 48–50.

24 I am indebted to Mr C. H. Gordon for communicating some of his recent discoveries about 'the physical Gentlemen' in regimental practice. For the career of Dr Munro of Fort St. George, see H. H. Dodwell, *The Nabobs of Madras* (1926), pp. 113–14.

25 JRL, B2/5/4 Colonel Anthony Ladeveze to Lieutenant–Colonel Samuel Bagshawe, 31 January 1754; JRL, B2/5/49 'Officers of the 39th Reg^t of Foot by Companys' 28 March 1754. For some harsh criticism of surgeons' mates, see Frey, op. cit., p. 50.

26 Kirkland's commission as adjutant was dated 17 January 1760. At first, this was his only commission in the 93rd, but he was promoted lieutenant on 23 June 1762. He retained the adjutantcy, as was usual.

27 Guy, *Oeconomy and Discipline*, p. 62.

28 JRL, B2/2/393 Captain Thomas Levett to Lieutenant-Colonel Samuel Bagshawe, 21 March 1751.

29 These developments are examined by Guy, *Oeconomy and Discipline*, *passim* and J. L. Pimlott, 'The Administration of the British Army, 1783–1793', unpublished PhD thesis (University of Leicester, 1975). See also an important overview by N. Baker, 'Changing Attitudes toward Government in Eighteenth Century Britain' in A. Whiteman et al, *Statesmen, Scholars and Merchants: Essays in Eighteenth Century History presented to Dame Lucy Sutherland* (Oxford, 1973), pp. 202–19.

30 Guy, *Oeconomy and Discipline*, pp. 137–61.

31 For these developments, see J. Childs, *The Army of Charles II* (1976); *The British Army of William III, 1689–1702* (Manchester, 1987); C. Clay, *Public Finance and Private Wealth: The Career of Sir Stephen Fox, 1627–1716* (Oxford, 1978); R. E. Scouller, *The Armies of Queen Anne* (Oxford, 1966) and Guy, *Oeconomy and Discipline*.

32 Hayes, 'Bagshawe Papers', p. 364.

33 NAM 8707–48–1 'Journal of an Expedition to the East Indies, Commanded by Colonel John Adlercron ...', p. 1.

34 For a discussion of regimental agents, see Hayes, 'Bagshawe Papers', pp. 373–80; A. J. Guy, 'Regimental Agency in the British

Standing Army, 1715–1763' *BJRL*, LXII (1980), pp. 423–53, LXIII (1980), pp. 31–57 and 'Minions of Fortune: The Regimental Agents of Early Georgian England, 1714–63', *Army Museum '85*, National Army Museum (1986), pp. 31–42.

35 J. Childs, *Armies and Warfare in Europe 1648–1789* (Manchester, 1982), pp. 97–100; Roy, op. cit., p. 212; Houlding, op. cit., pp. 1–98.

36 Hayes, 'Social and Professional Background' p. 220; M. Odintz, 'Expertise in the Eighteenth Century British Officer Corps', unpublished seminar paper (University of Michigan, 1979). The 'military section' of Samuel Bagshawe's library at Ford included two copies of General Humphrey Bland's *A Treatise of Military Discipline* (London and Dublin, 1727 and later editions), a book identified as 'King William's Campaigns', evidently Brigadier-General Richard Kane's *Campaigns of King William and Queen Anne from 1689 to 1712* (1745 and 1747), two editions of Vauban's works on fortification (one in French), and a six-volume set of the Chevalier de Folard's *Sentiments d'un Homme de Guerre sur le Polybius*. The collection also included a copy of Henry Fielding's 'military' novel *Amelia* (1751); JRL, B15/3/17 'Catalogue of Books' [1751].

37 Hayes, 'Social and Professional Background'; 'Bagshawe Papers'; 'Scottish Officers in the British Army 1714–63', *Scottish Historical Review*, XXXVII (1958), pp. 25–57; 'Two Soldier Brothers of the Eighteenth Century', *JSAHR* XL (1962), pp. 150–61.

38 W. Coxe, *The Administration of the Right Honourable Henry Pelham* (1829), I, pp. 192–95.

39 J. Cannon, *Aristocratic Century: The Peerage of Eighteenth Century England* (London, 1984), pp. 119–20.

40 Hayes, 'Social and Professional Background', pp. 27–63, is excellent on the purchase system, as is A. P. C. Bruce, 'The System of Purchase and Sale of Commissions in the British Army and the Campaign for its Abolition', PhD Thesis (University of Manchester, 1973), pp. 62–127. This unpublished version of Dr Bruce's work is to be preferred to his book, *The Purchase System in the British Army 1660–1870* (1980) in which the eighteenth century material is somewhat condensed.

41 As usual, Hayes, 'Social and Professional Background', pp. 101–10,

is excellent on the issues of social status and feeling. See also Guy, *Oeconomy and Discipline*, pp. 165–68.

42 This topic is explored by A. N. Gilbert, 'Law and Honour among Eighteenth Century British Army Officers', *Historical Journal*, XIX (1976), pp. 75–87 and, on a European basis, by C. Duffy, *The Military Experience in the Age of Reason* (1987), pp. 74–80.

43 A. J. Guy, 'The Stubborn English Spirit: Officer Discipline and Resistance to Authority, 1727–1750', *Army Museum '83*, National Army Museum (1984), pp. 9–18.

44 D. E. Leach, *Roots of Conflict: British Armed Forces and Colonial Americans, 1677–1763* (Chapel Hill (NC) and London, 1986), *passim*.

45 The dismissive phrase is Major John Mompesson's; NAM 8707–48–1, Adlercron Journal, p. 13.

46 Modern treatments of the rank and file and their families can be found in Houlding, op. cit., pp. 116–37; S. R. Frey, *The British Soldier in America: A Social History of Military Life in the Revolutionary Period* (Austin (Texas), 1981); G. A. Steppler, 'The Common Soldier in the Reign of George III, 1760–1793', unpublished DPhil thesis (University of Oxford, 1984); P. E. Kopperman, 'The British High Command and Soldiers' Wives in America, 1755–1783', *JSAHR*, LX (1982), pp. 14–34.

47 Frey, op. cit., p. 137.

48 JRL, B2/2/221 Lieutenant Archibald Grant to Major Samuel Bagshawe, 26 February 1748.

49 Kopperman, 'Soldiers' Wives', p. 14. Steppler's treatment of the women is less sympathetic than Kopperman's, op. cit., pp. 105–12. Dr Duffy's approach is distinctly hostile, op. cit., pp. 127–28.

50 JRL, B2/3/753 Lieutenant-Colonel Samuel Bagshawe to Mr John Lodge of Halifax, October 1752.

51 Frey, op. cit., pp. 6–16; Steppler, op. cit., pp. 23–36.

52 Houlding, op. cit., p. 116.

53 Steppler is excellent on the mechanics of recruiting, op. cit., pp. 8–29. See also Guy, *Oeconomy and Discipline*, pp. 123–36.

54 Guy, 'Recruiting for Rank', pp. 32–34.

55 JRL, B2/4/96 Order for Drafts, 7 January 1744.

56 Drafting is discussed in detail by Houlding, op. cit., pp. 120–25 and Guy, *Oeconomy and Discipline* pp. 119–20, 126–27.

57 Houlding, op. cit., pp. 116–17.

58 Duffy, op. cit., pp. 151–266, provides an exhaustive account of the degrading influences of campaign and battle on an eighteenth century regiment.

59 S. H. F. Johnston, 'The Irish Establishment', *The Irish Sword: The Journal of the Military Historical Society of Ireland*, I (1949), pp. 33–36; Guy, *Oeconomy and Discipline*, p. 171.

60 Ferguson, 'The Army in Ireland', *passim*; 'Military Manuscripts in the Public Record Office of Ireland', *The Irish Sword*, XV (1982), pp. 112–115.

61 Hayes, 'Bagshawe Papers', pp. 365–73.

62 See the interesting account of a visit from 'the Fairies', who demolished enclosures and terrorized Protestant inhabitants, sent to Colonel Bagshawe by one of his Tallagh constituents; JRL, B15/1/38, Mr John Kirby of Tallowbridge to Bagshawe, 2 April 1762. Kirby insisted that the mob was organized by 'Irish officers in foreign service', and pleaded for military assistance.

63 James, op. cit., pp. 181–290.

64 JRL, B2/3/226 Lieutenant-Colonel Samuel Bagshawe to William Bagshawe of the Inner Temple, 10 February 1750.

65 JRL, B2/2/730 Lieutenant-Colonel Samuel Bagshawe to Mr Thomas Waite, Secretary to the Lords Justices of Ireland, 10 April 1753.

66 Sir James Caldwell's campaigns are summarized by J. B. Cunningham, *A History of Castle Caldwell and its Families*, (Belleek, 1980), pp. 56–58.

67 A. J. Guy, 'A Whole Army Absolutely Ruined in Ireland: Aspects of the Irish Establishment, 1715–1773', *Annual Report of the National Army Museum* (1978–79), pp. 30–43.

Notes to Part 1

1 Much of the information in this section is gleaned from W. H. G. Bagshawe, *The Bagshawes of Ford: A Biographical Pedigree*, London, (1886). Extra copies of the first hundred pages were printed in memory of Samuel Bagshawe's most famous ancestor, the Presbyterian divine William Bagshawe, the 'Apostle of the Peak'

(1628–1702); *A Memoir of William Bagshawe of Ford Hall, styled 'The Apostle of the Peak'* (1887).

2 S. Glover, *The History and Gazetteer of the County of Derby* (Derby, 1831), II, p. 240.

3 Bagshawe, *Bagshawes of Ford*, p. 13.

4 Ibid, p. 388.

5 Dr Joseph Clegg, quoted by Bagshawe, op. cit., p. 109.

6 Ibid, p. 132.

7 Ibid. p. 145.

8 G. D. H. Cole, D. C. Browning eds; Daniel Defoe, *A Tour through the Whole Island of Great Britain* (1974), p. 174.

9 Bagshawe, op. cit., p. 131; R. Sedgwick ed., *The History of Parliament: The House of Commons, 1715–1754* (1970), I, p. 223. It was also usual at this period for the Cavendishes to return one of the two M.P.s for Derby.

10 R. W. Chapman ed., James Boswell, *Life of Johnson* (Oxford, 1976), p. 865.

11 JRL, B14/1/6 Reverend Henry Winder to William Bagshawe of Ford, 3 October 1740; B14/1/7 Bagshawe to Winder, 11 November 1740.

12 In a will dated 20 September 1746, Bagshawe left Rothwell a legacy of £30; increased to £20 per annum, plus a lump sum of £50, in a will dated 29 May 1754; JRL, B24/2/65a, b. Rothwell does not appear in later wills.

13 Guy, *Oeconomy and Discipline*, p. 118.

14 Deputy Commissaries of the Musters were part-time, locally-based officials of the Commissary General of the Musters' office. They carried out a manpower audit of troops quartered in their areas six times per annum; ibid. pp. 74–80.

15 Bagshawe, op. cit., p. 156. Bagshawe's discharge certificate, dated 14 April 1738, reveals that he had served for six years and 11 months as a private, corporal, sergeant and quartermaster-sergeant, '... in which Stations he behaved himself honestly and faithfully'; JRL, B15/2/9.

16 Bagshawe, op. cit., p. 156.

17 Ibid, pp. 156–157. Only a few pious fragments of this journal survive; JRL, B15/3/1. W. H. G. Bagshawe '... most foolishly destroyed the greater part of this diary many years ago.'

18 JRL, B15/1/5 Lieutenant-Colonel Samuel Bagshawe to Henry Caldwell [1753].

19 See, for example JRL, B2/3/23 Lieutenant-Colonel Samuel Bagshawe to his wife, Catherine, ('Kitty'), 17 September 1755.

20 The commission is dated 15 January 1740: JRL, B15/2/11. It was equivalent to an ensigncy.

21 The commission is dated 13 March 1741; JRL, B15/2/12.

22 Bagshawe, op. cit., p. 158.

23 JRL, B2/3/81 Lieutenant Samuel Bagshawe to William Bagshawe of Ford, 24 November 1741.

24 JRL, B15/3/1 Fragments of a journal, 1740–41, 42; Constantia Maxwell, *Dublin under the Georges, 1714–1830* (1956), describes the amazing contrasts between squalor and opulence in Ireland's capital at this time.

25 JRL, B2/3/83 Lieutenant Samuel Bagshawe to William Bagshawe of Ford, 29 April 1742.

26 The commission in Battereau's regiment, '... to be forthwith raised' on the Irish Establishment, is dated 28 April 1742; JRL, B15/2/13. The 62nd was disbanded in 1748.

27 The commission is dated 20 April 1743; JRL, B15/2/14.

28 JRL, B2/3/90 Captain Samuel Bagshawe to William Bagshawe of Ford, 12 November 1743.

29 Atkinson, *Dorsetshire Regiment*, I, pp. 1–41.

30 JRL, B2/3/99 Captain Samuel Bagshawe to his aunt, Mary Bagshawe, 28 December 1745.

31 William Bagshawe took advantage of the slump in property prices caused by the '45 to buy land at a discount; Bagshawe, op. cit., p. 135.

32 For the Hawkhurst gang, see C. Winslow, 'Sussex Smugglers' in Douglas Hay, Peter Linebaugh, E. P. Thompson eds., *Albion's Fatal Tree; Crime and Society in Eighteenth Century England* (1975), pp. 119–166.

33 The commission is dated 26 March 1746; JRL, B15/2/15. The brigade, commanded by Richbell as brigadier-general, comprised his own regiment, the 39th (992 strong), and Major-General Philip Bragg's 28th Foot (700 strong); JRL, B2/4/15, Return, 22 June 1746. For Bagshawe's salary, see JRL, B2/4/222 'Captain Bagshaw's Account' to 24 June 1747.

34 JRL, B15/2/22 List of men who carried Major Bagshawe to 'Plymieur' and to the shore, n.d. He gave gratuities to all those who assisted him. The best account of the L'Orient expedition is in *British Minor Expeditions 1746 to 1814*, compiled in the Intelligence Branch of the Quartermaster-General's Department (1884), pp. 7–10. Sir John Fortescue's account of this 'pointless' and 'comtemptible' operation is disappointingly brief: *A History of the British Army*, II (1910), p. 156. Bagshawe's unlucky part in the raid is described by an eye witness, James Wood, a Royal Artillery mattross; R. H. Whitworth ed. *Gunner at Large: The Diary of James Wood RA 1746–1765* (1988), p. 21 and Bagshawe, op. cit., pp. 172–79. His journal of the expedition is at JRL, B15/2/20, together with an informative account by an unidentified officer, JRL, B15/2/21. For the rout of the 39th on 21 September see Atkinson, op. cit., pp. 52–53 and Royal Archives, Windsor; Cumberland Papers, (Microfilm), C18/337, St. Clair to Colonel Robert Napier, Adjutant General, 19 October 1746.

35 JRL, B15/2/8 Mr Daniel Wright, Surgeon, to Major Samuel Bagshawe, 8 October 1747.

36 JRL, B2/3/548 Major Samuel Bagshawe to Mr Anthony Garmonsway, 26 February 1747.

37 JRL, B2/3/221 Major Samuel Bagshawe to William Bagshawe of the Inner Temple, 28 December 1747.

38 Dorset Record Office; DRO. D86/x/3, Out-Letter Book of Henry Fox; Fox to Colonel Robert Napier, 16 October 1747.

39 Hayes, 'Bagshawe Papers' pp. 385–86.

40 NAM, 8707–48–1, Adlercron Journal, p. 2.

41 RA Cumberland (M), C18/337 St. Clair to Napier, 19 October 1746.

42 PRO. WO71/20/22–45 General Court Martial of Captain Edward Williams and others, 23–24 July 1747.

43 Atkinson, op cit., pp. 56–59.

44 Bagshawe's company was heavily engaged in the action; three of the seven men of the 39th killed and six of the twelve wounded belonged to it; JRL, B2/4/103 Return, 14 October 1747.

45 Guy, *Oeconomy and Discipline*, pp. 128–31.

46 Hayes, 'Bagshawe Papers', p. 378.

47 JRL, B2/2/393 Captain Thomas Levett to Lieutenant-Colonel

Samuel Bagshawe, 21 March 1751. Bagshawe's scrupulous honesty led him to take personal responsibility for some dubious charges and overpayments, including one of £10. 1s. 4½d. to Captain Edward Williams, since dead. 'It is certain they are charges that could never have been found out' he told Levett, 'but I am acting before a Being that I cannot impose upon and I had rather wrong myself than wrong the Dead'; JRL, B2/2/388, Bagshawe to Levett, 28 September 1750.

48 The commission is dated 15 April 1749; JRL, B15/2/16.

49 The career of Sir James Caldwell, Bart. is described by Cunningham op. cit., pp. 46–101.

50 Bagshawe, op. cit., p. 192.

51 William Bagshawe junior died in Manchester, where his mother had taken him for medical advice, in April 1755, during his father's absence in India. He was buried in St. Anne's, Manchester, on 17 April; ibid, p. 379. 'Ye Doctor told me his Mass of Blood was intirely Corrupt'd,' reported Kitty to William Bagshawe of Ford, '... we ought to be thankful to providence for taking yᵉ Dear little innocent Creature out of pain & misery & wᵗ can be a greater Consolation than to be certain he's now happy ...' JRL, B1/1/72 Kitty to William, 4 May 1755.

52 The extant wills of William Bagshawe of Ford suggest that these fears were unfounded; JRL, B24/2/64, (i)–(vi), 1741–56.

53 Captain Alexander Wilson, regimental agent, of Queen Street, Westminster.

54 Major the Honourable William St. Clair, officer commanding Anstruther's 26th Regiment of Foot (the Cameronians).

55 Captain Adam Ferguson, 26th Foot.

56 Major William Hooke, 26th Foot.

57 Sir Peter Davenport, a deputy commissary of the musters.

58 The 1st or Royal Regiment of Foot (The Royal Scots) was a two-battalion regiment. Both were quartered in Ireland. In October, a service battalion, drawn from both battalions of the regiment, was formed at Cork for service in the West Indies, where the war against Spain was going badly. J. C. Leask and H. M. McCance, *The Regimental Records of the Royal Scots* (Dublin, 1915), pp. 130–32, believe that the 2nd battalion was brought up to strength for this duty by drafts from the 1st, and that 'no vital disturbance

or reformation took place'. The survivors of the expedition reached England in December 1742 and returned to Ireland in 1743, ibid, pp. 133–35.

59 There was a constitutional requirement to remove troops from a borough at election times, and it was customary to march them out of town during annual fairs and the assizes; C. M. Clode, *The Military Forces of the Crown; their Administration and Government* (1869), I, p. 194, Houlding, op. cit., p. 42.

60 Handel arrived in Dublin in November 1741 and remained there for ten months. The season included performances of 'L'Allegro, il Penseroso, & il Moderato', 'Esther', 'Alexander's Feast', and the 'new Grand Oratorio call'd the MESSIAH'; C. Hogwood, *Handel* (1984), pp. 167–77.

61 Colonel John Battereau's 'new Reg!' was the 62nd Foot, (disbanded, 1748).

62 Major Walter Wolfe, uncle of the conqueror of Quebec, joined the 39th in April 1743 and retired in April 1746.

63 Captain Theophilus Desbrisay, regimental agent, of Cork Hill, Dublin.

64 From a captain's point of view, the most important source of company income was a routine payment equal to the subsistence of two non-effective or 'warrant men'. The money was used for recruiting and other contingencies; Guy, *Oeconomy and Discipline*, p. 64.

65 A number of regimental contingencies, as well as loss of, or damage to, a man's 'necessaries'—his shoes, stockings, linen, etc—were paid for by stoppages from the troops' subsistence. They were a constant source of discontent, and were strictly regulated; ibid, pp. 65–70.

66 Mr John Jolliffe, M.P. for Petersfield, 1741–54, 1761–68.

67 East Meon, Hants; five miles west of Petersfield.

68 The words 'I ... Reg!' are struck through in the manuscript.

69 The fall of the Engish base at Ostend in August 1745 was a result of the desperate battle of Fontenoy, fought the previous April; Fortescue, op. cit., II, pp. 122–123.

70 Captain Henry Fox had served in the 39th since 1732, becoming a captain in July 1740. He was commissioned major in April 1746 and died in October 1747.

71 Sir William Yonge, Secretary at War, May 1735–July 1746.

72 Bagshawe was probably thinking of the recent campaigns against the Spanish in the Caribbean, but in view of the latest expedition's semi-secret objective of Cape Breton, he may also have had in mind Brigadier-General John Hill's disastrous Canadian filibuster of 1711; Leach, op. cit., pp. 31–41.

73 'Mr Barber'. William Bagshawe rode down to Gosport to see his nephew, attended by a groom; Bagshawe, op. cit., p. 180.

74 The bulk of St. Clair's expeditionary force, including a contingent from the 39th, landed first in Ireland, where many men died from 'an ugly fever'. The remainder of the 39th disembarked at Portsmouth; Atkinson, op. cit., p. 55.

75 The 30th Foot (Lieutenant-General Charles Frampton).

76 Brigadier-General Richard O'Farrell; Brigadier-General William Graham.

77 The 42nd Foot (ranked 43rd in 1746), the Royal Highland Regiment, (Colonel Lord John Murray).

78 Ensign Charles Philips, 29th Foot (Major-General Francis Fuller).

79 Captain John Cunningham, 1st Foot (Lieutenant-General the Hon. James St. Clair).

80 This was Mr James Butler, afterwards a captain in the Royal Regiment of Artillery. 'As an acknowledgement of the numerous tokens of gratitude with which he was favoured by Colonel Bagshawe, he named his eldest son Samuel, and the second James Bagshawe'; Bagshawe, op. cit., pp. 179–80.

81 Lieutenant John Lyons, 39th Foot.

82 Lieutenant Francis Forde, 39th Foot. Forde was shortly to become a captain in the regiment, (30 April 1746). He was commissioned major in 1755.

83 Captain the Hon. Augustus Keppel, R.N.

84 Captain Thomas Townsend, 39th Foot.

85 Captain Edward Williams, 39th Foot.

86 Captain Henry Keene, the regimental 'bad hat', was a long-serving officer. He had been commissioned into the 39th as an ensign as early as July 1716 and was promoted captain in July 1731. Rather than face the rigours of a campaign in the East Indies, he retired to the captaincy of a company of invalids in February 1754.

87 The 11th Foot (Brigadier-General William Graham).

88 'Lord Semple' was Lieutenant the Hon. John Sempill (12th Lord Sempill, 1746), 39th Foot.

89 Sir John Cope, the defeated commander at the battle of Prestonpans in October 1745, was colonel of the 39th from November 1730 to December 1732.

90 Enlistment was signified by a recruit accepting a shilling as part of his enlistment money. Following this, after a period of 24 hours had elapsed but within four days, the man had to be attested before a chief magistrate or justice of the peace; Steppler, op. cit., p. 16.

91 Bagshawe is referring to the action near Plomeur on 21 September 1746, during the L'Orient raid.

92 General Sir Philip Honeywood.

93 George Brydges, M.P. for Winchester, 1714–51. Sewell's home was in Winchester.

94 The three men returned on the evening of 14 December saying that '... they were only on an Intriguing scheme'; JRL, B2/2/198 Lieutenant Archibald Grant to Major Samuel Bagshawe, 15 December 1747.

95 Rear-Admiral James Stewart, R.N.

96 Lieutenant Henry Wray, 39th Foot.

97 Vice-Admiral Sir Peter Warren, R.N., captor of Louisbourg in 1745 and now Commander-in-Chief of the Western Squadron. David Hepburne was lucky to be going to sea with Warren, who made a fortune from prizes; DNB, 'Warren, Sir Peter, 1703–1752.'

98 JRL, B2/2/210 Major Samuel Bagshawe to Lieutenant Archibald Grant, 23 January 1748.

99 Captain William Lloyd, R.N.

100 Lieutenant Samuel Tobell, 39th Foot.

101 Ensign James Perrin, 39th Foot.

102 The 23rd Foot or 'Royal Welch Fuzileers', (Brigadier-General John Huske).

103 Mr Henry Fox, later 1st Baron Holland, Secretary at War, July 1746–November 1755.

104 Probably Major Cecil Forrester, 46th Foot, (Colonel the Hon. Thomas Murray).

105 The 'Devil's Arse' was a natural feature on the road from Buxton

to Castleton, Derbyshire, so there is more to Dawkin's crude remark than meets the eye; Defoe, *Tour*, II, p. 172.

106 Lieutenant-Colonel Thomas Weld of Sir Richard Temple's Regiment of Foot, (disbanded, 1713).

107 Probably Sherborne St. John, Hants.

108 Lieutenant Rowland Lewis, 39th Foot. He was commissioned captain-lieutenant in February 1751 and captain in June 1752. One of Bagshawe's close friends, he died suddenly at Cuddalore on 18 October 1754 while Bagshawe was lying ill at Fort St. George, Madras. 'I was in a Fever at the same time with your Brother' he told Mr Lewis, an apothecary on Ludgate Hill, 'mine took a turn for Life on the same Day his for Death' JRL, B2/5/145, Bagshawe to Lewis, 8 November 1754.

109 Captain David Dumont, 41st Foot, (Invalids), (Colonel Tomkyns Wardour).

110 Soldiers were subject to stoppages on account of 'slops' required for sea-service or voyages. Slops included bedding, a canvas jacket, trousers, check shirts, a cloth cap, shoes, linen, shipping and packing costs. The stoppage was as much as £2: 9s: 8d a man, and £2: 13s: 8d from a sergeant; NAM 8707–48–3, Orderly Book, 39th Foot, p. 8.

111 Major George Sawyer, regimental agent, of Brewer St, London.

112 Lieutenant Robert Supple, 39th Foot.

113 William Stanhope, 1st Earl of Harrington, Lord Lieutenant of Ireland, 1746–50.

114 Lieutenant-Colonel Philip Savage had entered the 39th as an ensign in November 1707 and had retired as lieutenant-colonel in May 1745.

115 Lieutenant-Colonel John Warburton, 5th (or Royal Irish) Dragoons, (Lieutenant-General Viscount Molesworth).

116 Lieutenant-Colonel Charles Edward Pearce, 5th Foot, (Colonel Alexander Irwin).

117 Lieutenant-General Richard, 3rd Viscount Molesworth. He was appointed Commander-in-Chief in Ireland in September 1751.

118 See note 110 above.

119 The battle of Cape Finisterre, 14 October 1747.

120 The sick officer was Captain Edward Williams. He died in February 1750.

121 Mr Thomas Sherwin, First Clerk in the War Office, 1745–55 and Deputy Secretary at War, 1755–56.

122 'Contingent Men' were a second category of 'non-effective' soldiers whose subsistence could be applied to the contingent charges of a company; Guy, *Oeconomy and Discipline*, pp. 64–65. Levett suggests here that the captains were only entitled to claim the money if their companies were already complete to the establishment, but the usual custom and practice seems to have been that outlined in Letter 168, below.

123 The 15th Foot, (Colonel John Jordan).

124 Samuel's sister Frances had made an unfortunate marriage to a Mr Stephen Peters in 1733. Peters got badly into debt and was forced to flee abroad, where he later died. In 1755, Frances married Mr Arnold Barroll, a merchant in Hereford, 'of high character but no great wealth.'. Samuel paid her an allowance throughout his life and charged his estate with an annuity to her of £30 per annum; Bagshawe, op. cit., pp. 377–79; JRL, B24/2/65d Will of Colonel Samuel Bagshawe, 16 August 1762.

125 The words 'And the favour …' to 'promote' are struck through in the manuscript. The letter ends abruptly, as transcribed.

126 Lieutenant Nicholas Weller, 39th Foot.

127 JRL, B2/4/186 Regimental Court Martial, Belfast, 28 August 1750.

128 Probably Mr Thomas Gore, M.P. for Portsmouth, 1746–47, M.P. for Bedford, 1747–54 and Commissary General of the Musters, 1746–77.

129 Belleek, Co. Fermanagh, was the Caldwell family's proprietary township.

130 The word 'wantonness' is struck through in the manuscript.

131 See note 130 above.

132 The word 'plumpish' is struck through in the manuscript.

133 Lieutenant Mordecai Abbot, 39th Foot.

134 Ensign Caleb Powell, 39th Foot.

135 Colonel Lord George Sackville, Chief Secretary, Ireland, 1751–55.

136 Mrs Elizabeth Adlercron.

137 Mr Samuel Evatt of Ashford, Derbyshire, estate steward at Ford.

138 Captain Patrick Wemyss, 39th Foot.

139 Lieutenant-Colonel George Munro, 35th Foot, (General Charles Otway).

140 Major James Gisborne, 29th Foot, (Lieutenant-General Hon. George Boscawen).

141 It was common, even essential, for soldiers to supplement their meagre subsistence by labouring or plying a trade; Steppler, op. cit., pp. 85–94.

142 Samuel Walter Whitshed was colonel of the 39th from December 1740 to June 1743.

143 A Board of General Officers met to resolve the dispute on 13 October 1752. Richbell agreed to provide a set of swords for all but the grenadier company, plus 100 sets of buff accoutrements. Worn-out firelocks were to be replaced by Government, while the captains were to pay for those that had been lost. As Adlercron objected to the quality of the accoutrements offered by Richbell, the dispute dragged on for another year, but Bagshawe's name was not mentioned; JRL, B2/2/14 Adlercron to Bagshawe, 21 October 1752; B2/2/27, 36, same to same, 20 March, 1 November 1753.

144 Bagshawe had borrowed money from Captain Levett (his agent), Captain David Hepburne of the 39th and Mr Anthony Garmonsway of Lower Castle Yard, Dublin; JRL, B24/2/65b, Will of Lieutenant-Colonel Samuel Bagshawe, 29 May 1754.

145 Bagshawe was praised for his handling of the riot, advised to double the guard, organize a captain's piquet, prevent the soldiers from mixing with the townsfolk and to co-operate closely with the major; JRL, B2/2/732, Thomas Waite to Bagshawe, 4 August 1753; B2/4/70 Colonel Thomas Butler, Adjutant General, Ireland, to Bagshawe, 4 August 1753.

Notes to Part 2

1 Bagshawe, op. cit., p. 200.

2 Ibid, p. 202.

3 Dodwell, *Nabobs of Madras*, pp. 122–24.

4 JRL, B2/5/15 Major John Mompesson to Lieutenant-Colonel Samuel Bagshawe, 10 February 1754.

5 S. C. Hill ed., *Bengal 1756–1757: The Indian Records Series* (1905), III, p. 395.

6 He was the brother of Cyrus Trapaud, lieutenant-colonel of the 3rd Foot, and Alexander Trapaud, lieutenant-governor of Fort Augustus; NAM, 8707–48–1, Adlercron Journal, p. 4.

7 Notably by Dr J. Roach in an important article, 'The 39th Regiment of Foot and the East India Company, 1754–1757', *BJRL*, XLVI (1958), pp. 102–38; see also Sir Penderel Moon, *The British Conquest and Dominion of India* (1989), pp. 44–45.

8 NAM, 8707–48–1, Adlercron Journal, p. 3.

9 JRL, B2/2/691 Lieutenant-Colonel Matthews Sewell to Lieutenant-Colonel Samuel Bagshawe, 3 November 1752.

10 NAM, 8707–48–1, Adlercron Journal, p. 2.

11 JRL, B2/5/21, John Calcraft to Lieutenant-Colonel Samuel Bagshawe, 14 February 1754.

12 JRL, B2/5/2 Lieutenant-Colonel John Campbell, Adjutant-General, Ireland, to Colonel John Adlercron, 31 January 1754. Some of the drafts were 'very bad'; JRL, B2/5/26 'Return of Draughts' [February 1754].

13 'Instructions for Our Trusty and Wellbeloved Colonel John Adlercron', 2 March 1754; NAM, 8707–48–1, Adlercron Journal, p. 15.

14 The Indian background to Bagshawe's expedition is explored by Roach, op. cit. See also Robert Orme, *A History of the Military Transactions of the British Nation in Indostan, from the Year MDCCXLV*, (3rd Edition, 1780), I, Book V; H. H. Dodwell, ed., *The Cambridge History of India*, V, *British India, 1497–1858*, (Cambridge, 1928); Moon, op. cit.; L. S. Sutherland, *The East India Company in Eighteenth Century Politics* (Oxford, 1952), pp. 44–58.

15 JRL, B2/5/54 'Return of the Arrival of the Ships on the Coast' [December 1754].

16 The 39th Foot and a detachment from the Royal Regiment of Artillery travelled to India aboard a fleet of six warships and three East Indiamen; JRL, B2/5/49, 'Officers of the 39th Reg.^{t} of Foot by Companys ...', 28 March 1754.

17 Roach, op. cit., p. 114.

18 NAM, 8707–48–1, Adlercron Journal, p. 52.

19 JRL, B2/6/15 Lieutenant-Colonel Samuel Bagshawe to William, 3rd Duke of Devonshire, 16 February [1756]. The 3rd Duke had died in December 1755, a fact of which Bagshawe would have

been unaware. He was succeeded by his eldest son, William, Marquess of Hartington, already one of Samuel's patrons and now 4th Duke of Devonshire. The 1756 date for this letter is suggested by W. H. G. Bagshawe in a note on the manuscript.

20 On 13 October 1755, the Secretary at War, Henry Fox, who was noted for the brisk tone of his correspondence, informed Adlercron that; 'Some Complaints to the India Company having been laid before the Duke [of Cumberland], I am Commanded by His Royal Highness to let you know, The India Company being Sovereign & answerable to His Majesty & Parliament for their Forts &c, The Command of those Forts are in the Company's Governors, & not in you, nor the Officers of His Majestys Regiment under your Command.' Adlercron received this letter on 10 April 1756; NAM 8707–48–1, Adlercron Journal p. 225.

21 Although his eye was '... not quite dark I am afraid [it] is gone to all the purposes of Life.'; JRL, B2/6/9 Lieutenant-Colonel Samuel Bagshawe to Lieutenant John Corneille, 17 January 1756.

22 'The Disorders of the Country are of such a nature,' Adlercron informed the Duke of Cumberland, 'that when a Person is once attacked by them, he has little or no chance of recovering but by going home.'; NAM, 8707–48–1, Adlercron to Cumberland, 18 October 1755, Adlercron Journal, p. 182. See also Adlercron to Henry Fox, 21 November 1756, ibid, p. 248.

23 The detachment from the 39th which left Madras for Bengal on 10 October 1756 consisted of three captains, nine subalterns and 276 rank-and-file. Significantly, Adlercron remained behind; Roach, op. cit., pp. 127–29. A succinct account of the expedition can be found in Atkinson, op. cit., pp. 70–88.

24 JRL, B2/2/813 Lieutenant-Colonel Samuel Bagshawe to Mr Leonard Morse, 13 December 1757.

25 JRL, B2/5/143 Lieutenant-Colonel Samuel Bagshawe to Mr John Calcraft, 7 November 1754.

26 JRL, B2/6/15 Lieutenant-Colonel Samuel Bagshawe to William, 3rd Duke of Devonshire, 16 February [1756]; (see note 19 above).

27 NAM 8707–48–1, Adlercron Journal, p. 307. Adlercron negotiated with Major Francis Forde, now in the process of transferring to the Company's service, to get this demand waived. Eventually, the

captains and subalterns were allowed £28: 10s each from the regiment's non-effective fund towards the cost of their passage; JRL, B2/6/162, Allowances, [1758].

28 Bagshawe, op. cit., p. 306.

29 JRL, B15/1/31 Samuel Evatt to Lieutenant-Colonel Samuel Bagshawe, 29 January 1757. A 1763 rent-roll states that the annual income was £496: 10s: 4d, but not all the Ford properties were let at that date; JRL, B12/1/1, 2.

30 For the Newton connection and the Chancery suit, see Bagshawe, op. cit., pp. 140, 246. Some of Bagshawe's money was also lost in the collapse of the Manchester firm of Touchet's: JRL, B2/3/866, Mr John Touchet to Kitty Bagshawe, 26 April 1764.

31 JRL, B2/3/786 Lieutenant-Colonel Samuel Bagshawe to the Reverend Philip Skelton, 16 April 1758.

32 See the numerous letters to Samuel Evatt and his successor as estate steward at Ford, Samuel Bagshawe of Bowdenhead, the colonel's cousin, in JRL, B2/3.

33 JRL, B2/3/835 Sir Robert Wilmot, Resident Secretary in England to the Lords Lieutenant of Ireland, to Lieutenant-Colonel Samuel Bagshawe, 6 August 1757.

34 Bagshawe was warned that Devonshire '... interferes very little at present with respect to Promotions in the Army'; JRL, B2/3/837a, Wilmot to Bagshawe, 7 January 1758.

35 JRL, B2/4/167, Return, 28 October 1758.

36 JRL, B2/2/265 Major David Hepburne to Lieutenant-Colonel Samuel Bagshawe, 2 November 1758.

37 JRL, B2/2/43 Major-General John Adlercron to Lieutenant-Colonel Samuel Bagshawe, 20 November 1759.

38 Robert Darcy, Earl of Holdernesse, Secretary of State (Southern Department), 1751–54.

39 Letter in the hand of Lady Caldwell's amanuensis, her kinswoman Judith Cooke. (Lady Caldwell suffered badly from eye complaints).

40 Letter in the hand of Judith Cooke.

41 The salary of the governor of Kinsale was £1 per diem.

42 John Ponsonby, second son of the Earl of Bessborough, was Speaker of the Irish House of Commons. He had raised four independent troops of horse during the '45; *DNB* 'Ponsonby, John (1713–89)'.

43 Lionel Cranfield Sackville, 1st Duke of Dorset, Lord Lieutenant of Ireland (1730–37, 1750–55).

44 Letter in the hand of Judith Cooke.

45 The form of address 'My Lord' is the only clue to the identity of Bagshawe's correspondent. Lord George Sackville, Chief Secretary to his father, the Duke of Dorset, Lord Lieutenant of Ireland, is a likely candidate. The draft ends abruptly, as transcribed here.

46 Rear-Admiral Edward Boscawen, R.N. was Commander-in-Chief by Sea and Land of the King's forces in the East Indies (1747–50). He led an abortive attack on Pondicherry in 1748; *DNB* 'Boscawen, Edward, (1711–1761).'

47 'Palankine'—Palanquin, '... a covered machine with cushions in it, arched in the middle, to give more room, and air, and [it] is carried on the shoulders of four or six men; the expence attending it, is not less than thirty pounds sterling a year.'; Edward Ives, *A Voyage from England to India in the Year MDCCLIV* (1773), p. 21.

48 'Punes'—Peons, '... a kind of Foot Soldiers, they are also employed as Servants or attendants & generally wear a Sword or dagger or both, & some carry Matchlocks.'; NAM 8707–48–2, Adlercron Papers; Court Martial of Lieutenant-Colonel Alexander Heron, p. 191.

49 Mr Thomas Saunders, President of the Council at Fort St. George.

50 Lieutenant-Colonel Stringer Lawrence had served with great gallantry and distinction since his arrival in India as a major in January 1748. His commission as lieutenant-colonel in the East Indies only dated from February 1754. He was affronted by Adlercron's arrival, but served as a volunteer under him during the Bengal crisis of 1757; *DNB* 'Lawrence, Stringer, (1697–1775).'

51 Adlercron's instructions to Bagshawe were dated 8 October 1754. The second article stated; 'When you arrive at Fort St George, you shall as a Preliminary to your Procedings, require from the General Council appointed by the Court of Directors, whether they do acknowledge Colonel Adlercron's Power and Authority over both the King's and Company's Forces? And whether they will give him the Title with which His Majesty has thought fit to Honour him—Colonel in the King of Great Britain's Service & Commander in Chief of the Troops of the East India Company—

And if the General Council will consult him in all their Delibera-
tions as far as it is directed by His Majesty's Instructions?'; NAM
8707–48–1, Adlercron Journal, p. 54.

52 This letter was not sent (see Letter 96).

53 Alexander Heron was formerly lieutenant-colonel of Lieutenant-
General James Edward Oglethorpe's 42nd Foot, disbanded in
1749. He came out to India as a major in the Company's service in
September 1754, was cashiered in 1755 and fled to Pondicherry.
Bagshawe presided at his court martial; NAM 8707–48–2.

54 'Morattoes'—'Morattas or Mahrattas, These are a powerful people
and inhabit the Malabar as well as the Coromandel coast. They are
chiefly horsemen and may be justly termed the *Swiss* of India, for
they let out their troops to hire, and always fight in support of the
party that pays them best.'; Ives, op. cit., p. 25.

55 JRL, B2/5/130 Colonel John Adlercron to Bagshawe, 29 October
1754.

56 The forfeit was a bottle of brandy and a pound of sugar, or a half-
crown; John Corneille, *Journal of My Service in India* (Folio Society,
1966), p. 30. Corneille was lieutenant to Bagshawe's company.

57 See Part One, n. 108, above.

58 The 'two maimed Ships' were the *Eagle* and *Bristol* men-of-war,
dismasted off Kinsale on 10–11 March 1754. The troops were
embarked on the *Tyger* and *Cumberland* men-of-war, which arrived
on the coast of Coromandel on 21 December 1754; JRL, B2/5/54,
Return, [December] 1754.

59 JRL, B2/5/117 Colonel John Adlercron to Bagshawe, 17 October
1754.

60 JRL, B2/5/125 Adlercron to Bagshawe, 24 October 1754.

61 Robert Orme, member of the Council at Fort St. George and
historian of India; *DNB* 'Orme, Robert, (1728–1801).'

62 Colonel Robert Napier, Adjutant-General.

63 Possibly Captain Charles Campbell, of the Company's service.

64 Lieutenant John Caldwell, 7th Foot.

65 William Bagshawe, junior; died, April 1755.

66 Mrs Uniake of Woodhouse, Youghall, was the daughter of Kitty
Bagshawe's uncle, Frederick Trench of Mote.

67 Loose neck-cloths.

68 Lady Elizabeth Caldwell, Sir James's wife.

69 Mr George Pigot succeeded Thomas Saunders as President of the Council at Fort St. George in January 1755; *DNB* 'Pigot, George, (1719–77)'.

70 The petition was rebuffed, and Bagshawe was referred back to Adlercron as his commanding officer; JRL, B2/5/264, Henry Vansittart to Bagshawe, 27 November 1755.

71 'Seton'—a thread drawn through a fold of skin to maintain an issue for discharges.

72 An ore of mercury.

73 'Polygars ... are a set of people who live in the woods, and, we are told, make not the least scruple to plunder every one that comes in their way. They are all independant of the Mogul government.'; Ives, op. cit., p. 25.

74 Bagshawe may be referring here to James Kilpatrick, commissioned brevet-major in the Company's service in July 1754, and who, at the time of writing, was in the field against the Polygars, but later in the letter he seems to be speaking of Lieutenant-Colonel Heron, at whose court martial he had presided in October–November 1755.

75 The Revd Robert Palk, Chaplain at Fort St. George, carried out numerous diplomatic missions for the Company; *DNB*, 'Palk, Sir Robert, (1717–98)'.

76 Dr Andrew Munro, Surgeon at Fort St. George.

77 Colonel Edward Whitmore, 22nd Foot.

78 Stephen Fox, Earl of Ilchester, brother of Henry Fox.

79 Edward, Baron Digby, brother-in-law of Henry Fox.

80 Probably David Roberts, lately chief clerk to the deceased Captain Thomas Levett, and now working in the Calcraft office; Guy, 'Regimental Agency', p. 29. It is even possible that this letter was intended as a hint to Morse himself (see letter 129 below).

81 Charles Lennox, 3rd Duke of Richmond, 72nd Foot.

82 Field Marshal Jean Louis, Lord Ligonier, Commander-in-Chief, (1757–66).

83 Colonel John La Fausille, 66th Foot.

84 Lieutenant-General John, Earl of Rothes, Commander-in-Chief, Ireland, (1758–68).

85 John Russell, 4th Duke of Bedford, Lord Lieutenant of Ireland, (1756–61).

Notes to Part 3

1 The invasion scare is described by R. Middleton in *The Bells of Victory: The Pitt-Newcastle Ministry and the Conduct of the Seven Years' War, 1757–1762* (Cambridge, 1985), pp. 107–29.

2 PRO. SP63/416/119 John, Duke of Bedford, Lord Lieutenant of Ireland, to William Pitt, 1 November 1759.

3 JRL, B3/10/10 The Memorial of Sir James Caldwell, 7 November 1759.

4 JRL, B3/10/19 Sir James Caldwell to John, Lord Shelburne, 29 November 1759.

5 PRO. SP63/416/199 Pitt to Bedford, 7 December 1759.

6 PRO. SP63/416/201 Bedford to Pitt, 30 November 1759.

7 PRO. SP63/416/253 Bedford to Pitt, 18 December 1759.

8 PRO. SP63/418/65 Estimate of ... Annual Expence, [January 1760]. Elsewhere, only seven ensigns are mentioned; *Journals of the House of Commons of Ireland*, VI, Appendix xxxcxiii, but the *Army List* (1760), confirms the figure of eight. An additional company was added to the 93rd in January 1762; Bagshawe, op. cit., p. 278.

9 JRL, B15/2/17.

10 JRL, B2/3/349 Captain Henry Caldwell to Lieutenant-Colonel Samuel Bagshawe, 27 December 1759.

11 JRL, B2/1/8 An Estimate for Swords and Accoutrements, [1760]. The only money refunded to Kitty after her husband's death appears to have been £21: 4s: 6d on account of waistcoats taken away by 56 drafts from the 93rd; JRL, B2/1/401, Mrs Catherine Bagshaw her Accompt with [Capt] William Montgomery [1764].

12 Guy, *Oeconomy and Discipline*, pp. 147–57.

13 JRL, B2/1/15 Beating Order for Colonel Bagshawe's Regiment, 5 February 1760.

14 JRL, B2/1/14 Order for the Draughts, 4 February 1760.

15 JRL, B2/1/69 Return of Recruits, 25 April 1760.

16 JRL, B2/1/77 Return, 2 May 1760.

17 JRL, B2/1/91 Lieutenant-Colonel Edward Windus to Colonel Samuel Bagshawe, 22 May 1760.

18 Bagshawe, op. cit., pp. 267–68.

19 Hayes, 'Bagshawe Papers', p. 358.

20 Guy, 'Drafts for Portugal', pp. 31–34.

21 JRL, B2/1/105 Return of Men Unfit for Service, 8 June 1760.

22 JRL, B2/1/344 List of Men's names to be Discharged, 2 May 1762.

23 JRL, B2/1/157 Order for Draughts, 28 October 1760.

24 JRL, B2/1/342 Return, April 1762.

25 JRL, B2/1/333 Windus to Bagshawe, 4 April 1762.

26 Bagshawe, op. cit., p. 278.

27 F. Bickley, *The Cavendish Family* (1911), pp. 210–11.

28 JRL, B2/1/194 Windus to Bagshawe, 20 March 1761.

29 Paper in the handwriting of the Hon. John Ponsonby, Speaker of the Irish House of Commons, September–October 1758; Public Record Office of Northern Ireland, 'Chatsworth Papers: Selected vice-regal and Irish estate correspondence ... from among the Devonshire and Burlington papers at Chatsworth House, Derbyshire' (1982); T.3158/1601.

30 Reverend Thomas Dawson to William 4th Duke of Devonshire, 30 April 1761; PRONI 'Chatsworth Papers'; T.3158/1635.

31 McDowell, op. cit., p. 119. The franchise at Tallagh was vested in the £5 freeholders; E. M. Johnston, *Great Britain and Ireland 1760–1800—A Study in Political Administration* (Edinburgh, 1963), pp. 161–62.

32 Bagshawe, op. cit., p. 272.

33 JRL, B15/3/12 Prescription, 7 August 1762; *DNB*, 'Pringle, Sir John, (1707–1782)'.

34 JRL, B15/3/29 Account, 21 August 1762. Bagshawe's last journey cost his estate £137: 7s: 5.½d.

35 Bagshawe, op. cit., pp. 284–89; JRL, B24/2/65(d). Last Will and Testament of Colonel Samuel Bagshawe, 16 August 1762.

36 John Bagshawe was born on 16 May 1758. His relatives dissuaded him from entering the army; Bagshawe, op. cit., p. 449.

37 Richard Bagshawe was born on 20 September 1761. He died in Manchester and was buried at St. Ann's church on 8 September 1764; ibid, p. 465.

38 William Bagshawe was born, posthumously, on 6 January 1763; ibid, p. 466.

39 Ann Bagshawe, the colonel's only daughter and most talented of his children, was born on 7 May 1760; loc. cit.

40 Ibid, pp. 359–60. Trench assigned his half-pay as a captain in the

93rd to Kitty's young family; JRL, B15/2/6 Trench to an unknown correspondent, 2 May 1780.

41 The 91st Foot, (Lieutenant-Colonel-Commandant The Hon. Cadwallader Blayney).

42 The 92nd Foot, (Lieutenant-Colonel-Commandant Sir Ralph Gore, Bart.).

43 Probably Lieutenant William Whyte, 16th Foot, (Lieutenant-General Roger Handasyde).

44 John Ponsonby, Speaker of the Irish House of Commons.

45 Bagshawe would have liked Hepburne as lieutenant-colonel of the 93rd; JRL, B15/1/29(a), fragment of a memorandum, [December 1759–January 1760].

46 The 2nd (or Queen's Royal) Regiment of Foot, (Major-General the Hon. John Fitzwilliam).

47 There is a regimental tradition that the men of the 62nd Foot defending Carrickfergus fired their coat-buttons when ball ammunition ran out; N. C. E. Kenrick, *The Story of the Wiltshire Regiment* (Aldershot, 1963), pp. 14–19.

48 Lieutenant-Colonel John Jennings, officer commanding the 62nd Foot, (Colonel William Strode) at Carrickfergus.

49 Possibly Lieutenant-Colonel le Comte de Shordeck, or Major Du Soulier.

50 Brigadier N. de Flobert.

51 Thurot's force was destroyed in a naval action on 28 February; M. Beresford, 'François Thurot and the French Attack at Carrickfergus', *The Irish Sword*, X, (1971–72), pp. 255–74; G. V. C. Young, C. Foster *Captain François Thurot* (Peel, Isle of Man, 1986).

52 Lieutenant Charles Crawford, 93rd Foot.

53 Mr John Nixon of Dublin.

54 Lieutenant William Caulfield, 93rd Foot.

55 Ensign George Cooke, 93rd Foot.

56 The battle of Almanza was fought on 25 April 1707.

57 Mr Richard Rigby, Chief Secretary to the Duke of Bedford, Lord Lieutenant.

58 Lieutenant William Hazard, 93rd Foot.

59 Captain Henry Caldwell, 93rd Foot, Bagshawe's brother-in-law.

60 Major-General the Hon. John Fitzwilliam.

61 Captain Duncan Urquhart, 93rd Foot.

62 Captain Courtland Schuyler, 93rd Foot.

63 Captain William Power Keating Trench, 93rd Foot, kinsman of Kitty Bagshawe.

64 Probably Mr Thomas Truelock, Dublin gunmaker.

65 Ensign Taylor Croker, 93rd Foot.

66 Ensign Lovelace Lowe, 93rd Foot.

67 Mr Ford, Dublin lacemaker.

68 Lieutenant Anthony Daly, 93rd Foot.

69 George Stone, Archbishop of Armagh and one of the Lords Justices of Ireland.

70 Lieutenant John Meredyth, 93rd Foot, formerly an ensign in the 39th.

71 The 1st (or Royal) Regiment of Foot, (the Royal Scots), (General the Hon. James St. Clair).

72 The 16th Foot, (Lieutenant-General Roger Handasyde).

73 Lieutenant-Colonel James Molesworth was also lieutenant-colonel of the 2nd Foot, to which Windus had been major. It seems that these gentlemen did not get on very well.

74 Lieutenant-Colonel Alexander Mackay, 39th Foot.

75 The Right Hon. Sir Henry Cavendish, Bart., Clerk of the Pells and M.P. for Lismore.

76 The 76th Foot, (Colonel William Rufane, *vice* Colonel George, Lord Forbes).

77 The 26th Foot (Lieutenant-General Philip Anstruther).

78 The 76th Foot (Rufane's).

79 The 90th Foot (Lieutenant-Colonel-Commandant Hugh Morgan).

80 A balsam, extracted from the tolu tree.

81 Bagshawe had originally offered the majority in the 93rd to Captain Ned Hunt of the 39th; JRL, B2/2/284 Hunt to Bagshawe, 19 January 1760. Another potential major, Thomas Spencer Wilson, never joined the corps, *Army List* (1760).

82 This letter does not survive.

83 This letter does not survive.

84 Ensign Mathias Smith, 93rd Foot.

85 Ensign Palmes Spaight, 93rd Foot.

86 Mr Alexander Mangin.

87 Captain-Lieutenant Thomas Woolacombe, 93rd Foot.

88 Lieutenant Richard Lombard, 93rd Foot.

89 Lieutenant-General the Earl of Rothes was colonel of the 3rd Foot Guards.

90 The 18th (or Royal Irish) Foot (Lieutenant-General John Folliott).

91 This letter does not survive.

92 Probably Ensign Charles Watts, 16th Foot (General Roger Handasyde).

93 Meredyth had dangerously wounded a man in an affray; JRL, B2/1/195 Windus to Bagshawe, 27 March 1761.

94 This letter does not survive.

95 This letter does not survive.

96 Major David Erskine, 26th Foot, had been promoted lieutenant-colonel of the 76th Foot on 27 November 1760. Robert Preston was eldest captain in the 26th.

97 Major Sir Robert Arnott, Bart.

98 Captain John Morris was eldest captain in the 2nd Foot (Major-General Charles Montague). A major's commission became available when Edward Windus was promoted from the 2nd to the lieutenant-colonelcy of the 93rd.

99 The words 'which ... deserved' are struck through in the manuscript.

100 The 120th–124th Regiments of Foot; Colonels Elphinstone, Gisbourne, Mackay, Pomeroy and Cunninghame.

101 The 83rd Foot (Colonel Bigoe Armstrong).

102 The 91st Foot (Colonel Cadwallader, Lord Blayney).

103 The 10th Foot (Colonel Edward Pole).

104 The 52nd Foot (Major General Sir John Sebright, Bart.).

105 Lieutenant-Colonel Joseph Gabbet, 16th Foot.

106 George Montague Dunk, Earl of Halifax, Lord Lieutenant 1761–63.

107 Warden Flood was appointed Lord Chief Justice of Ireland in August 1760.

108 Lieutenant-General the Hon. George Boscawen.

109 Draft memorial in the hand of Dr John Hawkesworth of Bromley, friend and literary coadjutor of Sir James Caldwell,

associate and biographer of Dr Johnson; *DNB* 'Hawkesworth, John, LLD. (1715?–73)', F. Taylor, 'Johnsoniana from the Bagshawe Muniments' *BJRL*, XXV (1952), pp. 211–47. It will be noted that there are a number of errors of fact in this memorial, not least the date given for the colonel's demise.

Biographical Note of Correspondents

Other persons mentioned in the transcripts are identified in the Notes at the time of their first appearance.

Adlercron, Colonel John (d. 1766); of Huguenot descent, brother of Cyrus Trapaud, (lieutenant-colonel 3rd Foot) and Alexander Trapaud, (Lieutenant-Governor Fort Augustus). Commissioned ensign in John Trapaud's Portuguese Regiment of Foot during the War of the Spanish Succession; half-pay 1712; captain in the army 1722; major 1739 and lieutenant-colonel 1741 in the 7th Foot; colonel 39th 1752; major-general 1759; lieutenant-general 1760.

Bagshawe, Catherine, 'Kitty', née Caldwell (1725/32–1801), wife of Colonel Samuel Bagshawe of Ford; younger of two daughters of Sir John Caldwell, Bart. of Castle Caldwell, Co. Fermanagh; married Samuel Bagshawe, 25 March 1751; renowned in the family for her Irish wit and sarcasm, a 'giddy' but faithful and affectionate wife.

Bagshawe, Mary, née Wingfield (1682–1754), wife of William Bagshawe of Ford Hall; Samuel Bagshawe's aunt; '. . . an excellent woman, a pious, kind and charitable neighbour', (Dr Jospeh Clegg).

Bagshawe, Richard (1674/5–1750), of Castleton and the Oaks, JP: cousin of Samuel Bagshawe.

Bagshawe, William (1686–1756), of Ford Hall, uncle of Samuel Bagshawe, Deputy Lieutenant for the County of Derby.

Bagshawe, William (1713–85), of the Inner Temple, Wormhill Hall and the Oaks; son of Richard Bagshawe of Castleton, barrister at law, JP and Deputy Lieutenant for the County of Derby, Samuel Bagshawe's executor.

Barrington, William, 2nd Viscount (1717–93); Secretary at War 1755–61; he was renowned for showing sympathy to deserving officers, but it was impossible for him to help everyone, as Samuel Bagshawe discovered.

Calcraft, John (1726–72), regimental agent, of Channel Row; protegé of Henry Fox, Secretary at War; agent to the 39th Foot 1754–59.

Caldwell, Ann, Dowager Lady; widow of Sir John Caldwell of Castle Caldwell and mother of Kitty Bagshawe; '. . . she glories in being the Mother of Six sons that have been bred to Military Employments'.

Caldwell, Sir James, Bart. (d. 1784) of Castle Caldwell, Co. Fermanagh, Samuel Bagshawe's brother-in-law; Count of Milan in the Holy Roman Empire, colonel of a regiment of Militia in Co. Fermanagh, captain-commandant 20th Light Dragoons, the 'Enniskillen Light Horse' 1760–63, Fellow of the Royal Society, friend of Dr Johnson.

Cavendish, William, 3rd Duke of Devonshire (c. 1698–1755), Samuel Bagshawe's patron, '... plain of manners, negligent in his dress', a heavy drinker, disciple of Sir Robert Walpole, Lord Lieutenant of Ireland 1737–45.

Cavendish, William (1720–1764), eldest son of William, 3rd Duke of Devonshire; Marquess of Hartington, 4th Duke of Devonshire 1755; patron of Samuel Bagshawe.

Clegg, Dr Joseph (d. 1755), celebrated dissenting minister of the Presbyterian meeting-house at Chapel-en-le-Frith, tutor of William Bagshawe of Ford; the 3rd Duke of Devonshire paid him an annuity for political services in Derbyshire. He died during his friend Samuel Bagshawe's absence in India.

Cotes, James, of Woodcote, Shropshire; friend of Samuel Bagshawe; captain 37th Foot, succeeded Philip Savage as lieutenant-colonel of the 39th in May 1745 and sold out in favour of Samuel Bagshawe in April 1749.

Crane, Michael, King's Apothecary; he attended Colonel Samuel Bagshawe during his final illness, August 1762.

Crawford, Charles, lieutenant 93rd Foot; an Irishman, sold out in 1761.

Dawkin, William, of Eagle's Bush, Neath; lieutenant of Samuel Bagshawe's company in 39th Foot, which he had joined as an ensign 1734; promoted lieutenant 1741, sold out in August 1749.

Devonshire, William, 3rd Duke of; William, 4th Duke of; see Cavendish.

Ellis, Hercules, lieutenant 93rd Foot; an Irishman, aged 37 in 1760 with 18 years' service to his credit; captain-lieutenant in the regiment June 1762.

Fletcher, Dr Thomas (d. 1761); Dean of Down 1739–44, Bishop of Dromore 1744, translated to Kildare 1745–61, Dean of Christ Church, Dublin 1745–61. Probably one of the three sons of the poet and divine Thomas Fletcher (1666–1715), he was a confidant of William 3rd Duke of Devonshire and friend of Samuel Bagshawe.

Flood, Francis, lieutenant 93rd Foot, an Irishman, nephew of Warden Flood, Attorney General of Ireland; ensign 1758, he was put into the 93rd by the Duke of Bedford, Lord Lieutenant.

Flood, The Right Hon. Warden; uncle of Francis, Attorney General of Ireland 1751, Lord Chief Justice of Ireland 1760.

Forde, Francis (d. 1769–70), 39th Foot; ensign 1740; lieutenant 1742; captain 1746; appointed paymaster when the regiment sailed for India in 1754; he transferred into the East India Company's service as a lieutenant-colonel (without obtaining permission) in June 1758; victor of Condore and conqueror of Masulipatam (1759) he was lost aboard the frigate *Aurora* en route to India.

Fox, Henry (1705–74); subsequently 1st Baron Holland; Secretary at War, 1746–55, and Paymaster General, 1757–65; an effective administrator, but devoted to the pursuit of power and profit.

Garrard, The Right Hon. William; described by Samuel Bagshawe as 'Secretary of State & Secret^y at Warr' at Dublin Castle, but not listed as such in Johnston, op. cit.

Gaylard, Thomas, captain 93rd Foot; an Englishman, commissioned ensign in 1746; despite his 15 years' service he was a bad influence on the young officers of the 93rd.

Grant, Archibald, 'Archy', 39th Foot; ensign 1737; lieutenant 1742; adjutant, April 1747–February 1751; captain-lieutenant 1749; captain 1751; a friend of Samuel Bagshawe, and assisted him as paymaster during 1747–48; he took part in the conquest of Bengal in 1757 and made a fortune; he left the 39th in 1760.

Hepburne, David, 'Davy', 39th Foot; ensign 1730; lieutenant 1731; adjutant, Febuary 1739–July 1740; captain-lieutenant 1746; captain 1746; major 1758; a close friend of Samuel Bagshawe; the colonel owed him £367: 10s at his death, which was not paid until 1767. In the course of this correspondence, Hepburne declines from being the 'greatest beau' in the Portsmouth garrison (1747) to a querulous invalid; he went on half-pay in August 1760.

Joass, Alexander, captain 93rd Foot; a Scotsman, commissioned captain in the 93rd after 13 years' service; commissioned fort major at Stirling in 1761.

Kellet William, Regimental Surgeon, 39th Foot; son of an officer killed at Falkirk (1746), he purchased his appointment in 1753; in 1757 he was allowed to purchase an ensigncy, continuing also as surgeon until 1763, by which time he was a captain; he commanded the 39th as lieutenant-colonel during the Great Siege of Gibraltar (1779–83).

Ladeveze, Colonel Anthony, Regimental Agent, Dublin; agent to the 39th Foot, 1752–54.

Levett, Thomas (d. 1758), Regimental Agent, of Warwick Street, Golden Square; captain, agent to the 39th Foot, 1744–49, a friend of Samuel Bagshawe, he died worth £40,000.

Lovett, Verney, 39th Foot; ensign 1732; lieutenant 1739; adjutant, July 1740–May 1743; captain 1743; major 1754; a nephew of Lord Verney, he sold out in November 1755.

Montgomery, William, Regimental Agent, Dublin; captain, agent to the 93rd Foot, 1760–63.

Morse, Leonard, War Office clerk from 1757; a protegé of Samuel Bagshawe, he was appointed secretary to the commander and deputy judge advocate in Major-General Peregrine Hopson's expedition to the Caribbean in October 1758.

Murray, Lieutenant-Colonel James, 15th Foot (Colonel John Jordan).

Payne, John, Chairman of the Court of Directors of the Hon. East India Company.

Preston, Robert, 93rd Foot; a Scotsman, ensign 1736; lieutenant (26th Foot) 1741; captain 1746; major in the army 1759; major 93rd Foot 1760.

Richbell, Brigadier-General Edward (d. 1757), Colonel of the 39th Foot; captain Sir Richard Temple's Regiment of Foot 1708; served at Malplaquet 1709; half-pay 1713; captain of an independent company in New York 1719; major 37th Foot 1720; lieutenant-colonel May 1722; colonel 61st Foot 1742,; colonel 39th Foot 1743; brigadier-general 1745; colonel 17th Foot 1752.

Sackville, Colonel Lord George (1716–85); Chief Secretary to his father, the Duke of Dorset, Lord Lieutenant of Ireland, December 1750–April 1755, disgraced at the battle of Minden (1759).

Sempill, The Hon. John, 39th Foot, 12th Lord Sempill (1746); ensign 1732; lieutenant 1739; half-pay 1754.

Sewell, Lieutenant-Colonel Matthews; captain 10th Marines 1741; lieutenant-colonel of the Duke of Bolton's provincial regiment 'the Leicester Blues' 1745; major 39th Foot 1747; transferred to an independent company of invalids at Pendennis Castle, 1754.

Starke, Richard, Deputy Governor of the East India Company's settlement at Fort St. David, Cuddalore.

Symes, George, 39th Foot; ensign 1727; lieutenant 1732; captain-lieutenant 1739; captain 1746; half-pay 1751.

Waite, Thomas, Secretary to the Lords Justices of Ireland, who administered the country during the prolonged absences of the Lords Lieutenant.

Wilmot, Sir Robert (1708–72), of Osmaston, Derbyshire; resident secretary in England of the Lords Lieutenant of Ireland from 1736.

Windus, Lieutenant-Colonel Edward (d.c. 1792), 93rd Foot, an Englishman; ensign 2nd Foot 1729; captain by 1749; major 1756; lieutenant-colonel 93rd Foot 1760. In 1770 appointed Inspector of Recruits for the East India Company (based in London) and, from 1771 Inspector of Small Arms and Accoutrements for the several Presidencies. He retired on pension in 1787. From 1779 to his death he was the most senior lieutenant-colonel in the British Army.

Yonge, Sir William (c. 1693–1755); Secretary at War 1735–46; a superannuated crony of Sir Robert Walpole and unable to respond to the full demands of his post in wartime, he was succeeded by the efficient Henry Fox.

Bibliography

1 Manuscript Sources

(i) John Rylands University Library of Manchester, (Deansgate)

Col Samuel Bagshawe of Ford

JRL, B2/1/1/–403	Correspondence and papers, the 93rd Foot (1759–64).
B2/2/1–824	Correspondence, military (1727–62).
B2/3/1/881	Correspondence, personal (1738–64).
B2/4/1–751	Papers, military (1736–62).
B2/5, 6/1–573	East India papers (1754–57).
B2/7/1–436	Household and personal bills (c. 1730–62).
B12/1, 2	Rental of Ford and executors' accounts (1762–76).
B13/3/383	Will of Colonel Samuel Bagshawe of Ford, n.d. (1762).
B13/3/391	Papers in a legal dispute respecting the settlement, made for Colonel Bagshawe's wife and children.
B15/1/1–43	Correspondence, personal (1745–62).
B15/2/1–26	Correspondence and papers, military (1738–80).
B15/3/1–35	Papers, personal; journals, accounts (1740–64).
B24/2/65	Wills of Colonel Samuel Bagshawe (1746–62).

William Bagshawe of Ford (Uncle)

JRL, B1/1/1–737	Correspondence and papers (1703–56).
B14/1/1–31	Correspondence (1711–51).
B14/2/1–21	Papers and accounts (1706–50).
B24/2/64	Wills of William Bagshawe of Ford (1741–56).

Sir James Caldwell, Bart. (Brother-in-Law)

JRL, B3/10	Letter books (1759–64).
B3/16 (various)	Correspondence, non-peerage.
B3/21/6	'A Proposal for Increasing His Majesty's Revenue in Ireland' (1763).
B3/21/8	'An address to Lord Townshend … in favour of Sir James Caldwell's Light Dragoons' (1772).
B3/23/1–31	Papers relating to the 'Enniskillen Light Horse',

(the 20th Regiment [or Corps] of Light Dragoons)
(1759–65).

(ii) Dorset Record Office, Dorchester

DRO. D86/x/3 Out-letter book of Henry Fox, Secretary at War (1746–48).

(iii) National Army Museum, London

Adlercron Papers

NAM, 8708–48–1 Journal of an expedition to the East Indies, commanded by Colonel John Adlercron (1754–58); in the colonel's own hand.

8707–48–2 Court Martial of Lieutenant-Colonel Alexander Heron (1755).

8707–48–3 Orderly Book, 39th Foot (1752–58).

(iv) National Library of Ireland, Dublin

Adlercron Papers

NLI, P. 926 Microfilm copy of two Letterbooks of Lieutenant-General John Adlercron (1726–66) and regimental accounts, 39th Foot (1755–60). (There is a copy of this microfilm in the National Army Museum, London).

(v) Public Record Office, London

PRO. SP63/416, 417 Out-letters, Lord Lieutenant of Ireland (1759–60).

PRO. WO71/20 General Courts Martial (1746–51).

2 Official Publications and Works of Reference

Army List. Printed by Order of the House of Commons (1740).

Army Lists. Published by John Millan, '... by permission of the ... Secretary at War' (1754–63).

British Minor Expeditions, 1746 to 1804: Compiled in the Intelligence Branch of the Quartermaster General's Department (1884).

Cannon, R, *Historical Record of the Thirty-Ninth, or the Dorsetshire Regiment of Foot* (1853).

Clode, C. M., *The Military Forces of the Crown, their Administration and Government* (1869).

Gilbert, J. T., *A History of the City of Dublin* (Dublin, 1881).

Glover, S., *The History and Gazetteer of the County of Derby* (Derby, 1831).

Journals of the House of Commons of Ireland, Vols III–VII, (1757–63).

Lawson, C. C. P., *A History of the Uniforms of the British Army*, II (1949).

Lewis, S., *A Topographical Dictionary of Ireland* (1837, reprinted Port Washington (N.Y.) and London, 1970).

Moody, T. W., Martin F. X., Bryne, F. J., *A New History of Ireland*, IX, *Maps, Genealogies, Lists* (Oxford, 1984).

Namier, L., Brooke, J., *The History of Parliament: The Commons, 1754–1790*, (1964).

Sedgwick, R., *The History of Parliament: The Commons, 1714–1754* (1971).

Taylor, F., *Hand-List of the Bagshawe Muniments deposited in the John Rylands Library*, John Rylands University Library of Manchester (Manchester, 1955), reprinted from *BJRL* XXXVI–XXXVII (1953–55).

The Victoria History of the County of Derby, (1905).

3 Printed Primary Sources

Bagshawe, W. H. G., *The Bagshawes of Ford: A Biographical Pedigree* (1886): *A Memoir of William Bagshawe of Ford Hall, styled 'The Apostle of the Peak'* (1887).

Barrington, S., *The Political Life of William Wildman, Viscount Barrington* (1814).

Chatsworth Papers, 'Selected vice-regal and Irish estate correspondence … from among the Devonshire and Burlington papers at Chatsworth House, Derbyshire'. Public Record Office of Northern Ireland, typescript copy at the Royal Commission on Historic Manuscripts, London.

Corneille, Major J., (M. Edwardes ed.) *Journal of my Service in India*, (Folio Society, 1966).

Defoe, D., (G. D. C. Cole, D. C. Browning eds.), *A Tour through the Whole Island of Great Britain* (1974).

Hervey, John Lord, (R. Sedgwick ed.), *Some Materials towards Memoirs of the Reign of King George II* (1953).

Hill, S. C. (ed.), *Bengal, 1756–1757: The Indian Records Series* (1905).

Ives, E., *A Voyage from England to India in the Year MDCCLIV* (1773).

Orme, R., *A History of the Military Transactions of the British Nation in Indostan, from the Year MDCCXLV* (1780).

Wood, J., (R. H. Whitworth ed.), *Gunner at Large: The Diary of James Wood RA, 1746–1765* (1988).

4 Secondary Sources: unpublished Theses and Papers

Bruce, A. P. C., 'The System of Purchase and Sale of Commissions in the British Army and the Campaign for its Abolition 1660–1871', University of Manchester PhD thesis (1973).

Ferguson, K. P., 'The Army in Ireland from the Restoration to the Act of Union', Trinity College, Dublin, PhD thesis (1980).

Hayes, J. W., 'The Social and Professional Background of the Officers of the British Army 1714–1763', University of London, MA thesis (1956).

Odintz, M., 'Expertise in the Eighteenth Century British Officer Corps', University of Michigan, seminar paper (1979).

Pimlott, J. L., 'The Administration of the British Army 1783–1793', University of Leicester, PhD thesis (1975).

Steppler, G. A., 'The Common Soldier in the Reign of George III, 1760–1793', University of Oxford PhD thesis (1984).

5 Secondary Sources: Books

Atkinson, C. T., *The Dorsetshire Regiment*, I (Oxford (1952).

Bickley, F., *The Cavendish Family* (1911).

Bruce, A. P. C., *The Purchase System in the British Army 1660–1871* (1980).

Cannon, J., *Aristocratic Century: The Peerage of Eighteenth Century England* (Cambridge, 1984).

Childs, J., *The Army of Charles II* (1976).

——, *Armies and Warfare in Europe, 1648–1789* (Manchester, 1982).

——, *The British Army of William III 1689–1702* (Manchester, 1987).

Clay, C., *Public Finance and Private Wealth: The Career of Sir Stephen Fox, 1627–1716* (Oxford, 1978).

Corbett, J. S., *England in the Seven Years' War: A Study in Combined Strategy* (1918).

Coxe, W., *The Administration of the Right Honourable Henry Pelham* (1829).

Cunningham, J. B., *Castle Caldwell and its Families* (Belleek, 1980).

Dodwell, H. H., *The Nabobs of Madras* (1926).

——, *The Cambridge History of India*, V, *British India, 1497–1858* (Cambridge, 1929).

Duffy, C., *The Military Experience in the Age of Reason* (1987).

Forde, L., *Lord Clive's Right-Hand Man: A Memoir of Colonel Francis Forde* (1910).

Fortescue, J. W., *A History of the British Army*, II (1910).

Frey, S. R., *The British Soldier in America: A Social History of Military Life in the Revoluntionary Period* (Austin (Texas), 1981).

Guy, A. J., *Oeconomy and Discipline: Officership and Administration in the British Army, 1714–63* (Manchester, 1985).

Hayter, T., *The Army and the Crowd in Mid-Georgian England* (1978).

Hogwood, C., *Handel* (1984).

Houlding, J. A., *Fit for Service: The Training of the British Army, 1715–1795* (Oxford, 1980).

James, F. G., *Ireland in the Empire, 1688–1770: A History of Ireland from the Williamite Wars to the Eve of the American Revolution* (Cambridge (Mass), 1973).

Johnston, E. M., *Great Britain and Ireland 1760–1800—A Study in Political Administration* (Edinburgh, 1963).

Kenrick, N. C. E., *The Story of the Wiltshire Regiment* (Aldershot, 1963).

Leach, D. E., *Roots of Conflict: British Armed Forces and Colonial Americans, 1677–1763* (Chapel Hill (NC) and London, 1986).

Leask, J. C., McCance, H. M. *Regimental Records of the Royal Scots* (Dublin, 1915).

McDowell, R. B., *Ireland in the Age of Imperialism and Revolution, 1760–1801* (Oxford, 1979).

Maxwell, C., *Dublin under the Georges, 1714–1830* (1956).

Middleton, R., *The Bells of Victory: The Pitt-Newcastle Ministry and the Conduct of the Seven Years' War, 1757–1762* (Cambridge, 1985).

Moody, T. W., Vaughan, W. E., *A New History of Ireland*, IV, *Eighteenth Century Ireland, 1691–1800* (Oxford, 1986).

Moon, P., *The British Conquest and Dominion of India* (1989).

Schwoerer, L. G., *No Standing Armies! The Anti-Army Ideology in Seventeenth Century England* (Baltimore and London, 1974).

Scouller, R. E. , *The Armies of Queen Anne* (Oxford, 1966).

Stevens, P. L., *A King's Colonel at Niagara, 1774–1776: Lieutenant-Colonel John Caldwell and the beginnings of the American Revolution on the New York Frontier* (Old Fort Niagara Association, Youngstown (N.Y.), (1987).

Sutherland, L. S., *The East India Company in Eighteenth Century Politics* (Oxford, 1952).

Whitworth, R. H., *Field Marshal Lord Ligonier: A Story of the British Army, 1702–1770* (Oxford, 1958).

Williams, B., *The Whig Supremacy*, 2nd edn. (Oxford, 1965).

Young, G. V. C., Foster, C. *Captain François Thurot* (Peel, Isle of Man, 1986).

6 Secondary Sources: Articles

Baker, N. 'Changing Attitudes toward Government in Eighteenth Century Britain', A. Whiteman et al *Statesmen, Scholars and Merchants: Essays in Eighteenth Century History presented to Dame Lucy Sutherland* (Oxford, 1973), pp. 209–19.

Beresford, M. 'François Thurot and the French Attack at Carrickfergus, 1759–60', *The Irish Sword*, X (1971–72), pp. 255–74.

Ferguson, K. P. 'Military Manuscripts in the Public Record Office of Ireland', *The Irish Sword*, XV (1982), pp. 112–15.

Gilbert, A. N. 'Law and Honour among British Eighteenth Century Army Officers', *Historical Journal*, XIX (1976), pp. 75–87.

Guy, A. J. 'Reinforcements for Portugal, 1762: Recruiting for Rank at the End of the Seven Years' War', *Annual Report of the National Army Museum* (1977–78), pp. 29–34.

——, 'A Whole Army Absolutely Ruined in Ireland: Aspects of the Irish Establishment, 1715–1773', *Annual Report of the National Army Museum* (1979–80), pp. 30–43.

——, 'Regimental Agency in the British Standing Army 1715–1763: A Study in Georgian Military Administration, *BJRL*, LXII (1980), pp. 423–53, LXIII (1980), pp. 31–57.

——, 'The Stubborn English Spirit: Officer Discipline and Resistance to Authority, 1727–1750', *Army Museum '83*, National Army Museum (1984), pp. 9–18.

——, 'Minions of Fortune: The Regimental Agents of Early Georgian England, 1714–63', *Army Museum '85*, National Army Museum (1986), pp. 31–42.

Hayes, J. W., 'The Military Papers of Colonel Samuel Bagshawe, 1713–1762', *BJRL*, XXXIX (1956–57), pp. 356–89.

——, 'Scottish Officers in the British Army, 1714–63', *Scottish Historical Review*, XXXVII (1958), pp. 25–57.

——, 'Lieutenant-Colonel and Major Commandants of the Seven Years' War', *Journal of the Society for Army Historical Research*, XXXVI (1958), pp. 3–13, 38–39.

——, 'Two Soldier Brothers of the Eighteenth Century', *Journal of the Society for Army Historical Research*, XL (1962), pp. 150–61.

Johnson, S. H. F., 'The Irish Establishment', *The Irish Sword*, I (1949–53), pp. 33–36.

Kopperman, P. E., 'The British High Command and Soldiers' Wives in America, 1755–1783', *Journal of the Society for Army Historical Research*, LX (1982), pp. 14–34.

——, 'Religion and Religious Policy in the British Army c1700–1796', *The Journal of Religious History* (forthcoming).

Roach, J., 'The 39th Regiment of Foot and the East India Company, 1754–1757', *BJRL*, XLVI (1958), pp. 102–38.

Roy, I., 'The Profession of Arms', W. Prest, ed. *The Professions in Early Modern England* (1987), pp. 181–219.

Taylor, F. 'Johnsoniana from the Bagshawe Muniments in the John Rylands Library: Sir James Caldwell, Dr Hawkesworth, Dr Johnson, and Boswell's use of the Caldwell Minute', *BJRL*, XXXV (1952), pp. 211–47.

Winslow, C., 'Sussex Smugglers', D. Hay, P. Linebaugh, E. P. Thomson, *Albion's Fatal Tree: Crime and Society in Eighteenth Century England* (1975), pp. 119–66.

Index

Officers are shown with the rank they had attained at time of last mention in this correspondence.

Abbot, Lt. Modecai, 105, 287

Accounts, regimental, 42–4, 66–8, 76–7, 79–81, 87–8, 90–4, 100–2, 109, 111–13, 230–1, 236–8, 242, 253–4, 260–2

Adlercron, Mrs Elizabeth, 107, 192–4, 287

Adlercron, Col. John, 5, 10, 20, 106–7, 122–5, 127–8, 130–1, 133–4, 136–7, 139, 140–7, 151–7, 161–3, 165, 191, 192–4, 195–6, 288–9, 290–3, 301

Adlercron's, *see* Army: 39th Foot

Agents, regimental, 9–11, 178, 182–3

Aix-la-Chapelle, Peace of, 4, 77–8

Almanza, Battle of, 220

American Independence, War of, 9

Anne, Queen, 1, 36

Anstruthers's, *see* Army: 26th Foot

Armstrong, Col. Bigoe, 257–8, 260

Armstrong's, *see* Army: 83rd Foot

Army,
Parliamentary Estimates for, 2
proprietary command in, 8–11, 100–2
regimental organization, 4–8
Regiments
5th Dragoons, 86
20th (Light) Dragoons, 19, 200
Foot Guards, 3
3rd Foot Guards, 243
1st Foot, 24, 36–8, 53, 230–1, 234, 236–7, 240, 282–3
2nd Foot, 209, 248–9
5th Foot, 86, 97
7th Foot, 125
10th Foot, 261
11th Foot, 60
15th Foot, 93
16th Foot, 207, 230–1, 234, 236–7, 240, 261
18th Foot, 243
23rd Foot, 76, 285
26th Foot, 23, 33, 235, 248, 253, 261
28th Foot, 280
29th Foot, 53, 284

30th Foot, 6, 26, 53
38th Foot, 4
39th Foot, 2, 6, 13–17, 20,
 25–9, 42, 46–9, 51–4, 66,
 69, 75–7, 80–2, 84,
 86–94, 109–13, 122–8,
 130–1, 133–4, 138–40,
 158–9, 162–3, 191–6,
 209, 212–13, 231, 235,
 260, 289–90
41st Foot, 78
42nd Foot, 53, 284
46th Foot, 5
52nd Foot, 261
62nd Foot (disbanded
 1748), 25, 40, 283
62nd Foot, 3, 260, 297
76th Foot, 234–5, 240
83rd Foot, 255, 261
90th Foot, 234–5
91st Foot, 207, 255–6, 261
92nd Foot, 207, 260
93rd Foot, 4–5, 9, 13, 15,
 17, 200–6, 210–12,
 220–1, 225–8, 230–2,
 235–8, 245–62, 268
Arnott, Maj. Sir Robert, 248,
 299
Austrian Succession, War of the,
 2, 10, 28

Bagshawe's, see Army: 93rd Foot
Bagshawe Family, 21–3, 189–90,
 204–5, 278
Bagshawe, Miss Ann (b.1760),
 204, 296
Bagshawe, Mrs Catherine, 'Kitty'

née Caldwell, 28–9, 102–3,
 108, 115, 121, 125, 129–30,
 133, 136–8, 160, 166–7, 173,
 178, 190, 196–7, 201, 204–5,
 269–71, 282, 295, 301
Bagshawe, Mrs Frances, née
 Hardwar, 22
Bagshawe, Miss Frances, 22, 25,
 204, 287
Bagshawe, John (b.1758), 204,
 296
Bagshawe, Mrs Mary, née
 Wingfield, 39–40, 48–50, 52,
 57, 64, 108, 117, 121, 125, 301
Bagshawe, Richard (b.1761),
 204, 296
Bagshawe, Richard, of Castleton,
 23, 30, 301
Bagshawe, Samuel of Ford
 (d.1712), 22
Bagshawe, Col. Samuel of Ford,
 born, 22
runs away from school, 23
serves in the ranks, 23, 30–4,
 279
ransomed from the army, 23
first commissions, 24, 35
in Lord Lieutenant's
 household, 24–5, 39–40
commissioned captain, 25
attempts to purchase majority,
 46–9
thwarted in attempts to go on
 active service, 25–6, 49
on anti-smuggling duty, 26,
 49
commissioned major-of-
 brigade, 26, 51

loses leg at l'Orient, 26–7,
  51–2, 54–5
recovers, 27, 57
thwarted in new attempt to
  obtain majority, 58–64
loses money settling regimental
  accounts, 28, 87–8, 90–4
commissioned lieutenant-
  colonel, 28, 89
engagement and marriage, 28,
  102–3
clashes with his uncle over
  money, 29, 94–6, 107–8,
  113–17
in riots at Cork, 117–19, 288
ordered to India, 121, 128
ambitions in India, 121–2,
  138–40
voyage, 121–3, 148–50
frustrations of service in India,
  124, 163–9, 170–2, 175–6,
  179–80
negotiates abortive 'Convention' with the East India
  Company, 140–47, 151–7
quarrels with Col. Adlercron,
  161–6
is repeatedly sick, 125, 158–9,
  166–7, 173
loses sight in one eye, 126,
  169–70, 290
voyage home, 126, 179
inherits Ford Hall, 125–6
recovers his health, 125–6, 180
requests posting to active duty,
  126, 180
solicits colonelcy of an old
  regiment, 126, 176, 180–92

is reconciled with Col.
  Adlercron, 192–4
proposes to raise a new
  regiment, 127, 200, 206
raises and commands the 93rd
  Foot, 200–3, 206–7
protests against policy of
  drafting the 93rd, 202–3,
  236–8, 252–3
elected M.P. for Tallagh,
  203–4, 207–8, 233–4
final illness and death, 204,
  268–9
will, 204–5
Bagshawe, Samuel of Ford
  (b.1753), 21, 29, 160, 204–5
Bagshawe, Samuel of
  Bowdenhead, 291
Bagshawe, William of Ford, 'The
  Apostle of the Peak', 21, 24
Bagshawe, William of Ford,
  22–3, 26, 29, 30–2, 34–8,
  46–8, 51–2, 54, 82, 89, 94–6,
  107–8, 113–17, 121, 125,
  136–8, 160, 173, 280, 282, 301
Bagshawe, William (b.1752,
  d.1755), 29, 137, 160, 173,
  282, 293
Bagshawe, William (b.1763),
  204, 296
Bagshawe, William of the Inner
  Temple and Castleton, 23,
  31–2, 35–6, 48, 189–90, 301
Bagshawe, W. H. G., 203, 278–9
Barber, Mr, 52, 284
Barrington, William, Viscount,
  180, 185–8, 190, 192–3, 201,
  301

Barroll, Arnold, 287

Bath, Col. Bagshawe's treatment at, 204, 268–9

Battereau, Col. John, 25, 40, 283

Battereau's, *see* Army: 62nd Foot (disbanded 1748)

Bedford, John, Duke of, 193, 200–1, 206, 216–17, 222–3, 248

Belleek, Co. Fermanagh, 28, 102

Bever, Capt. Samuel, 5

Bland, Gen. Humphrey, 276

Bissett's, *see* Army: 30th Foot

Blayney, Lt.-Col.-Commdt. the Hon. Cadwallader, 207, 297

Blayney's, *see* Army: 91st Foot

Board of General Officers, 111–13, 242, 288

Bolton's Provincial Regiment, 27, 63, 86

Boscawen, Rear-Admiral Edward, 121, 139–40, 292

Boscawen, Lt.-Gen. George, 268, 299

Boyle, Charlotte, Duchess of Devonshire, 203

Bragg's, *see* Army: 28th Foot

Brydges, George, MP, 63, 285

Burlington, Richard, Earl of, 203

Butler, Dr James, 27, 54–5, 284

Buxton Spa, Col. Bagshawe takes the cure at, 126, 178, 194

Byng, Admiral Sir George, 25

Calcraft, John, MP, 10, 126, 133–4, 175, 180–3, 193, 196, 301

Caldwell Family, 12, 20, 28, 108

Caldwell, Ann, Dowager Lady, 28, 129, 130–2, 135, 160–1, 301

Caldwell, Miss Catherine, *see* Bagshawe, Catherine

Caldwell, Elizabeth, Lady, 164, 293

Caldwell, Capt. Henry, 201, 223, 227, 246–7

Caldwell, Sir James of Castle Caldwell, 19, 28, 121, 128–33, 148–50, 177, 200, 204, 207, 301

Caldwell, Sir John of Castle Caldwell, 28

Caldwell, Lt. John, 125, 137, 160, 293

Cameronians, *see* Army: 26th Foot

Campo Mayor, Battle of, 25

Carrickfergus, Thurot's raid on, 3, 19, 202, 213–15

Caulfield, Lt. William, 218–22, 228, 297

Cavendish Family, 10, 12, 22–3, 175–6

Cavendish, Sir Henry, 204, 233, 298

Cavendish, William, 3rd Duke of Devonshire, 7, 13–14, 20, 22–3, 24–5, 26–7, 35–6, 39–42, 48–9, 61, 64, 74–5, 89, 119–20, 124, 130–1, 175–6, 289, 301

Cavendish, William, Marquess of Hartington and 4th Duke of Devonshire, 22, 27, 48–9, 64,

89, 126, 131, 175–6, 178, 183,
185, 188, 190–2, 199, 203–4,
207–8, 232–3, 290–1, 301
Chapel-en-le-Frith, 21, 41
Chaplains, regimental, 7
Chatsworth, 22, 174
Chief Secretary to the Lord
Lieutenant of Ireland, 9–10,
19, 242
Clare Castle, 251–2
Clegg, Dr Joseph, 113–17, 160,
301
Clive, Col. Robert, 123
Commissions, purchase and sale
of, 13–14, 38, 81–9, 240–5,
249–50, 262–3
Cook, Ens. George, 218–22, 297
Cooke, Miss Judith, 291–2
Cope, Lt.-Gen. Sir John, 62, 285
Cork, military affairs in, 1, 4, 16,
19, 117–19, 202, 223–4,
230–1, 234–5, 239, 246,
253–62, 288
Corneille, Lt. John, 290, 293
Coromandel, Coast of, 7, 29, 121
140
Cotes, Lt.-Col. James, 26, 72,
76–7, 81–4, 89–90, 301
Crane, Dr Michael, 204, 269,
301
Crawford, Lt. Charles, 217,
221–2, 197, 301
Croker, Lt. Taylor, 225, 240, 298
Cuddalore, Fort St. David, 123,
138–40, 146, 151–3, 155–6,
162–3
Cumberland, William Augustus,
Duke of, Captain-General, 19,

27, 57, 74–5, 79, 85–6, 122,
134, 136–7, 290
Cunningham, Capt. John, 53,
284
Curzon Family, 22

Daly, Lt. Anthony, 229–30, 298
Davenport, Sir Peter, 23, 36
Dawkin, Lt. William, 14, 55–6,
74–8, 82, 301
Dawson, the Revd. Thomas, 204
Deane, Sir Robert, 204
Degge, Col. William, 24
Derbyshire, 12, 21–4, 119, 233,
239
Desbrisay, Capt. Theophilus, 10,
44, 106–7, 111, 193
Devonshire, Dukes of, *see*
Cavendish Family
Devonshire House, 196
Digby, Edward, Lord, 175, 294
'Disbanding Act', 3
Dorset, John, Duke of, 19, 132
Drafting, policy of, 17, 202–3,
230–1, 235–8, 242, 252–7,
260–2
Dublin,
military command in, 85–6
regimental agents in, 9–10
vice-regal court, 40–41
Dumont, Capt. David, 78, 286
Dupleix, Joseph, 123, 150

East India Company, 7, 14–15,
122–5, 132, 138–47, 151–7,

163–8, 170–3, 175–6, 179–80, 189, 193, 290, 292–3

Ellis, Lt. Hercules, 199, 213–15, 217, 225, 244, 251, 263, 265–6, 301

Enniskillen Light Horse, see Army: 20th (Light) Dragoons

Erskine, Major David, 248, 299

Evatt, Samuel, 107, 160, 287

Ferguson, Capt. Adam, 23, 33, 282

Ferguson, Dr Kenneth, 18

Fielding, Henry, 276

Finisterre, Battle of Cape, 28, 88, 91, 281

Fitzwilliam, Maj.-Gen. the Hon. John, 223, 297

Fitzwilliam's, see Army: 2nd Foot

Fletcher, Dr Thomas, Dean of Down, Bishop of Kildare, 35–6, 40–2, 46–51, 89, 301

Flood, Lt. Francis, 14, 201, 215–17, 220–1, 232–3, 238, 240–1, 243–5, 249–52, 256, 258–9, 262–7, 301

Flood, Warden, 201, 216–17, 220–1, 233, 238, 243–4, 250, 266–7, 299, 301

Folard, the Chevalier de, 276

Forbes, Col. George, Lord, 234, 298

Forbes's, see Army: 76th Foot

Ford, Mr, 228, 298

Ford Hall, Derbyshire, 15, 21–2, 79, 115, 121, 125–6, 184–5, 194, 204–5, 291

Forde, Maj. Francis, 8, 16, 56, 71, 97–8, 100–2, 126, 134, 155–6, 181–3, 193, 195–6, 290, 302–3

Forrester, Maj. Cecil, 75, 285

Fort St. David, see Cuddalore

Fort St. George, see Madras

'Forty-Five' Rebellion, 25–6, 48–9, 165, 280

Fox, Henry, MP, 10, 27, 170–2, 175, 290, 303

Fox, Maj. Henry, 6, 48, 53, 56, 58–9, 90, 283

Frampton's, see Army: 30th Foot

Frederick II, 'the Great' of Prussia, 11

Frey, Dr Sylvia, 15–16

Fuller's, see Army: 29th Foot

Gabbet, Lt.-Col. Joseph, 261, 299

Germonsway, Anthony, 288

Gaylard, Capt. Thomas, 222–5, 302

George I, King, 13

George II, King, 1, 134, 184, 186, 190–2, 199

George III, King, 269–71

Gibraltar, 2, 16, 23, 25, 30–4, 72, 191

Gisborne, Maj. James, 110, 288

Gore, Lt.-Col.-Commdt. Sir Ralph, 207, 260, 297

Gore's, see Army: 92nd Foot

Gore, Thomas, MP, 100, 287

Graham, Brig.-Gen. William, 53, 284

Grant, Lt. Archibald, 'Archy', 8, 28, 64–8, 73, 76–8, 81–3, 87, 104–6, 122, 302
Green, Sgt. John, 28

Halifax, George, Earl of, 262–6, 299
Handasyde, Gen. Roger, 207
Handasyde's, see Army: 16th Foot
Handel, George Frederick, 39, 283
Hardwar, John of Bromborough Court, 22
Harrington, William, Earl of, 82–6, 286
Hartington, William, Marquess of see Cavendish, William, 4th Duke of Devonshire
Hawke, Admiral Edward, 28, 202
Hawkesworth, Dr John, 299–300
Hayes, James, 9, 11, 202
Hazard, Lt. William, 222, 224, 230
Hepburne, Maj. David, 52–4, 56, 66, 68–73, 82, 183, 189, 193, 195–6, 208–9, 212–13, 288, 303
Heron, Lt.-Col. Alexander, 144, 171, 293
Hervey, John, Lord, 1
Highlanders, see Army: 42nd Foot
Holdernesse, Robert, Earl of, 128, 153, 193, 291
Honeywood, Gen. Sir Philip, 63, 285

Hooke, Maj. William, 34, 282
Houlding, Dr J. A., 4, 6–7, 18
Hunt, Capt. Edward, 'Ned', 298
Huske's, see Army: 23rd Foot

Ilchester, Stephen, Earl of, 175, 294
Invalids, see Army: 41st Foot
Invasions of Britain and Ireland, French plans for, 199–200, 202
Ireland,
    efficiency of the army in, 19–20
    military life in, 4, 18–20, 73, 94–6, 109–11, 117–19
    Parliament of, 12, 41, 203–4, 208, 233, 250
Irish Establishment, 2–3, 5, 9–10, 17, 18–20, 195, 200
Irwin's, see Army: 5th Foot

Jamaica, 7, 25
James, Dr F. G. 18
Jennings, Lt.-Col. John, 214–15
Joass, Capt. Alexander, 228, 234, 242–5, 249–50, 258, 263, 265, 303
Johnson, Dr Samuel, 22–3, 299–300
Johnston, Maj. S. H. F., 18
Joliffe, John, MP, 45, 283
Jordan's, see Army: 15th Foot

Kane, Brig.-Gen. Richard, 276

Keene, Capt. Henry, 60, 62–3, 81, 284

Kellet, Dr William, 7, 158–9, 169–70, 174, 303

Keppel, Capt. the Hon. Augustus, R.N., 56, 284

Kilpatrick, Maj. James, 170, 294

Kinsale, governorship of, 121, 132, 291

Kirby, John, 278

Kirkland, Sgt. Joseph, 8, 27, 275

Kopperman, Dr Paul, 16

Ladeveze, Col. Anthony, 106, 128, 303

La Fausille, Col. John, 189–90, 294

Lawrence, Lt.-Col. Stringer, 123, 139, 153, 292

Leeward Isles, 4

Levett, Capt. Thomas, 10, 28, 42–4, 46–7, 59, 61, 63, 79–81, 85, 87–94, 282, 303

Lewis, Capt. Rowland, 14, 77, 80, 150, 286

Ligonier, Field Marshal Jean Louis, Lord, Commander-in-Chief, 187–8, 190–3, 199

Lloyd, Capt. William, RN, 69, 285

Lombard, Lt. Richard, 243, 299

Lord Lieutenant of Ireland, 11, 14, 19, 35, 82, 200, 207, 222–3, 237, 252, 262–3, 267

Lords Justices of Ireland, 14, 82, 85–6, 117–19, 236–8, 264

L'Orient Expedition, 14, 26–7, 50–6, 165, 191, 269, 281

Louisbourg, 199

Lovett, Maj. Verney, 72–4, 81, 106, 109, 156, 303

Lowe, Ens. Lovelace, 227, 298

Lyons, Lt. John, 56, 73, 284

Macartney, Sgt., 16, 97–100

Mackay, Lt.-Col. Alexander, 231, 235, 298

Madras, Fort St. George, 14–15, 121–4, 130, 138–44, 146, 151–2, 156–8, 161, 171

Mangin, Alexander, 242, 298

McDowell, Prof. R. B., 3

Marathas, 123, 144, 294

Marines, 27, 51, 60, 77

Marlborough, John, 1st Duke of, 1, 55

Meredyth, Lt. John, 229, 245–8, 298

Minorca, 2, 25, 72

Molesworth, Lt.-Col. James, 203, 230–2, 235–6, 254–8, 298

Molesworth, Lt.-Gen. Richard, Viscount, 86

Molesworth's, see Army: 5th Dragoons

Mompesson, Maj. John, 252, 277

Montague, Maj.-Gen. Charles, 248–9, 299

Montgomery, Capt. William,

206–7, 228–30, 233, 242, 244, 255, 263, 303
Morgan, Lt.-Col.-Commdt. Hugh, 235, 298
Morgan's, *see* Army: 90th Foot
Morris, Capt. James, 248, 299
Morse, Leonard, 174–5, 178, 183–5, 187–8, 303
Munro, Dr Andrew, 7, 174, 275
Munro, Lt.-Col. George, 110, 288
Murray, Lt.-Col. James, 128–33, 304
Muster Master General and Clerk of the Cheque, 10, 242

Napier, Maj-Gen. Robert, 154, 191–2, 195, 293
Newcastle, Thomas Pelham Holles, Duke of, 199
Newton, Robert, 125–6, 271, 291
Nixon, John, 218, 228–9, 234, 244, 297

O'Farrell, Brig.-Gen. Richard, 53, 284
Officers, 11–15
Orme, Robert, 153, 172, 289, 293
Ostend, siege of, 25, 48, 283

Palk, The Revd Robert, 172, 294
Parker, Corpl., 73–4

Passaro, Battle of Cape, 25
Paymaster General, 9–10
Payne, John, 179–80, 304
Pearce, Lt.-Col. Charles, 86, 97, 286
Pelham, the Hon. Henry, MP, 11–12
Perrin, Ens. James, 26, 70, 285
Peters, Stephen, 287
Philips, Ens. Charles, 53, 284
Pigot, George, 167, 294
Pitt, William, MP, 199–200
Plassey, Battle of, 122
Pole's, *see* Army: 10th Foot
Polygars, 170, 294
Pondicherry, 121, 123, 292–3
Ponsonby, the Hon. John, 132, 220, 291
Powell, Ens. Caleb, 105–6, 287
Preston, Maj. Robert, 6, 203, 225 227, 235, 239, 246, 248–9, 253, 264–8, 304
Pringle, Sir John, 204
Prize Money, 73

Queen's *see* Army: 2nd Foot
Quiberon Bay, Battle of, 202

Rank and File, 15–18
Ray, Job, 235
Recruiting service, 16–17, 73–4, 104–6, 210–12, 215–20, 234, 236–8, 253–5, 261, 268
Religion in the army, 7

Richbell, Brig.-Gen. Edward, 5,
25–6, 42, 46–9, 51, 55, 58–63,
65, 71–3, 76–81, 85, 106,
111–13, 122, 288, 304
Richbell's, *see* Army: 39th Foot
Richmond, Charles, Duke of,
183, 186, 294
Rigby, Richard, MP, 221, 297
Roberts, David, 178, 183, 294
Roman Catholics, recruitment of,
3, 202, 218–20
Rothes, Lt.-Gen. John, Earl of,
192, 207, 219, 234, 242–3,
257–8, 294
Rothwell, Sgt. Thomas, 23, 279
Royals, *see* Army: 1st Foot
Royal Irish, *see* Army: 18th Foot
Royal Welch Fuzileers, *see* Army:
23rd Foot
Rufane, Col. William, 234, 298
Rufane's, *see* Army: 76th Foot

Sabine, Lt.-Gen. Joseph, 33
Sackville, Col. Lord George, 19,
106, 132, 135–6, 304
Sailors, straggling and deserting,
44–5
St. Clair, Lt-Gen the Hon. James,
24, 26, 51–4, 191–2
St. Clair, Maj the Hon. William,
23, 32–3, 282
Saunders, Thomas, 140–44, 292
Savage, Lt.-Col. Philip, 84, 286
Sawyer, Maj. George, 80, 286
Schuyler, Capt. Courtland, 223,
228, 231, 256, 298

Sea service, 16, 25, 28, 56,
59–60, 64–6, 68–73, 76–7, 79,
87–8, 90–4
Sebright's *see* Army: 52nd Foot
Secretary at War, 10, 27, 74–5,
81–2, 87–8, 90–4, 126, 170–2,
180, 185–7, 192, 201
Sempill, Lt. John, Lord, 14,
60–2, 66, 304
Seven Years' War, 2, 5–6, 12, 17,
126, 199–200, 202–3
Sewell, Lt.-Col. Matthews,
13–14, 27–8, 63–6, 68–72,
75–9, 81–7, 97–100, 106,
109–11, 122, 131, 199, 304
Shearer, Sgt., 64
Sherwin, Thomas, 92, 287
Shields, Sgt., 97–8, 110
Smith, Ens. Mathias, 241, 298
Spaight, Ens. Palmes, 241, 298
Spanish Succession, War of the,
1, 25
Speaker of the House of
Commons of Ireland, 85–6,
208, 250
Starke, Richard, 138–40, 304
Steppler, Dr Glenn, 16
Stewart, Rear-Admiral James,
66, 68–72, 285
Stone, the Very Revd. George,
229–30, 298
Street, Sgt., 73–4
Strode's *see* Army: 62nd
Foot
Supple, Lt. Robert, 81, 83, 85–6,
286
Surgeons, regimental, 7, 158–9,
169–70

Sussex, operations against smugglers in, 26, 49
Symes, Capt. George, 16, 72, 81, 85, 304

Tallagh (or Tallow), Co Waterford, 203–4, 232–4, 239, 278
Thurot, Commodore François, 3, 19, 199, 202
Tobell, Lt. Samuel, 70, 285
Townsend, Capt. Thomas, 59, 109, 284
Townshend, Maj. Gen. George, Viscount, 19
Trapaud, Lt.-Govr. Alexander, 289
Trapaud, Lt.-Col. Cyrus, 289
Trench, Capt. William, 305, 223, 296–7
Trichinopoly, 144, 161
Truelock, Thomas, 225, 298

Uniake, Mrs 160, 293
Urquhart, Capt. Duncan, 223, 298

Vauban, Sebastien le Prestre, Seigneur de, 276

Waite, Thomas, 117–19, 304
Walpole, Sir Robert, MP, 1

Walsh, Lt. Anthony, 98
War Office, 9, 74, 90
Warburton, Lt.-Col. John, 86, 286
Warren, Vice-Admiral Sir Peter, 66–8, 71–2, 78, 285
Watts, Ens. Charles, 245, 299
Weld, Lt.-Col. Thomas, 75, 286
Weller, Lt. Nicholas, 97, 287
Wemyss, Capt. Patrick, 109, 287
Whiting (or Whyte), Lt. William, 207, 297
Whitmore, Col. Edward, 175, 294
Whitshed, Col. Samuel, 25, 112
Whitshed's, see Army: 39th Foot
William III, King, 1, 9
Williams, Capt. Edward, 28, 59, 73, 81, 90, 282, 284
Wilmot, Sir Robert, 10–11, 175–6, 178, 183–5, 188, 191, 196, 233–4, 304
Wilson, Capt. Alexander, 32, 282
Windus, Lt.-Col. Edward, 6, 24, 202–4, 209–12, 217–20, 222–8, 230–2, 234–6, 238–9, 244–9, 253–62, 265–6, 298, 304
Wolfe, Maj. Walter, 42, 283
Wollacombe, Capt.-Lt. Thomas, 243, 298
Women and children of the regiments, 16, 85, 135–6
Wray, Lt. Henry, 66, 285

Yonge, Sir William, MP, 48–9, 304

ARMY RECORDS SOCIETY
(FOUNDED 1984)

Members of the Society are entitled to purchase back
volumes at reduced prices.
Orders should be sent to the Hon. Treasurer, Army Records Society,
c/o National Army Museum,
Royal Hospital Road,
London SW3 4HT.

The Society has already issued:

Vol. I:
*The Military Correspondence of
Field Marshal Sir Henry Wilson 1918–1922*
Edited by Dr Keith Jeffery

Vol. II:
*The Army and the
Curragh Incident, 1914*
Edited by Dr Ian F. W. Beckett

Vol. III:
*The Napoleonic War Journal of
Captain Thomas Henry Browne, 1807–1816*
Edited by Roger Norman Buckley

Vol. IV:
*An Eighteenth-Century Secretary at War
The Papers of William, Viscount Barrington*
Edited by Tony Hayter

Vol. V:
*The Military Correspondence of Field
Marshal Sir William Robertson 1915–1918*
Edited by David R. Woodward